# ANT-MAN



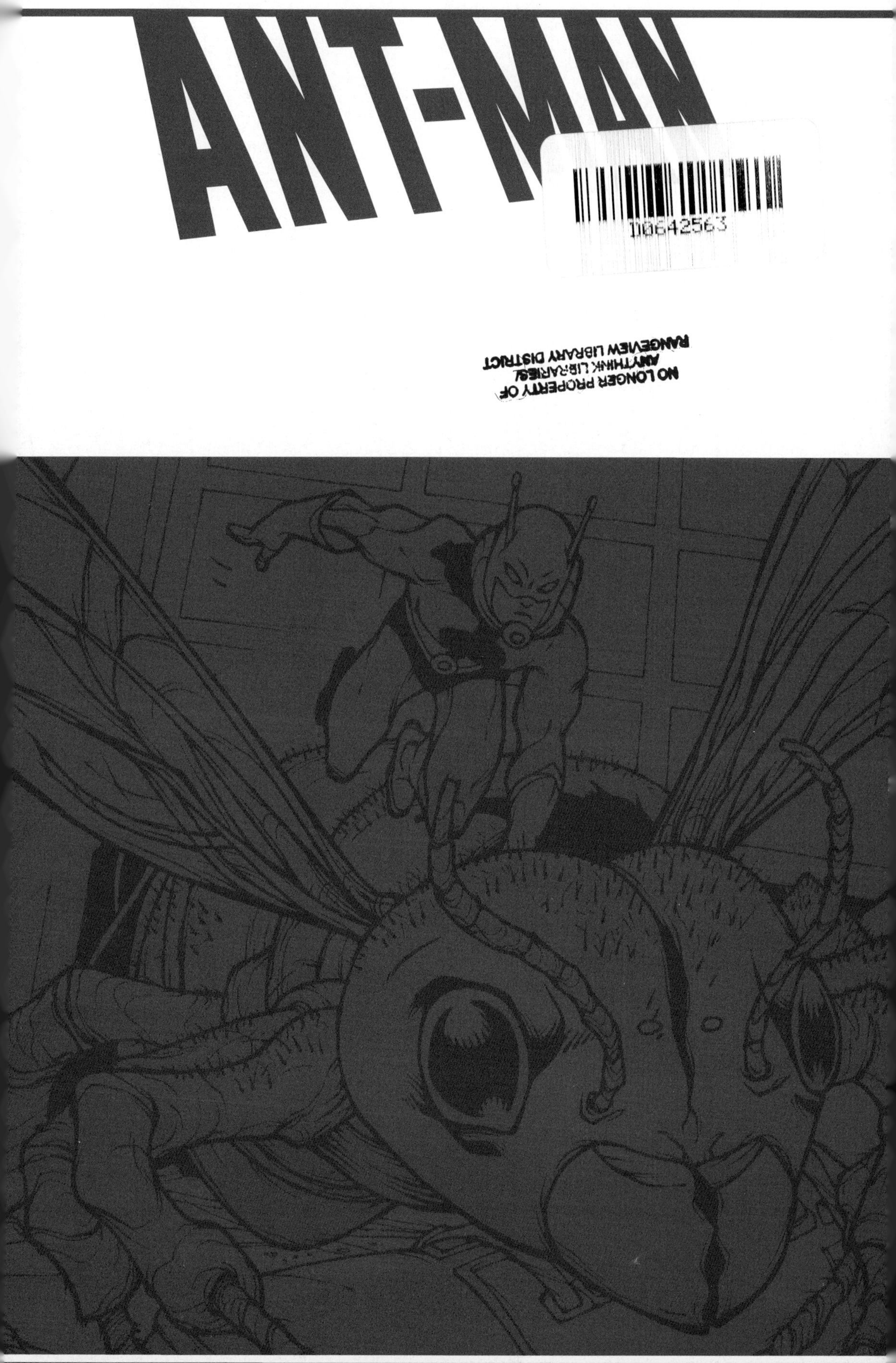

COLLECTION EDITOR: **JENNIFER GRÜNWALD**
ASSISTANT EDITOR: **CAITLIN O'CONNELL**
ASSOCIATE MANAGING EDITOR: **KATERI WOODY**
EDITOR, SPECIAL PROJECTS: **MARK D. BEAZLEY**
VP PRODUCTION & SPECIAL PROJECTS: **JEFF YOUNGQUIST**
SVP PRINT, SALES & MARKETING: **DAVID GABRIEL**
BOOK DESIGN: **JEFF POWELL**

EDITOR IN CHIEF: **C.B. CEBULSKI**
CHIEF CREATIVE OFFICER: **JOE QUESADA**
PRESIDENT: **DAN BUCKLEY**
EXECUTIVE PRODUCER: **ALAN FINE**

**ANT-MAN: ASTONISHING ORIGINS.** Contains material originally published in magazine form as ANT-MAN: SEASON ONE and ANT-MAN #1. First printing 2018. ISBN 978-0-7851-6390-9. Published by MAR WORLDWIDE, INC., a subsidiary of MARVEL ENTERTAINMENT, LLC. OFFICE OF PUBLICATION: 135 West 50th Street, New York, NY 10020. Copyright © 2018 MARVEL No similarity between any of the names, charact persons, and/or institutions in this magazine with those of any living or dead person or institution is intended, and any such similarity which may exist is purely coincidental. **Printed in the U.S.A.** DAN BUCKLEY, Presid Marvel Entertainment; JOHN NEE, Publisher; JOE QUESADA, Chief Creative Officer; TOM BREVOORT, SVP of Publishing; DAVID BOGART, SVP of Business Affairs & Operations, Publishing & Partnership; DAVID GABRIEL, SV Sales & Marketing, Publishing; JEFF YOUNGQUIST, VP of Production & Special Projects; DAN CARR, Executive Director of Publishing Technology; ALEX MORALES, Director of Publishing Operations; DAN EDINGTON, Mana Editor; SUSAN CRESPI, Production Manager; STAN LEE, Chairman Emeritus. For information regarding advertising in Marvel Comics or on Marvel.com, please contact Vit DeBellis, Custom Solutions & Integrated Advertis Manager, at vdebellis@marvel.com. For Marvel subscription inquiries, please call 888-511-5480. **Manufactured between 4/13/2018 and 5/15/2018 by LSC COMMUNICATIONS INC., KENDALLVILLE, IN, USA.**

10 9 8 7 6 5 4 3 2 1

# ANT-MAN

WRITER
## TOM DeFALCO
ARTIST
## HORACIO DOMINGUES
ART ASSISTANTS
## RUBEN GONZALEZ
## & ANDRES PONCE
COLOR ARTIST
## CHRIS SOTOMAYOR
LETTERERS
## VC'S CHRIS ELIOPOULOS
## & JOE SABINO

COVER ARTIST
## JULIAN TOTINO TEDESCO

EDITOR
## TOM BRENNAN
EXECUTIVE EDITOR
## TOM BREVOORT

ANT-MAN CREATED BY STAN LEE,
LARRY LIEBER & JACK KIRBY

## ASTONISHING
## ORIGINS

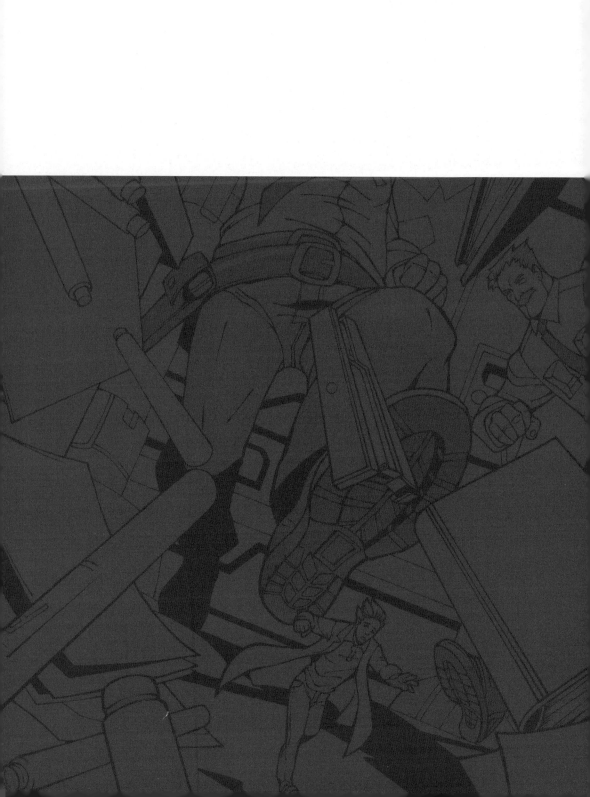

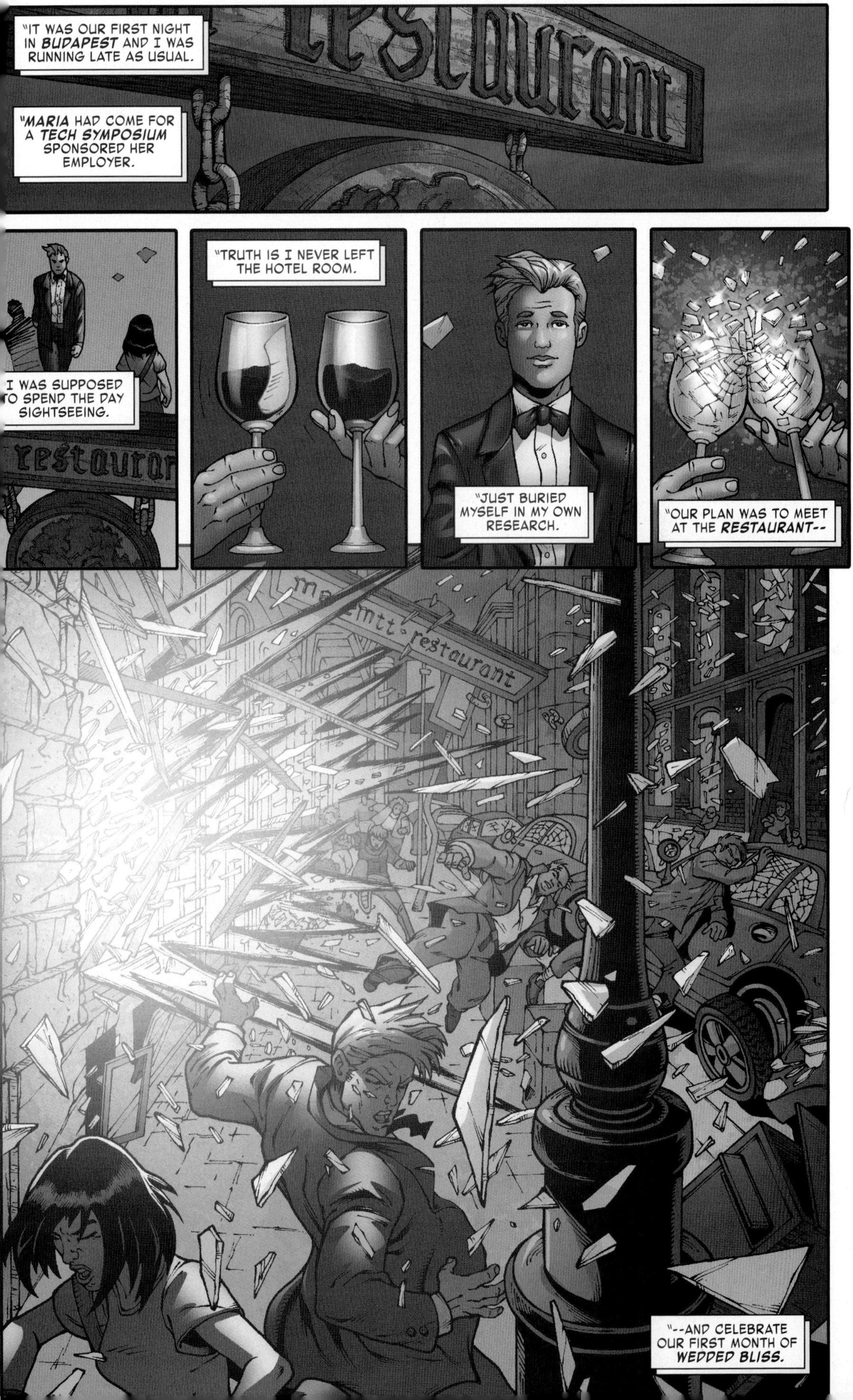
"IT WAS OUR FIRST NIGHT IN *BUDAPEST* AND I WAS RUNNING LATE AS USUAL.
"*MARIA* HAD COME FOR A *TECH SYMPOSIUM* SPONSORED HER EMPLOYER.
I WAS SUPPOSED TO SPEND THE DAY SIGHTSEEING.
"TRUTH IS I NEVER LEFT THE HOTEL ROOM.
"JUST BURIED MYSELF IN MY OWN RESEARCH.
"OUR PLAN WAS TO MEET AT THE *RESTAURANT*--
restaurant
"--AND CELEBRATE OUR FIRST MONTH OF *WEDDED BLISS.*

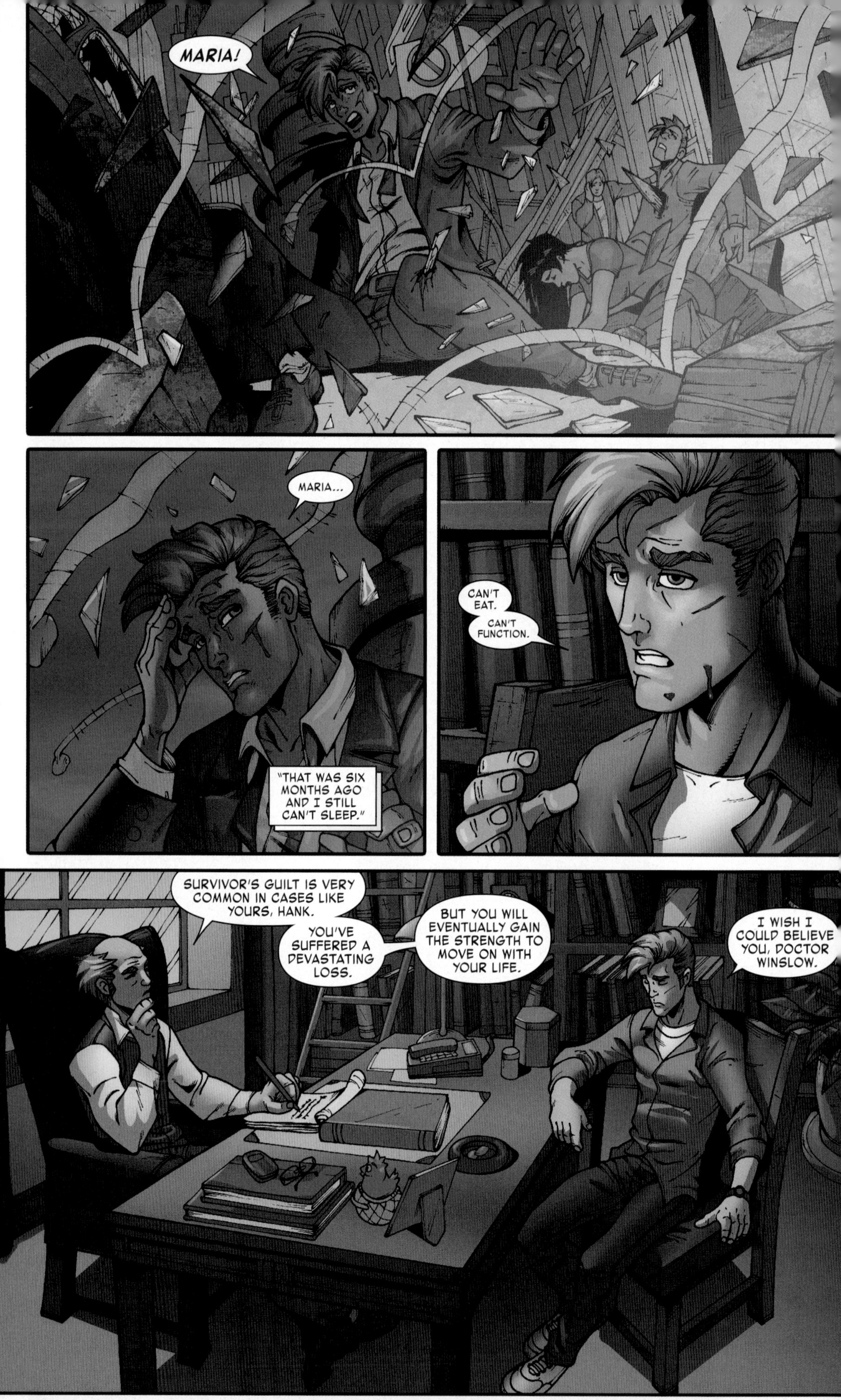
MARIA!
MARIA...
"THAT WAS SIX MONTHS AGO AND I STILL CAN'T SLEEP."
CAN'T EAT.
CAN'T FUNCTION.
SURVIVOR'S GUILT IS VERY COMMON IN CASES LIKE YOURS, HANK.
YOU'VE SUFFERED A DEVASTATING LOSS.
BUT YOU WILL EVENTUALLY GAIN THE STRENGTH TO MOVE ON WITH YOUR LIFE.
I WISH I COULD BELIEVE YOU, DOCTOR WINSLOW.

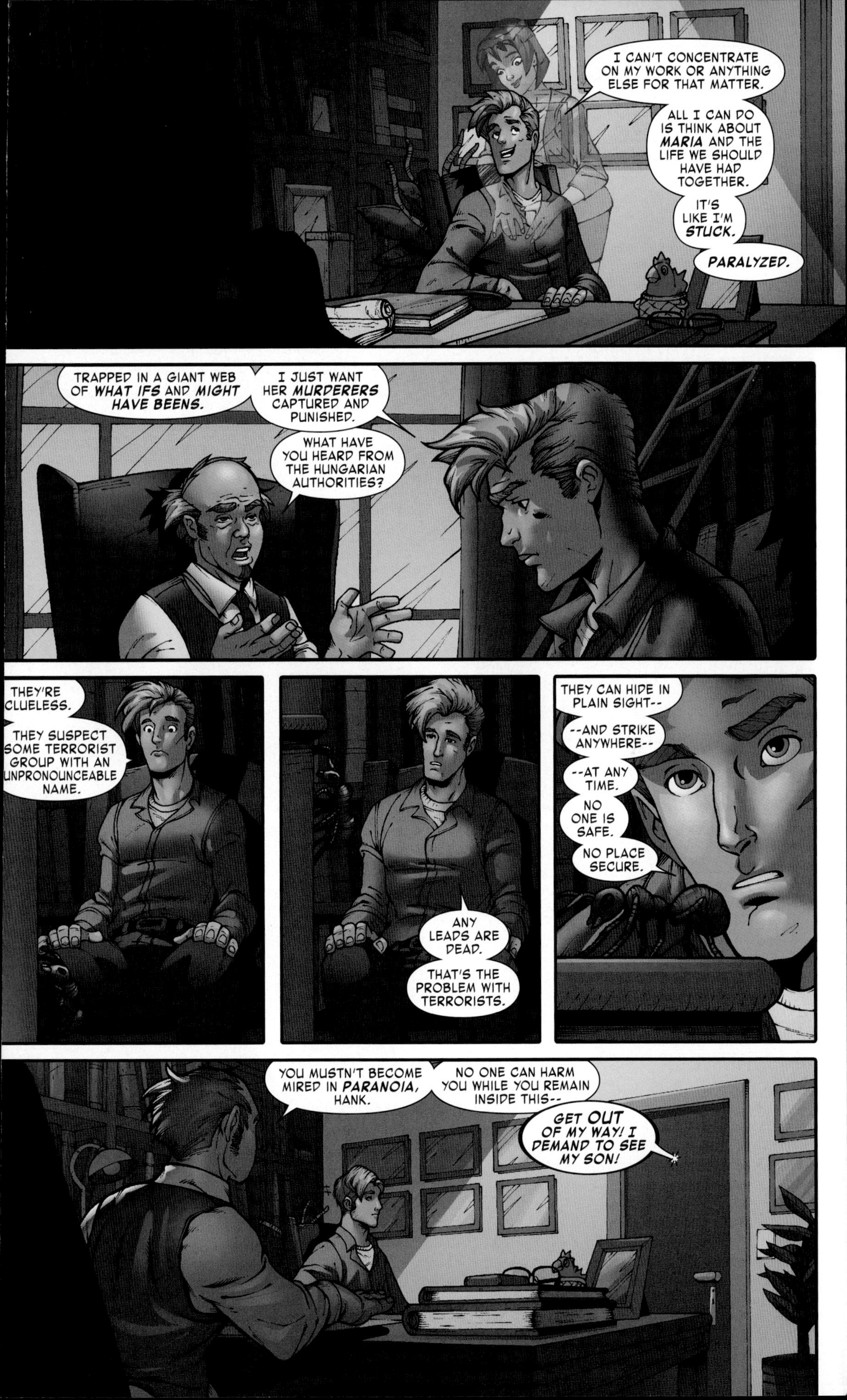

I CAN'T CONCENTRATE ON MY WORK OR ANYTHING ELSE FOR THAT MATTER.
ALL I CAN DO IS THINK ABOUT MARIA AND THE LIFE WE SHOULD HAVE HAD TOGETHER.
IT'S LIKE I'M STUCK.
PARALYZED.
TRAPPED IN A GIANT WEB OF WHAT IFS AND MIGHT HAVE BEENS.
I JUST WANT HER MURDERERS CAPTURED AND PUNISHED.
WHAT HAVE YOU HEARD FROM THE HUNGARIAN AUTHORITIES?
THEY'RE CLUELESS.
THEY SUSPECT SOME TERRORIST GROUP WITH AN UNPRONOUNCEABLE NAME.
ANY LEADS ARE DEAD.
THAT'S THE PROBLEM WITH TERRORISTS.
THEY CAN HIDE IN PLAIN SIGHT--
--AND STRIKE ANYWHERE--
--AT ANY TIME.
NO ONE IS SAFE.
NO PLACE SECURE.
YOU MUSTN'T BECOME MIRED IN PARANOIA, HANK.
NO ONE CAN HARM YOU WHILE YOU REMAIN INSIDE THIS--
GET OUT OF MY WAY! I DEMAND TO SEE MY SON!

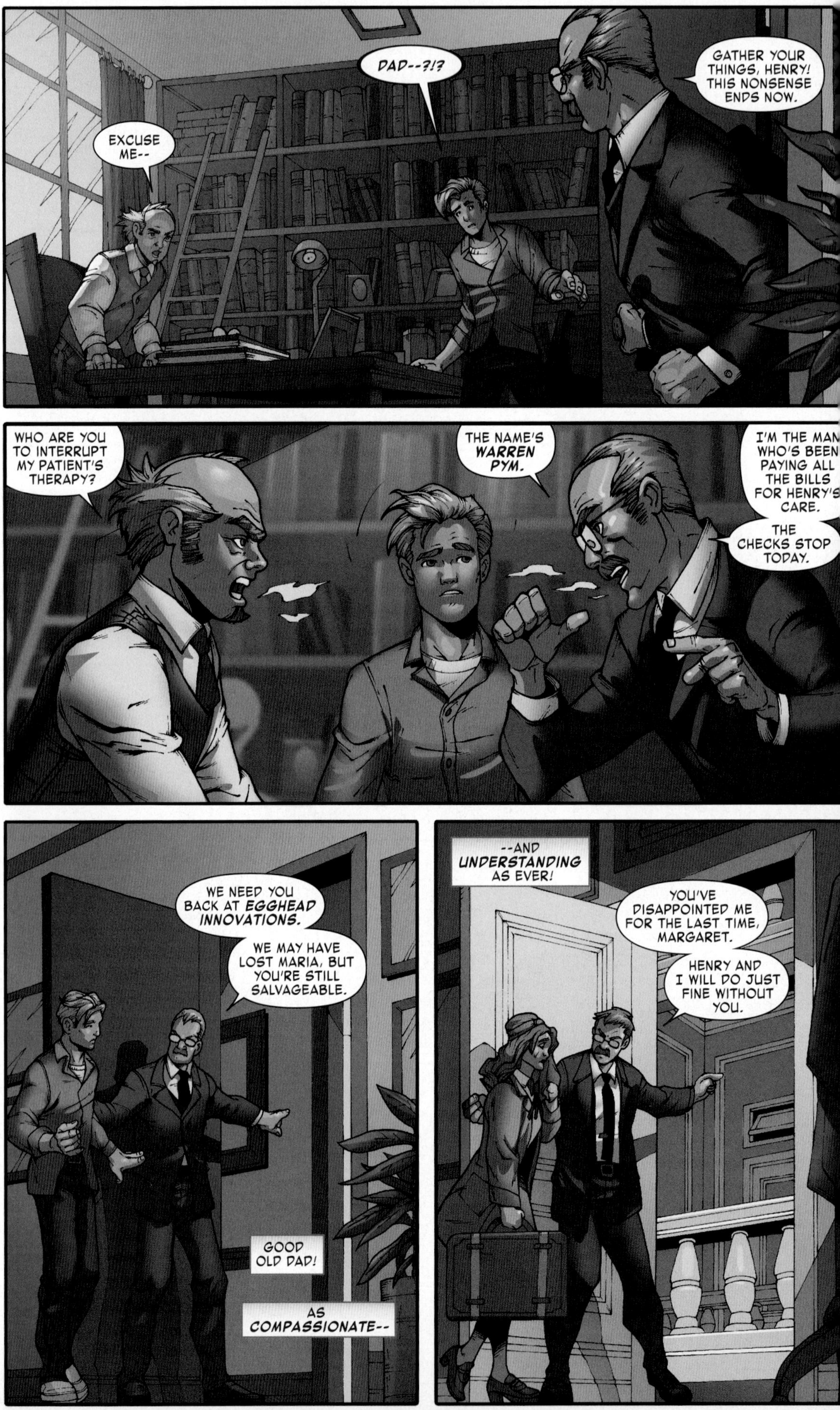
EXCUSE ME--
DAD--?!?
GATHER YOUR THINGS, HENRY! THIS NONSENSE ENDS NOW.
WHO ARE YOU TO INTERRUPT MY PATIENT'S THERAPY?
THE NAME'S WARREN PYM.
I'M THE MAN WHO'S BEEN PAYING ALL THE BILLS FOR HENRY'S CARE.
THE CHECKS STOP TODAY.
WE NEED YOU BACK AT EGGHEAD INNOVATIONS.
WE MAY HAVE LOST MARIA, BUT YOU'RE STILL SALVAGEABLE.
GOOD OLD DAD!
AS COMPASSIONATE--
--AND UNDERSTANDING AS EVER!
YOU'VE DISAPPOINTED ME FOR THE LAST TIME, MARGARET.
HENRY AND I WILL DO JUST FINE WITHOUT YOU.

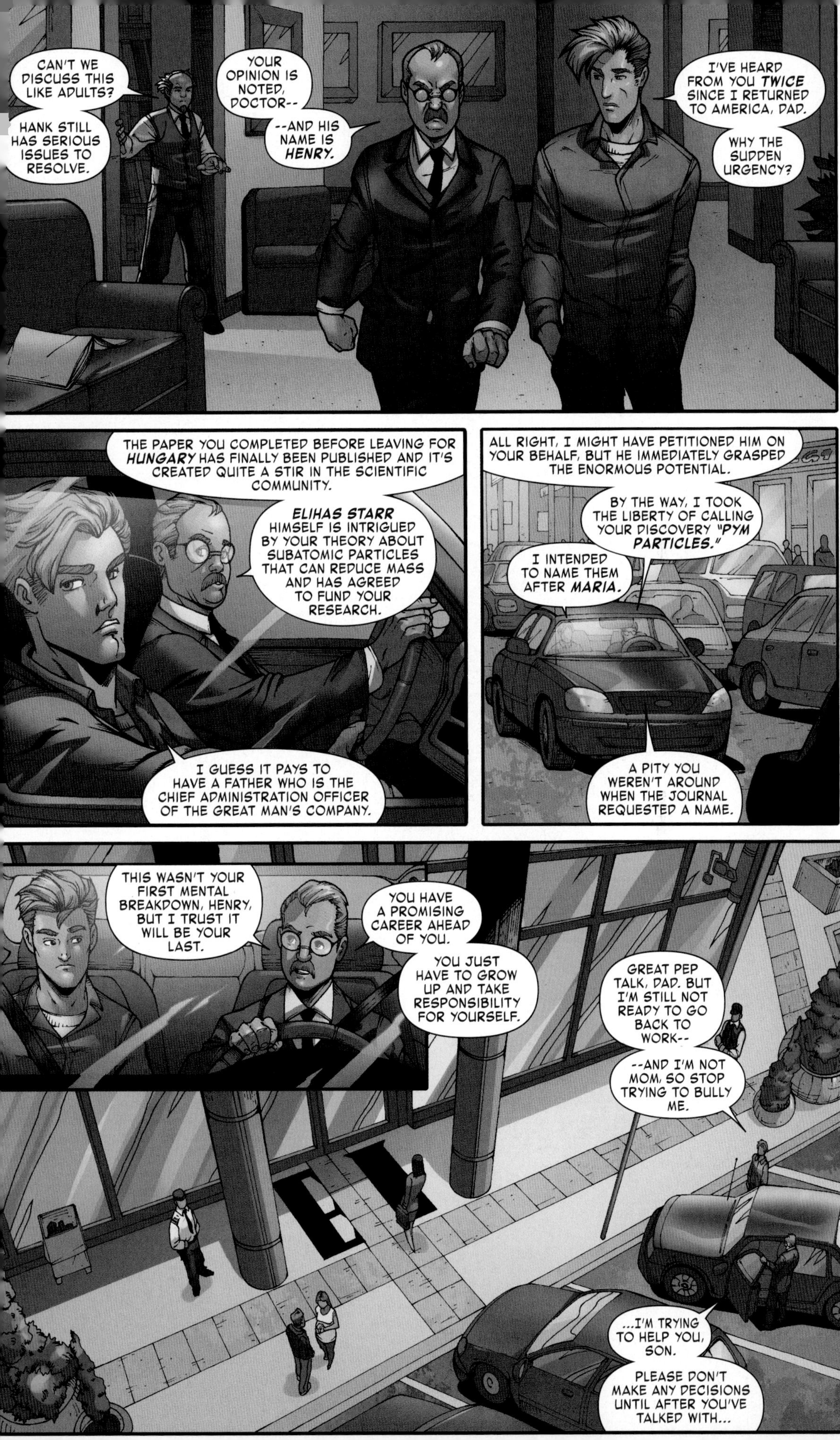
CAN'T WE DISCUSS THIS LIKE ADULTS?
HANK STILL HAS SERIOUS ISSUES TO RESOLVE.
YOUR OPINION IS NOTED, DOCTOR--
--AND HIS NAME IS HENRY.
I'VE HEARD FROM YOU TWICE SINCE I RETURNED TO AMERICA, DAD.
WHY THE SUDDEN URGENCY?
THE PAPER YOU COMPLETED BEFORE LEAVING FOR HUNGARY HAS FINALLY BEEN PUBLISHED AND IT'S CREATED QUITE A STIR IN THE SCIENTIFIC COMMUNITY.
ELIHAS STARR HIMSELF IS INTRIGUED BY YOUR THEORY ABOUT SUBATOMIC PARTICLES THAT CAN REDUCE MASS AND HAS AGREED TO FUND YOUR RESEARCH.
I GUESS IT PAYS TO HAVE A FATHER WHO IS THE CHIEF ADMINISTRATION OFFICER OF THE GREAT MAN'S COMPANY.
ALL RIGHT, I MIGHT HAVE PETITIONED HIM ON YOUR BEHALF, BUT HE IMMEDIATELY GRASPED THE ENORMOUS POTENTIAL.
BY THE WAY, I TOOK THE LIBERTY OF CALLING YOUR DISCOVERY "PYM PARTICLES."
I INTENDED TO NAME THEM AFTER MARIA.
A PITY YOU WEREN'T AROUND WHEN THE JOURNAL REQUESTED A NAME.
THIS WASN'T YOUR FIRST MENTAL BREAKDOWN, HENRY, BUT I TRUST IT WILL BE YOUR LAST.
YOU HAVE A PROMISING CAREER AHEAD OF YOU.
YOU JUST HAVE TO GROW UP AND TAKE RESPONSIBILITY FOR YOURSELF.
GREAT PEP TALK, DAD. BUT I'M STILL NOT READY TO GO BACK TO WORK--
--AND I'M NOT MOM, SO STOP TRYING TO BULLY ME.
...I'M TRYING TO HELP YOU, SON.
PLEASE DON'T MAKE ANY DECISIONS UNTIL AFTER YOU'VE TALKED WITH...

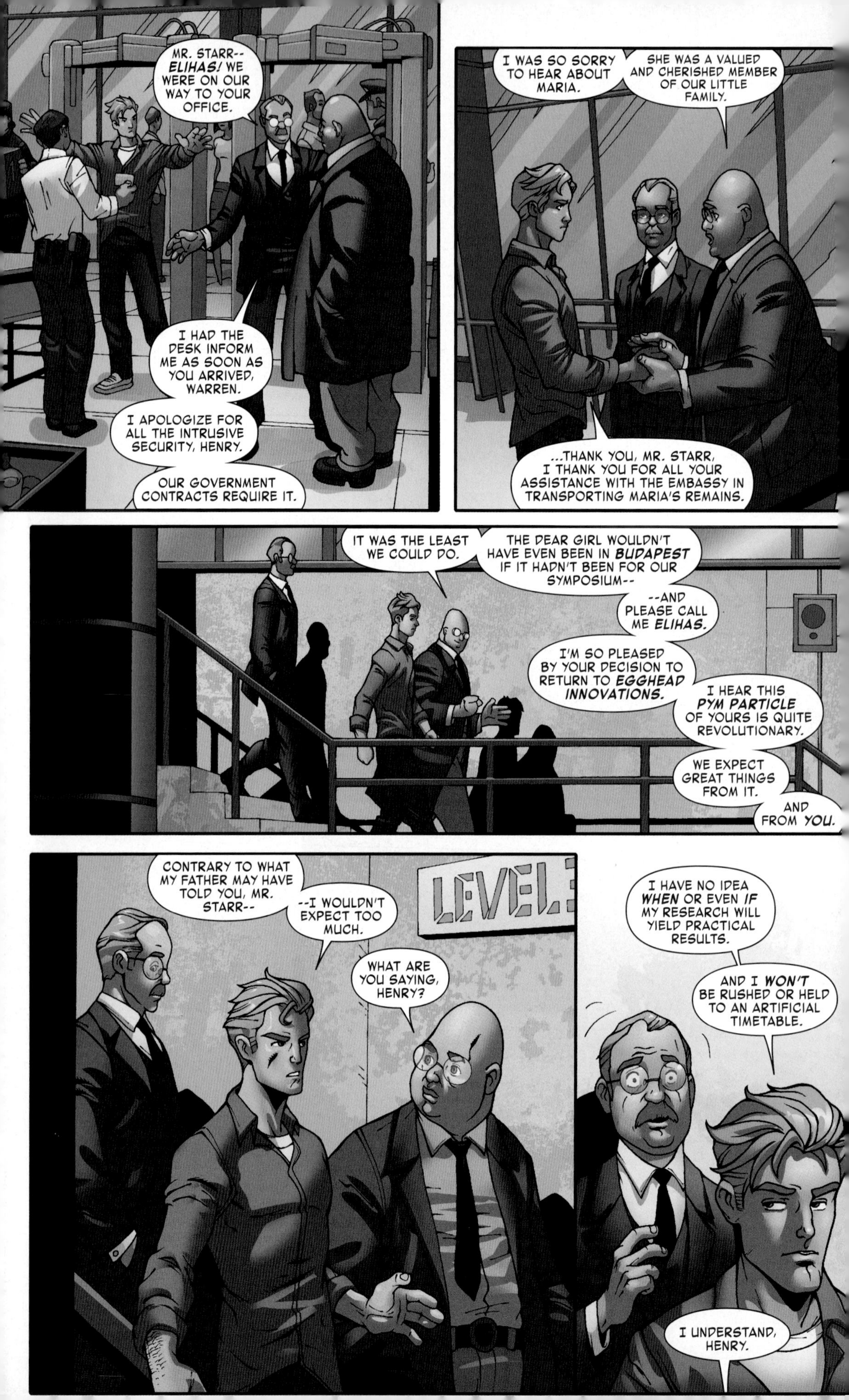

MR. STARR-- ELIHAS! WE WERE ON OUR WAY TO YOUR OFFICE.
I HAD THE DESK INFORM ME AS SOON AS YOU ARRIVED, WARREN.
I APOLOGIZE FOR ALL THE INTRUSIVE SECURITY, HENRY.
OUR GOVERNMENT CONTRACTS REQUIRE IT.
I WAS SO SORRY TO HEAR ABOUT MARIA.
SHE WAS A VALUED AND CHERISHED MEMBER OF OUR LITTLE FAMILY.
...THANK YOU, MR. STARR, I THANK YOU FOR ALL YOUR ASSISTANCE WITH THE EMBASSY IN TRANSPORTING MARIA'S REMAINS.
IT WAS THE LEAST WE COULD DO.
THE DEAR GIRL WOULDN'T HAVE EVEN BEEN IN BUDAPEST IF IT HADN'T BEEN FOR OUR SYMPOSIUM--
--AND PLEASE CALL ME ELIHAS.
I'M SO PLEASED BY YOUR DECISION TO RETURN TO EGGHEAD INNOVATIONS.
I HEAR THIS PYM PARTICLE OF YOURS IS QUITE REVOLUTIONARY.
WE EXPECT GREAT THINGS FROM IT.
AND FROM YOU.
CONTRARY TO WHAT MY FATHER MAY HAVE TOLD YOU, MR. STARR--
--I WOULDN'T EXPECT TOO MUCH.
LEVEL 3
WHAT ARE YOU SAYING, HENRY?
I HAVE NO IDEA WHEN OR EVEN IF MY RESEARCH WILL YIELD PRACTICAL RESULTS.
AND I WON'T BE RUSHED OR HELD TO AN ARTIFICIAL TIMETABLE.
I UNDERSTAND, HENRY.

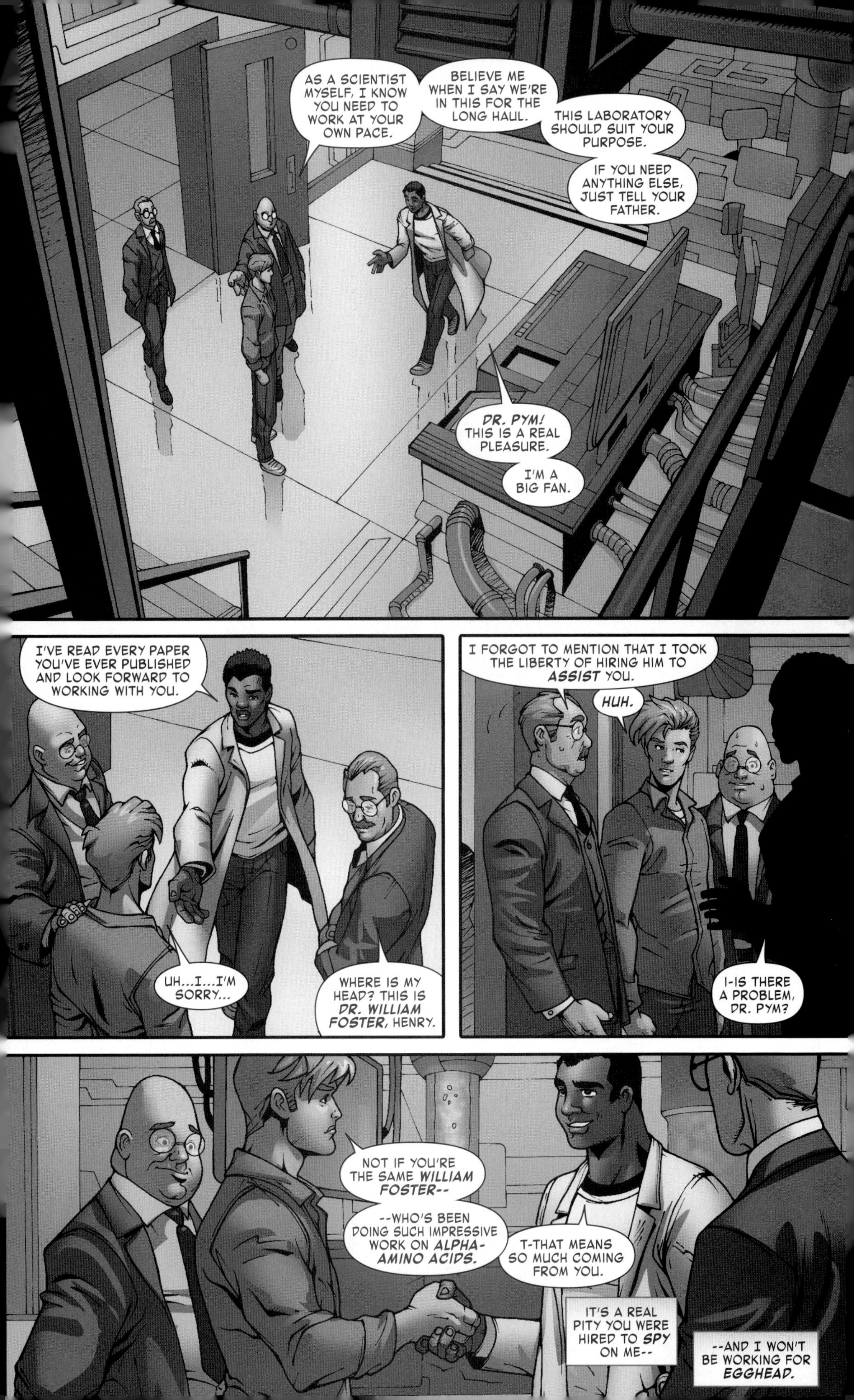
AS A SCIENTIST MYSELF, I KNOW YOU NEED TO WORK AT YOUR OWN PACE.
BELIEVE ME WHEN I SAY WE'RE IN THIS FOR THE LONG HAUL.
THIS LABORATORY SHOULD SUIT YOUR PURPOSE.
IF YOU NEED ANYTHING ELSE, JUST TELL YOUR FATHER.
DR. PYM! THIS IS A REAL PLEASURE.
I'M A BIG FAN.
I'VE READ EVERY PAPER YOU'VE EVER PUBLISHED AND LOOK FORWARD TO WORKING WITH YOU.
UH...I...I'M SORRY...
WHERE IS MY HEAD? THIS IS DR. WILLIAM FOSTER, HENRY.
I FORGOT TO MENTION THAT I TOOK THE LIBERTY OF HIRING HIM TO ASSIST YOU.
HUH.
I-IS THERE A PROBLEM, DR. PYM?
NOT IF YOU'RE THE SAME WILLIAM FOSTER--
--WHO'S BEEN DOING SUCH IMPRESSIVE WORK ON ALPHA-AMINO ACIDS.
T-THAT MEANS SO MUCH COMING FROM YOU.
IT'S A REAL PITY YOU WERE HIRED TO SPY ON ME--
--AND I WON'T BE WORKING FOR EGGHEAD.

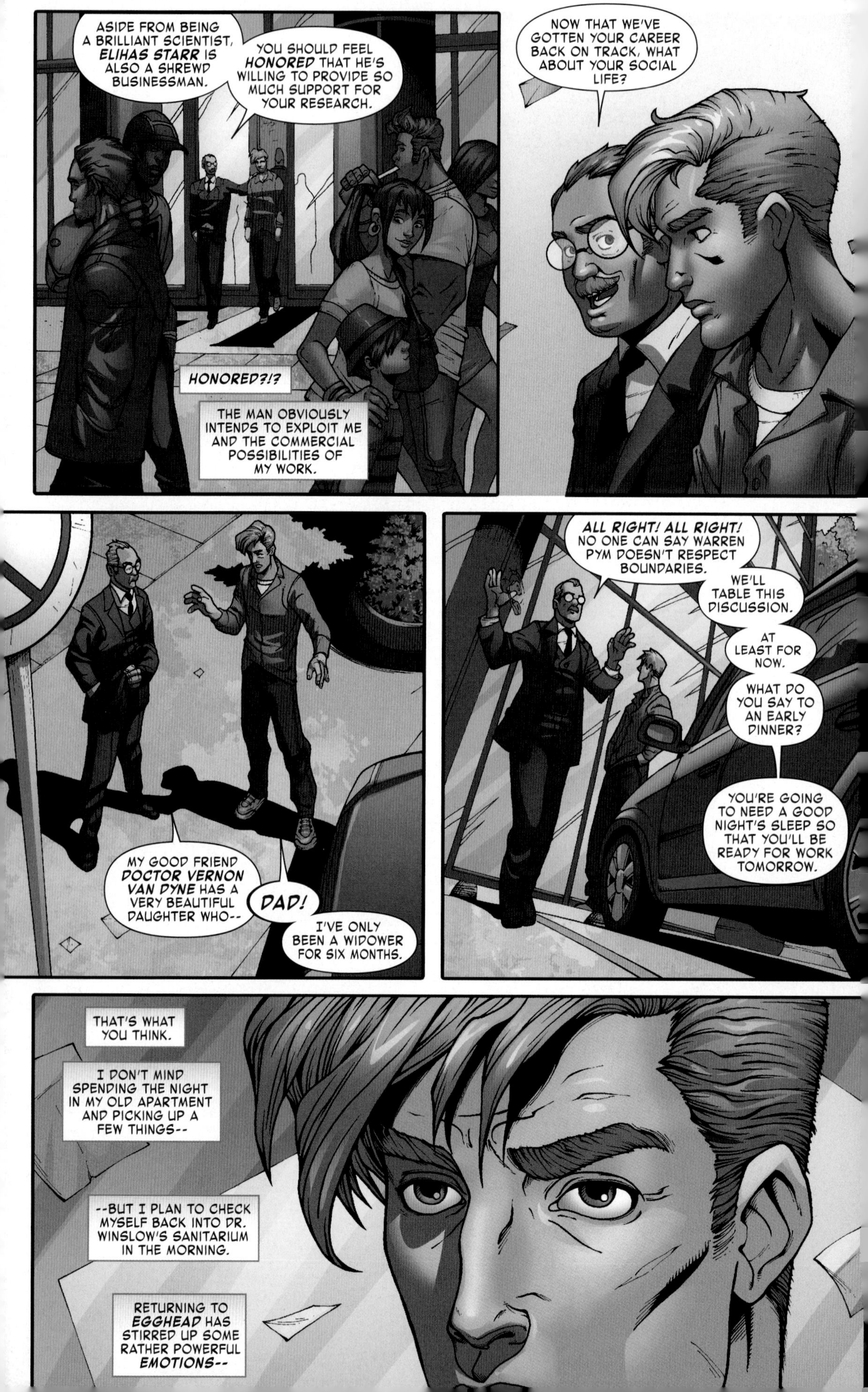

ASIDE FROM BEING A BRILLIANT SCIENTIST, ELIHAS STARR IS ALSO A SHREWD BUSINESSMAN.
YOU SHOULD FEEL HONORED THAT HE'S WILLING TO PROVIDE SO MUCH SUPPORT FOR YOUR RESEARCH.
HONORED?!?
THE MAN OBVIOUSLY INTENDS TO EXPLOIT ME AND THE COMMERCIAL POSSIBILITIES OF MY WORK.
NOW THAT WE'VE GOTTEN YOUR CAREER BACK ON TRACK, WHAT ABOUT YOUR SOCIAL LIFE?
MY GOOD FRIEND DOCTOR VERNON VAN DYNE HAS A VERY BEAUTIFUL DAUGHTER WHO--
DAD!
I'VE ONLY BEEN A WIDOWER FOR SIX MONTHS.
ALL RIGHT! ALL RIGHT! NO ONE CAN SAY WARREN PYM DOESN'T RESPECT BOUNDARIES.
WE'LL TABLE THIS DISCUSSION.
AT LEAST FOR NOW.
WHAT DO YOU SAY TO AN EARLY DINNER?
YOU'RE GOING TO NEED A GOOD NIGHT'S SLEEP SO THAT YOU'LL BE READY FOR WORK TOMORROW.
THAT'S WHAT YOU THINK.
I DON'T MIND SPENDING THE NIGHT IN MY OLD APARTMENT AND PICKING UP A FEW THINGS--
--BUT I PLAN TO CHECK MYSELF BACK INTO DR. WINSLOW'S SANITARIUM IN THE MORNING.
RETURNING TO EGGHEAD HAS STIRRED UP SOME RATHER POWERFUL EMOTIONS--

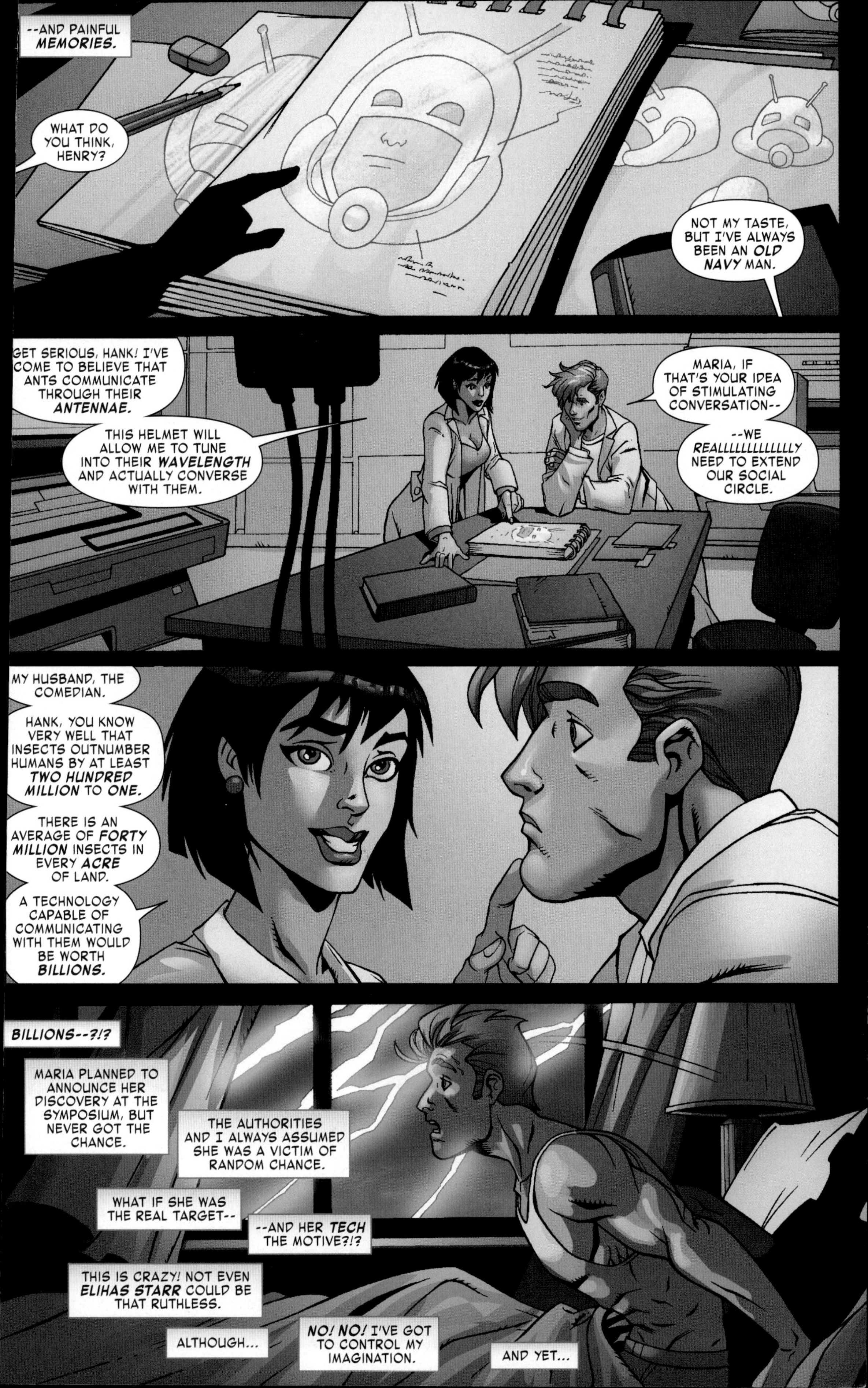
--AND PAINFUL MEMORIES.
WHAT DO YOU THINK, HENRY?
NOT MY TASTE, BUT I'VE ALWAYS BEEN AN OLD NAVY MAN.
GET SERIOUS, HANK! I'VE COME TO BELIEVE THAT ANTS COMMUNICATE THROUGH THEIR ANTENNAE.
THIS HELMET WILL ALLOW ME TO TUNE INTO THEIR WAVELENGTH AND ACTUALLY CONVERSE WITH THEM.
MARIA, IF THAT'S YOUR IDEA OF STIMULATING CONVERSATION--
--WE REALLLLLLLLLLLLLY NEED TO EXTEND OUR SOCIAL CIRCLE.
MY HUSBAND, THE COMEDIAN.
HANK, YOU KNOW VERY WELL THAT INSECTS OUTNUMBER HUMANS BY AT LEAST TWO HUNDRED MILLION TO ONE.
THERE IS AN AVERAGE OF FORTY MILLION INSECTS IN EVERY ACRE OF LAND.
A TECHNOLOGY CAPABLE OF COMMUNICATING WITH THEM WOULD BE WORTH BILLIONS.
BILLIONS--?!?
MARIA PLANNED TO ANNOUNCE HER DISCOVERY AT THE SYMPOSIUM, BUT NEVER GOT THE CHANCE.
THE AUTHORITIES AND I ALWAYS ASSUMED SHE WAS A VICTIM OF RANDOM CHANCE.
WHAT IF SHE WAS THE REAL TARGET--
--AND HER TECH THE MOTIVE?!?
THIS IS CRAZY! NOT EVEN ELIHAS STARR COULD BE THAT RUTHLESS.
ALTHOUGH...
NO! NO! I'VE GOT TO CONTROL MY IMAGINATION.
AND YET...

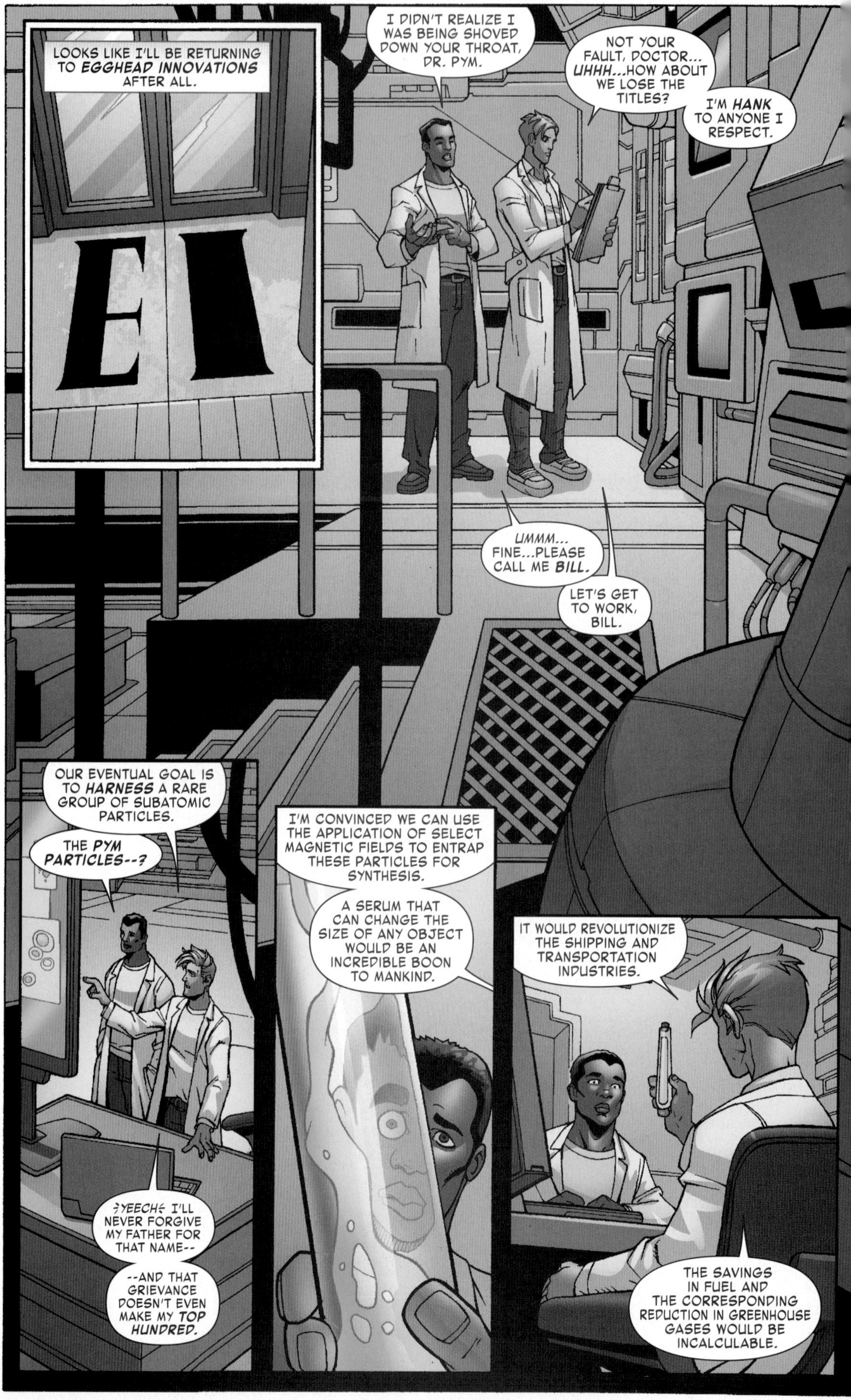
LOOKS LIKE I'LL BE RETURNING TO EGGHEAD INNOVATIONS AFTER ALL.
EI
I DIDN'T REALIZE I WAS BEING SHOVED DOWN YOUR THROAT, DR. PYM.
NOT YOUR FAULT, DOCTOR... UHHH...HOW ABOUT WE LOSE THE TITLES?
I'M HANK TO ANYONE I RESPECT.
UMMM... FINE...PLEASE CALL ME BILL.
LET'S GET TO WORK, BILL.
OUR EVENTUAL GOAL IS TO HARNESS A RARE GROUP OF SUBATOMIC PARTICLES.
THE PYM PARTICLES--?
≠YEECH≠ I'LL NEVER FORGIVE MY FATHER FOR THAT NAME--
--AND THAT GRIEVANCE DOESN'T EVEN MAKE MY TOP HUNDRED.
I'M CONVINCED WE CAN USE THE APPLICATION OF SELECT MAGNETIC FIELDS TO ENTRAP THESE PARTICLES FOR SYNTHESIS.
A SERUM THAT CAN CHANGE THE SIZE OF ANY OBJECT WOULD BE AN INCREDIBLE BOON TO MANKIND.
IT WOULD REVOLUTIONIZE THE SHIPPING AND TRANSPORTATION INDUSTRIES.
THE SAVINGS IN FUEL AND THE CORRESPONDING REDUCTION IN GREENHOUSE GASES WOULD BE INCALCULABLE.

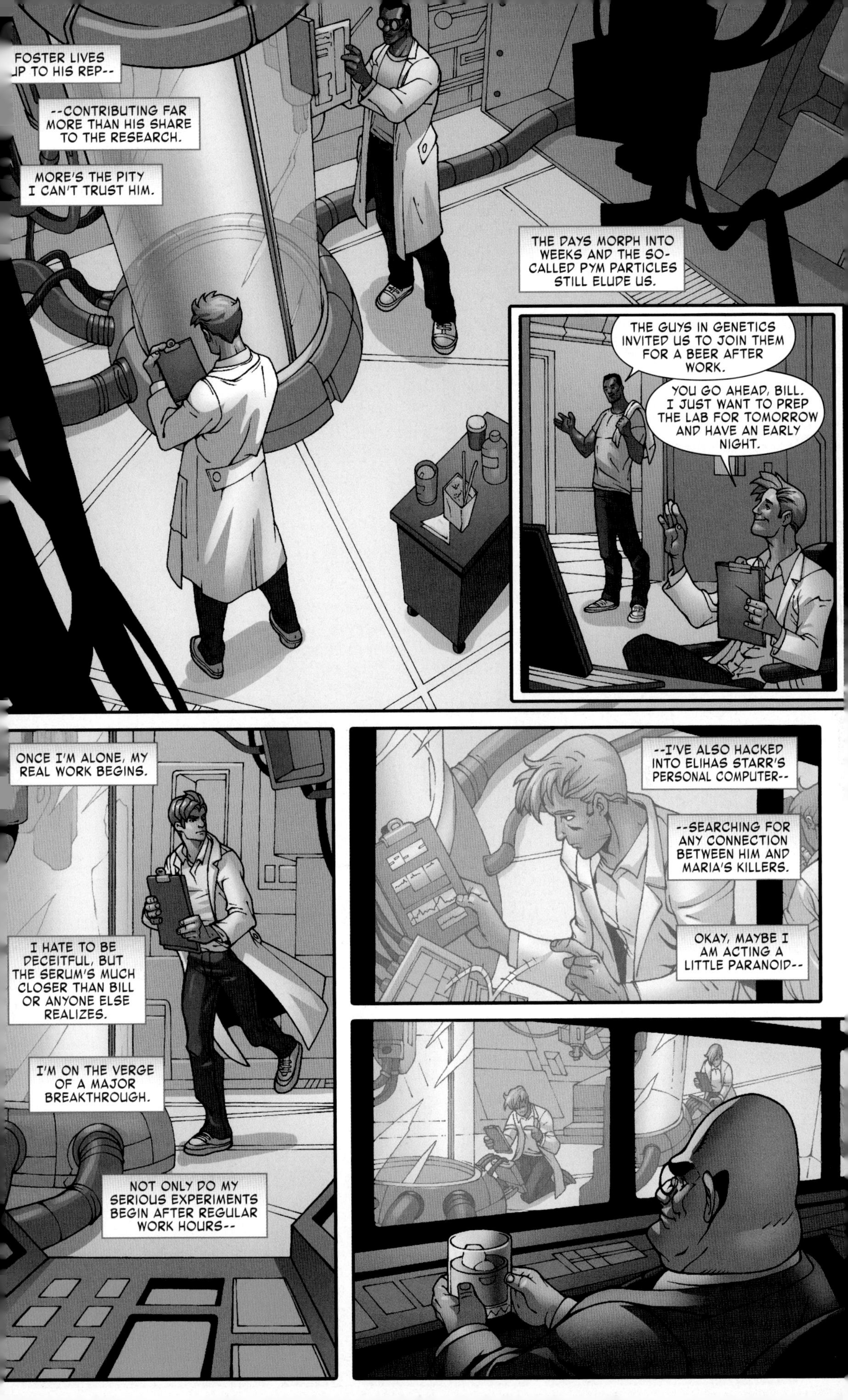

FOSTER LIVES UP TO HIS REP--
--CONTRIBUTING FAR MORE THAN HIS SHARE TO THE RESEARCH.
MORE'S THE PITY I CAN'T TRUST HIM.
THE DAYS MORPH INTO WEEKS AND THE SO-CALLED PYM PARTICLES STILL ELUDE US.
THE GUYS IN GENETICS INVITED US TO JOIN THEM FOR A BEER AFTER WORK.
YOU GO AHEAD, BILL. I JUST WANT TO PREP THE LAB FOR TOMORROW AND HAVE AN EARLY NIGHT.
ONCE I'M ALONE, MY REAL WORK BEGINS.
I HATE TO BE DECEITFUL, BUT THE SERUM'S MUCH CLOSER THAN BILL OR ANYONE ELSE REALIZES.
I'M ON THE VERGE OF A MAJOR BREAKTHROUGH.
NOT ONLY DO MY SERIOUS EXPERIMENTS BEGIN AFTER REGULAR WORK HOURS--
--I'VE ALSO HACKED INTO ELIHAS STARR'S PERSONAL COMPUTER--
--SEARCHING FOR ANY CONNECTION BETWEEN HIM AND MARIA'S KILLERS.
OKAY, MAYBE I AM ACTING A LITTLE PARANOID--

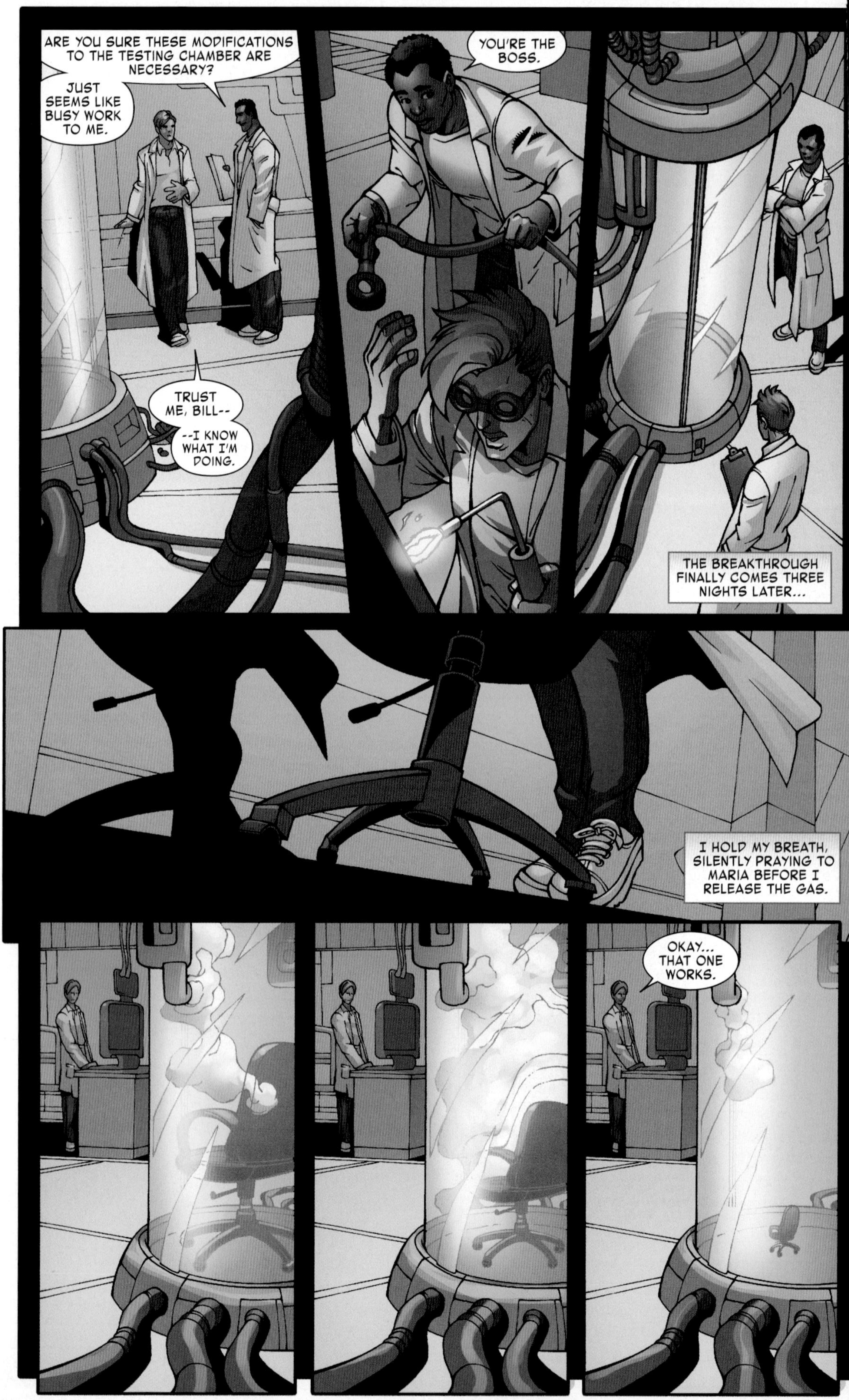
ARE YOU SURE THESE MODIFICATIONS TO THE TESTING CHAMBER ARE NECESSARY?
JUST SEEMS LIKE BUSY WORK TO ME.
TRUST ME, BILL--
--I KNOW WHAT I'M DOING.
YOU'RE THE BOSS.
THE BREAKTHROUGH FINALLY COMES THREE NIGHTS LATER...
I HOLD MY BREATH, SILENTLY PRAYING TO MARIA BEFORE I RELEASE THE GAS.
OKAY... THAT ONE WORKS.

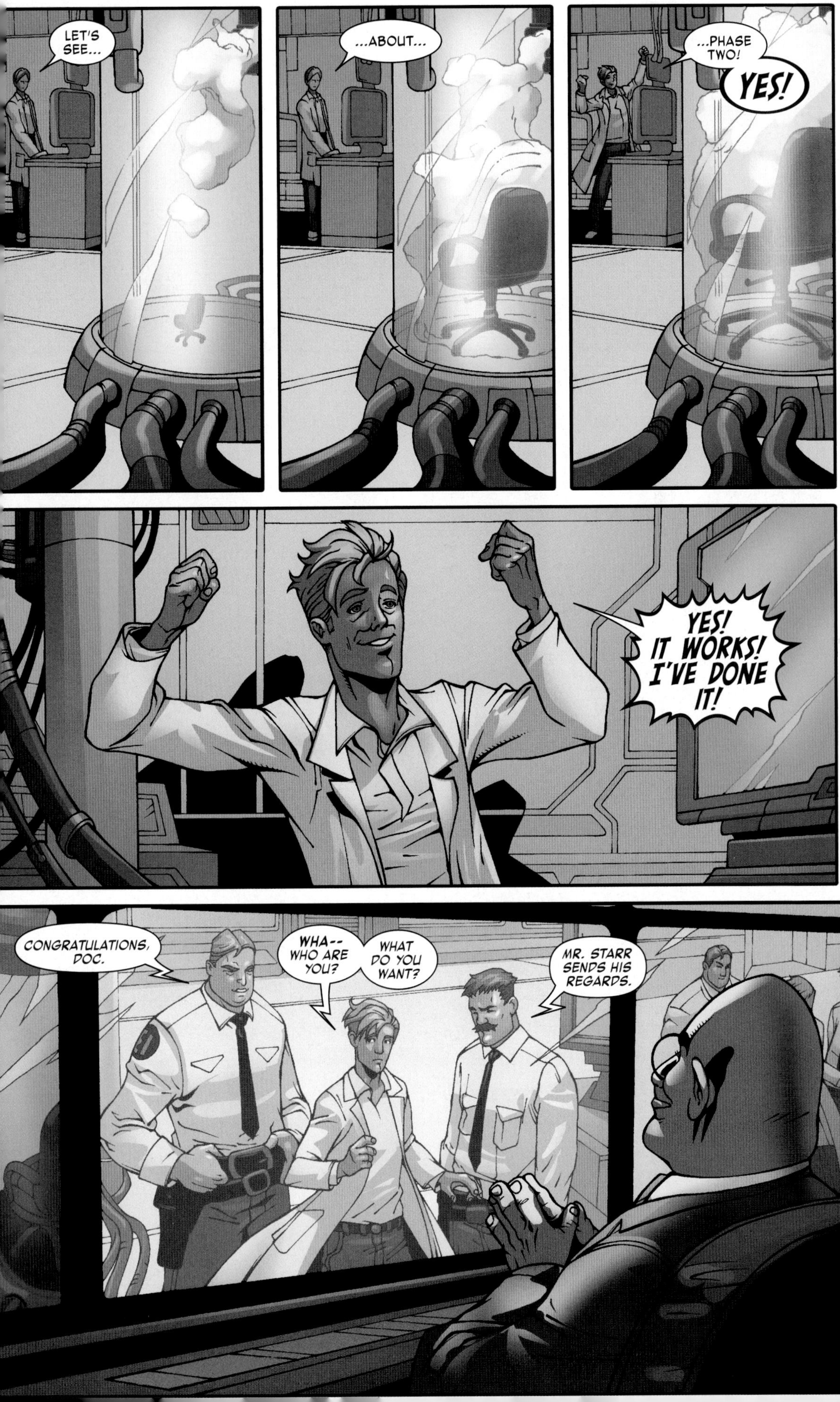
LET'S SEE...
...ABOUT...
...PHASE TWO!
YES!
YES! IT WORKS! I'VE DONE IT!
CONGRATULATIONS, DOC.
WHA-- WHO ARE YOU?
WHAT DO YOU WANT?
MR. STARR SENDS HIS REGARDS.

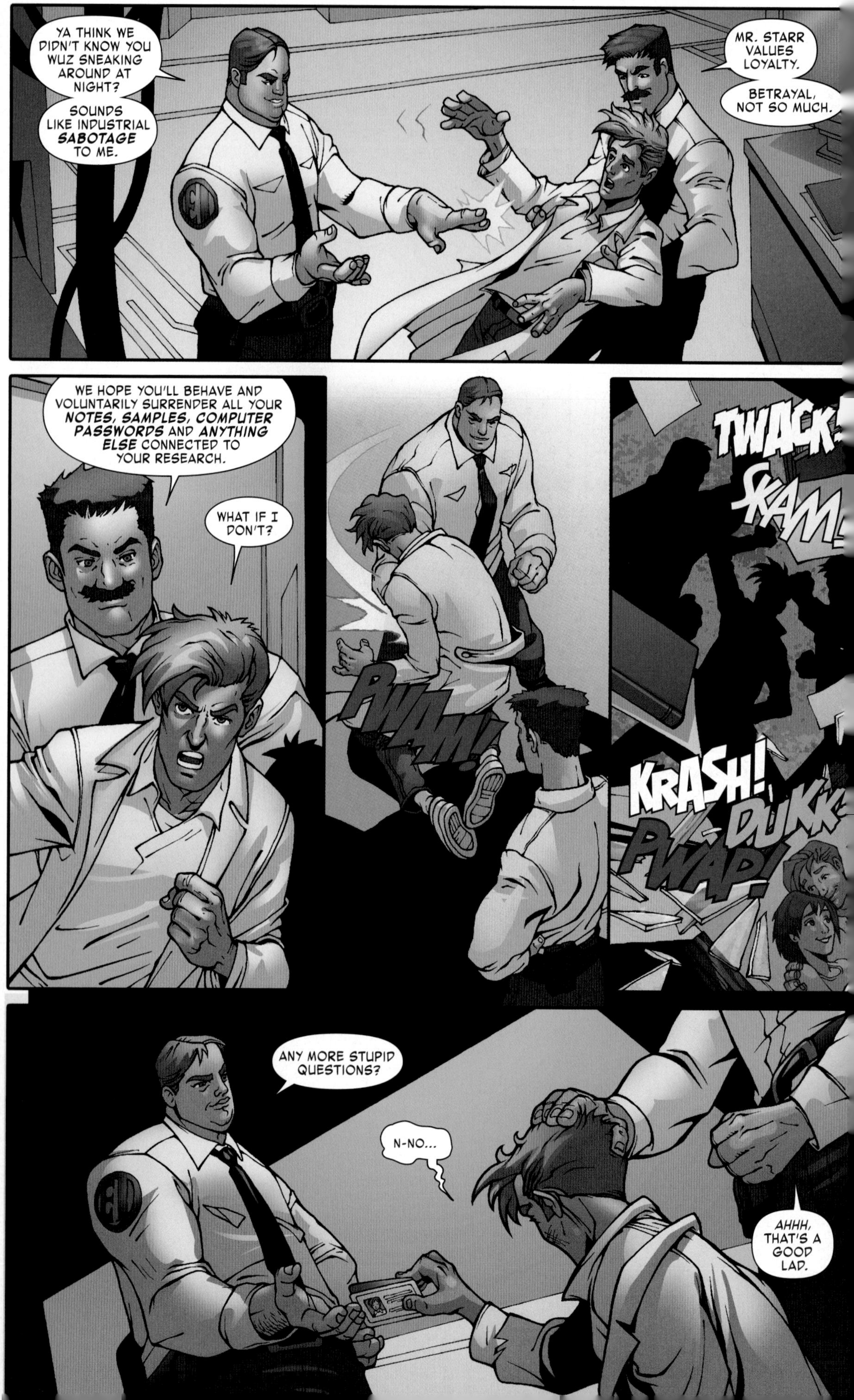
YA THINK WE DIDN'T KNOW YOU WUZ SNEAKING AROUND AT NIGHT?
SOUNDS LIKE INDUSTRIAL **SABOTAGE** TO ME.
MR. STARR VALUES LOYALTY.
BETRAYAL, NOT SO MUCH.
WE HOPE YOU'LL BEHAVE AND VOLUNTARILY SURRENDER ALL YOUR **NOTES, SAMPLES, COMPUTER PASSWORDS** AND **ANYTHING ELSE** CONNECTED TO YOUR RESEARCH.
WHAT IF I DON'T?
PWAM!
TWACK!
SKAM!
KRASH!
DUKK
PWAP!
ANY MORE STUPID QUESTIONS?
N-NO...
AHHH, THAT'S A GOOD LAD.

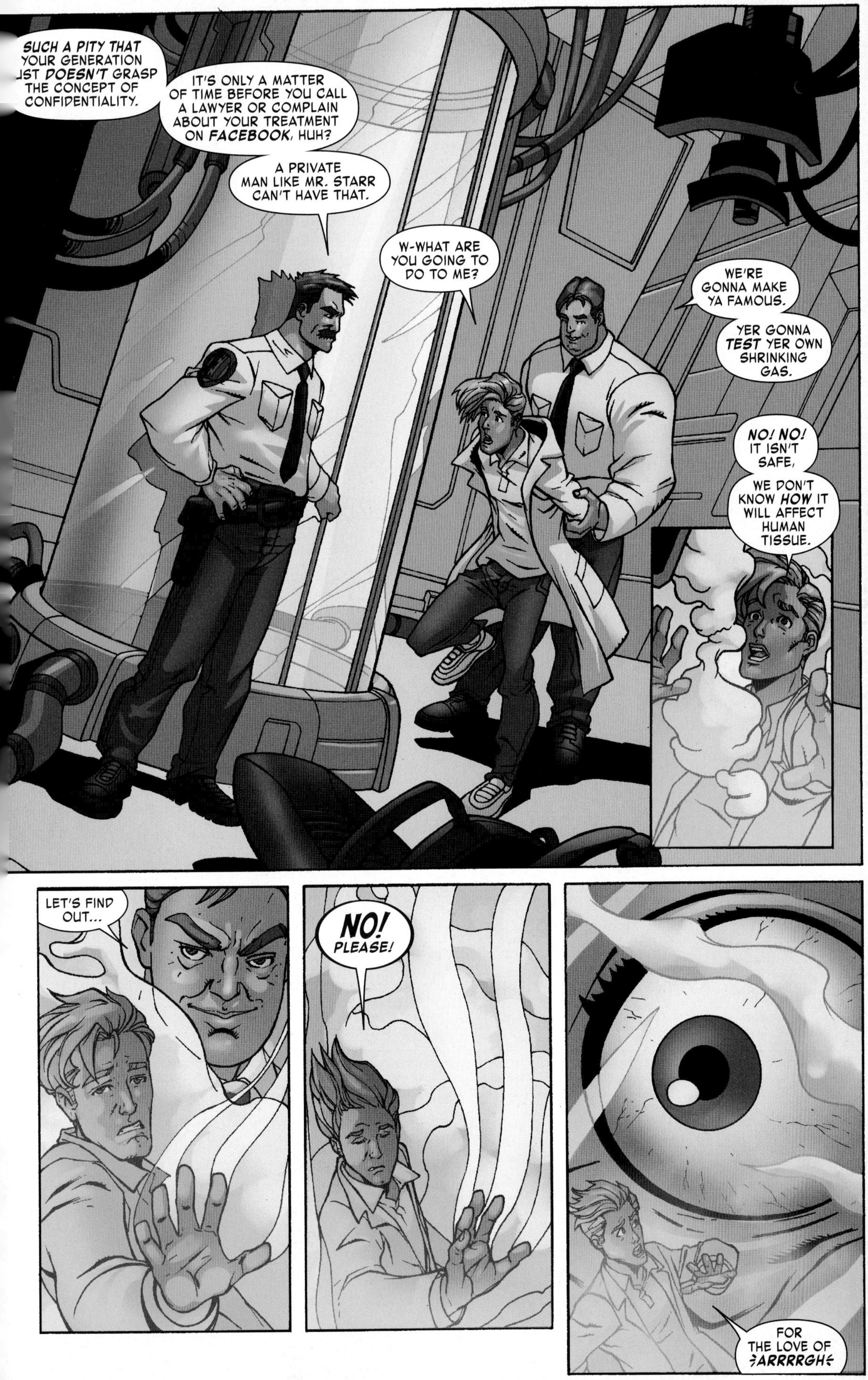
SUCH A PITY THAT YOUR GENERATION JUST DOESN'T GRASP THE CONCEPT OF CONFIDENTIALITY.
IT'S ONLY A MATTER OF TIME BEFORE YOU CALL A LAWYER OR COMPLAIN ABOUT YOUR TREATMENT ON FACEBOOK, HUH?
A PRIVATE MAN LIKE MR. STARR CAN'T HAVE THAT.
W-WHAT ARE YOU GOING TO DO TO ME?
WE'RE GONNA MAKE YA FAMOUS.
YER GONNA TEST YER OWN SHRINKING GAS.
NO! NO! IT ISN'T SAFE,
WE DON'T KNOW HOW IT WILL AFFECT HUMAN TISSUE.
LET'S FIND OUT...
NO! PLEASE!
FOR THE LOVE OF
ARRRRGH

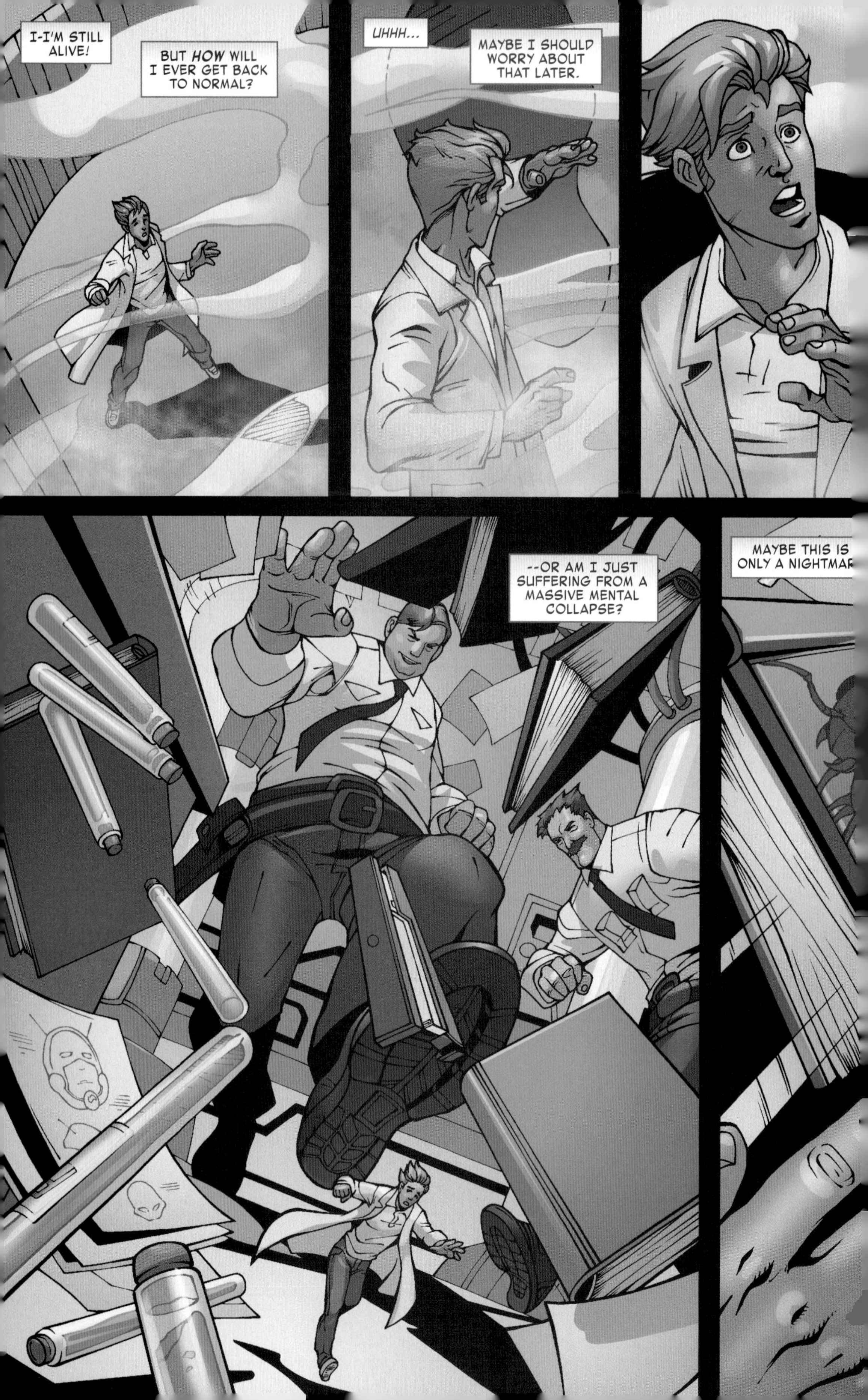
I-I'M STILL ALIVE!
BUT HOW WILL I EVER GET BACK TO NORMAL?
UHHH...
MAYBE I SHOULD WORRY ABOUT THAT LATER.
--OR AM I JUST SUFFERING FROM A MASSIVE MENTAL COLLAPSE?
MAYBE THIS IS ONLY A NIGHTMAR

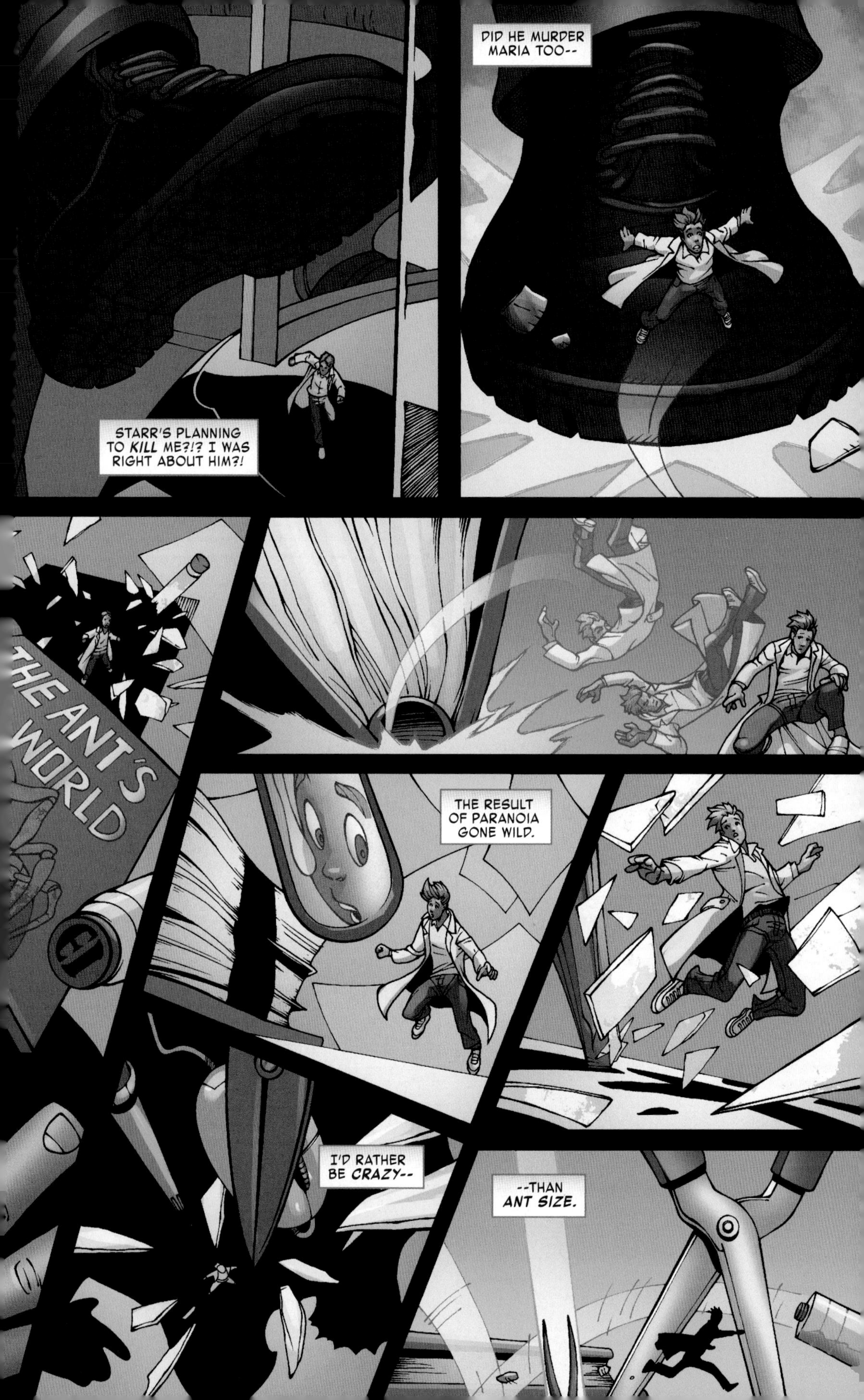
STARR'S PLANNING TO KILL ME?!? I WAS RIGHT ABOUT HIM?!
DID HE MURDER MARIA TOO--
THE ANT'S WORLD
THE RESULT OF PARANOIA GONE WILD.
I'D RATHER BE CRAZY--
--THAN ANT SIZE.

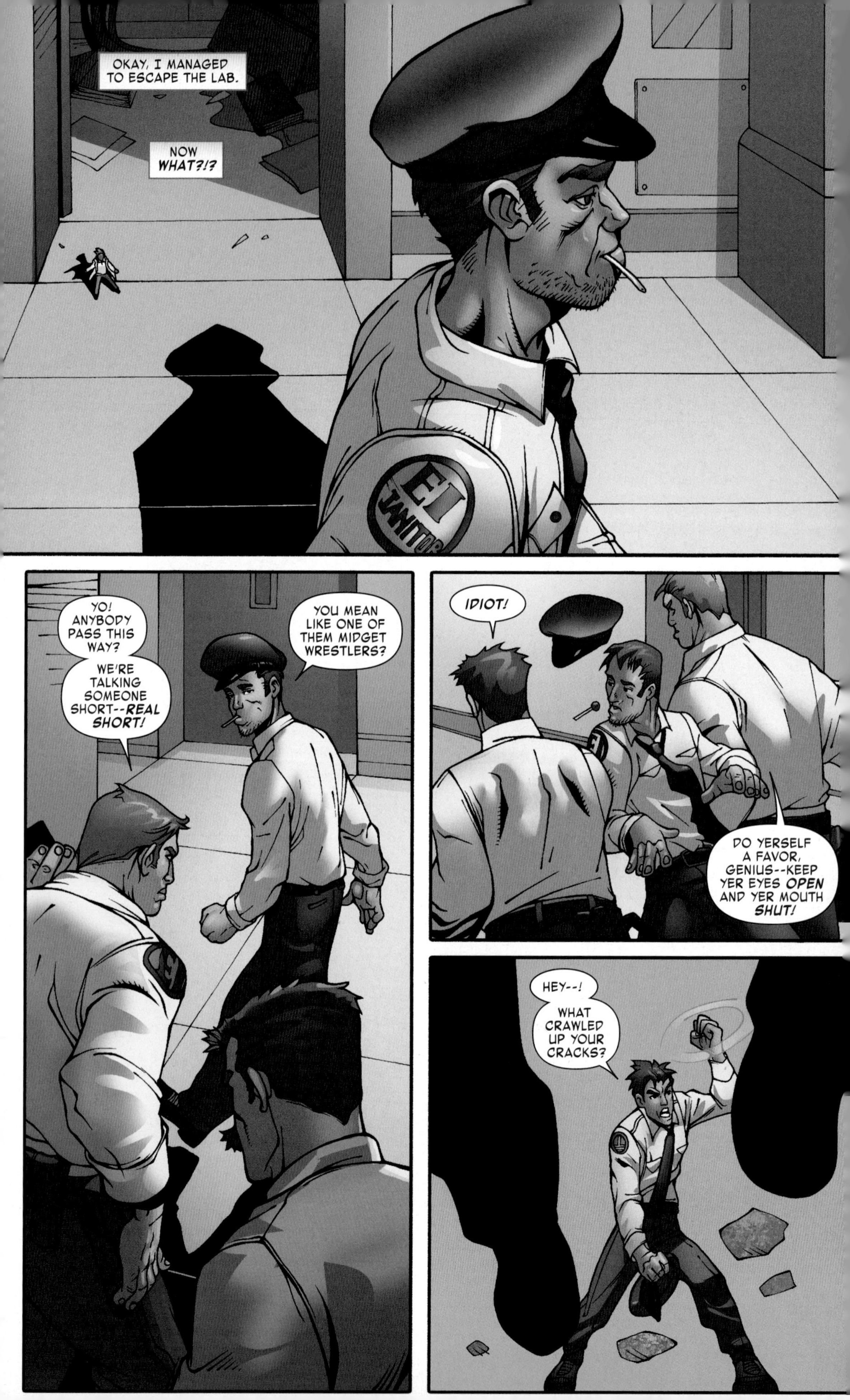
OKAY, I MANAGED TO ESCAPE THE LAB.
NOW WHAT?!?
YO! ANYBODY PASS THIS WAY?
WE'RE TALKING SOMEONE SHORT--REAL SHORT!
YOU MEAN LIKE ONE OF THEM MIDGET WRESTLERS?
IDIOT!
DO YERSELF A FAVOR, GENIUS--KEEP YER EYES OPEN AND YER MOUTH SHUT!
HEY--!
WHAT CRAWLED UP YOUR CRACKS?

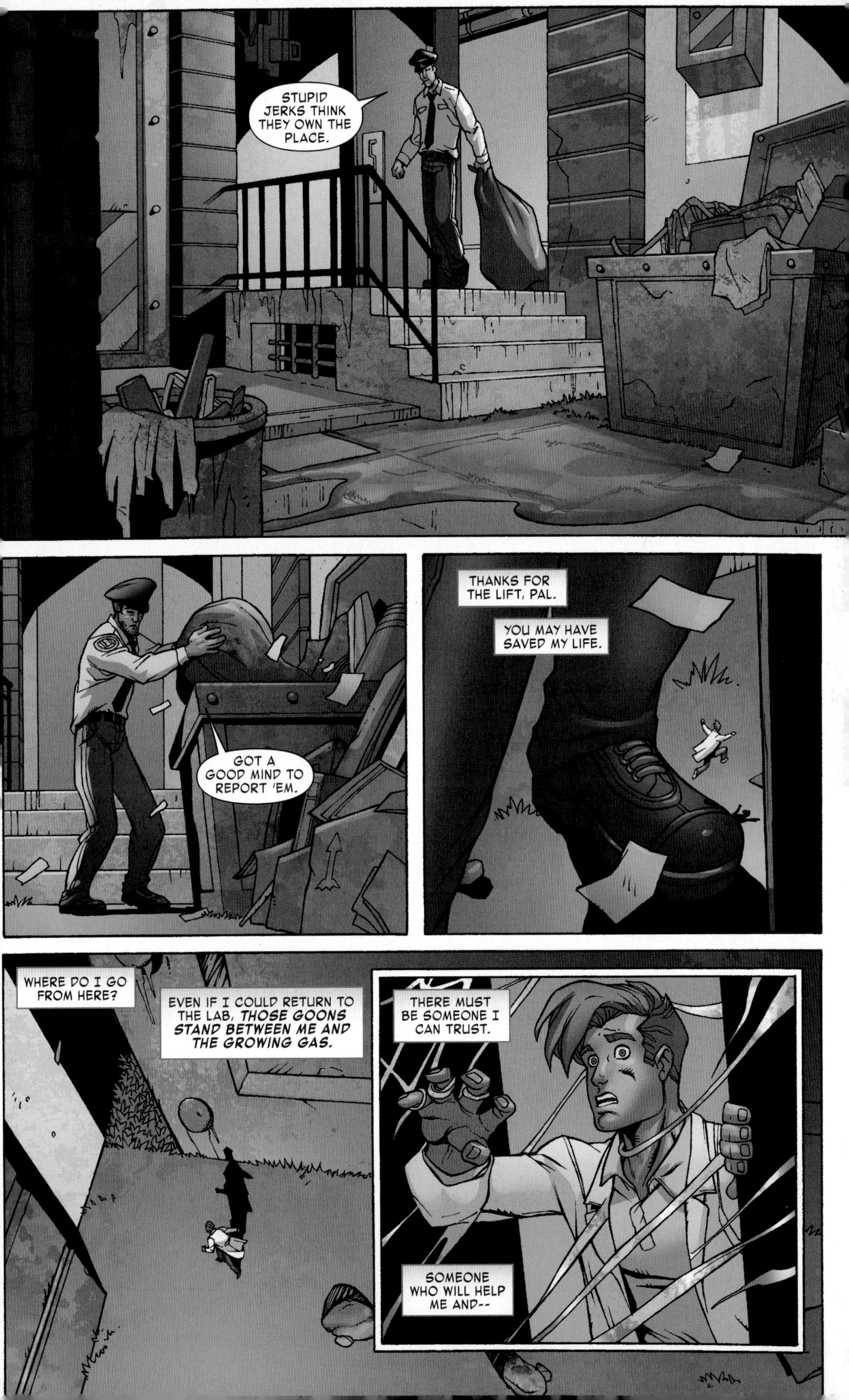
STUPID JERKS THINK THEY OWN THE PLACE.
GOT A GOOD MIND TO REPORT 'EM.
THANKS FOR THE LIFT, PAL.
YOU MAY HAVE SAVED MY LIFE.
WHERE DO I GO FROM HERE?
EVEN IF I COULD RETURN TO THE LAB, THOSE GOONS STAND BETWEEN ME AND THE GROWING GAS.
THERE MUST BE SOMEONE I CAN TRUST.
SOMEONE WHO WILL HELP ME AND--

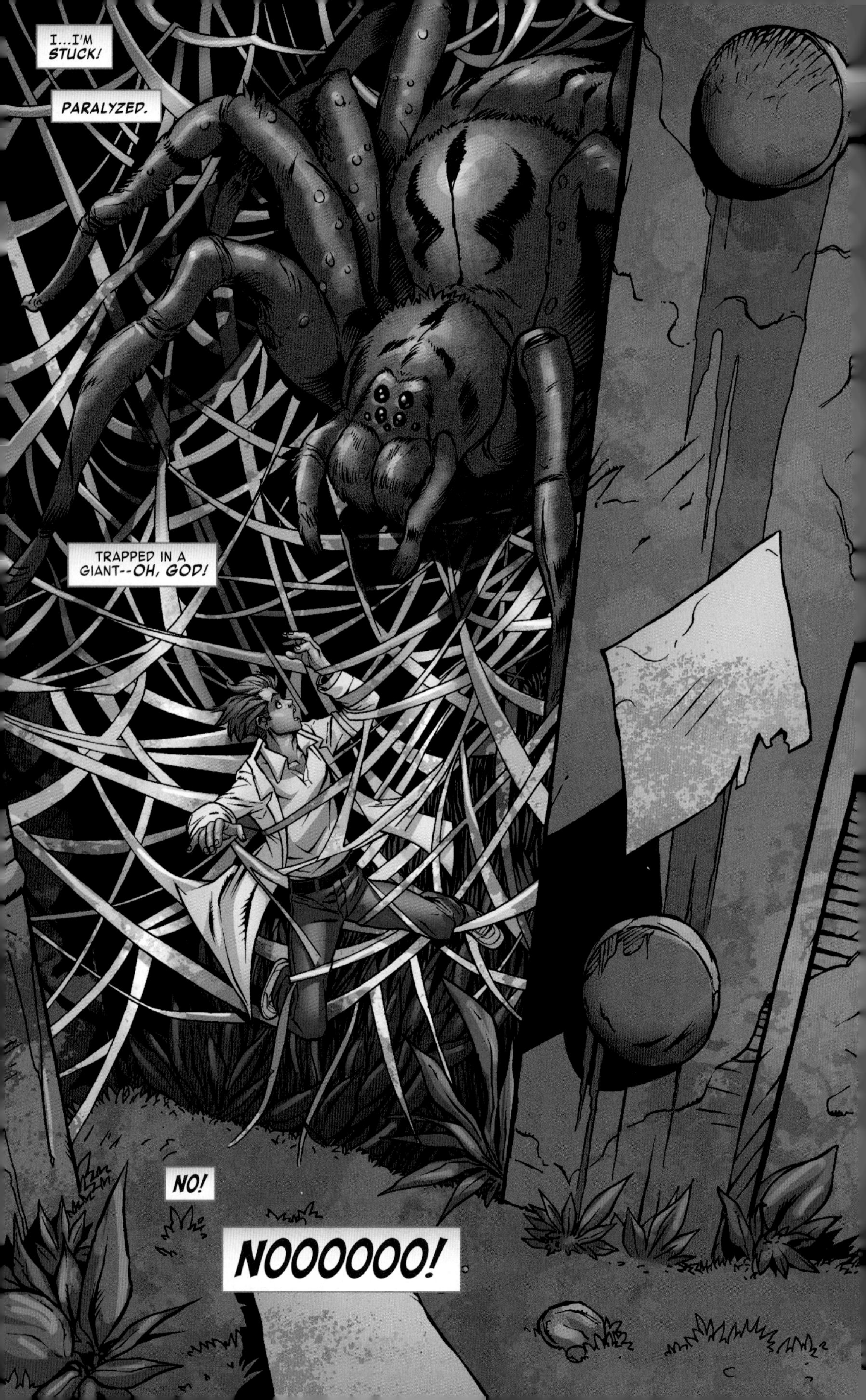
I...I'M STUCK!
PARALYZED.
TRAPPED IN A GIANT--OH, GOD!
NO!
NOOOOOO!

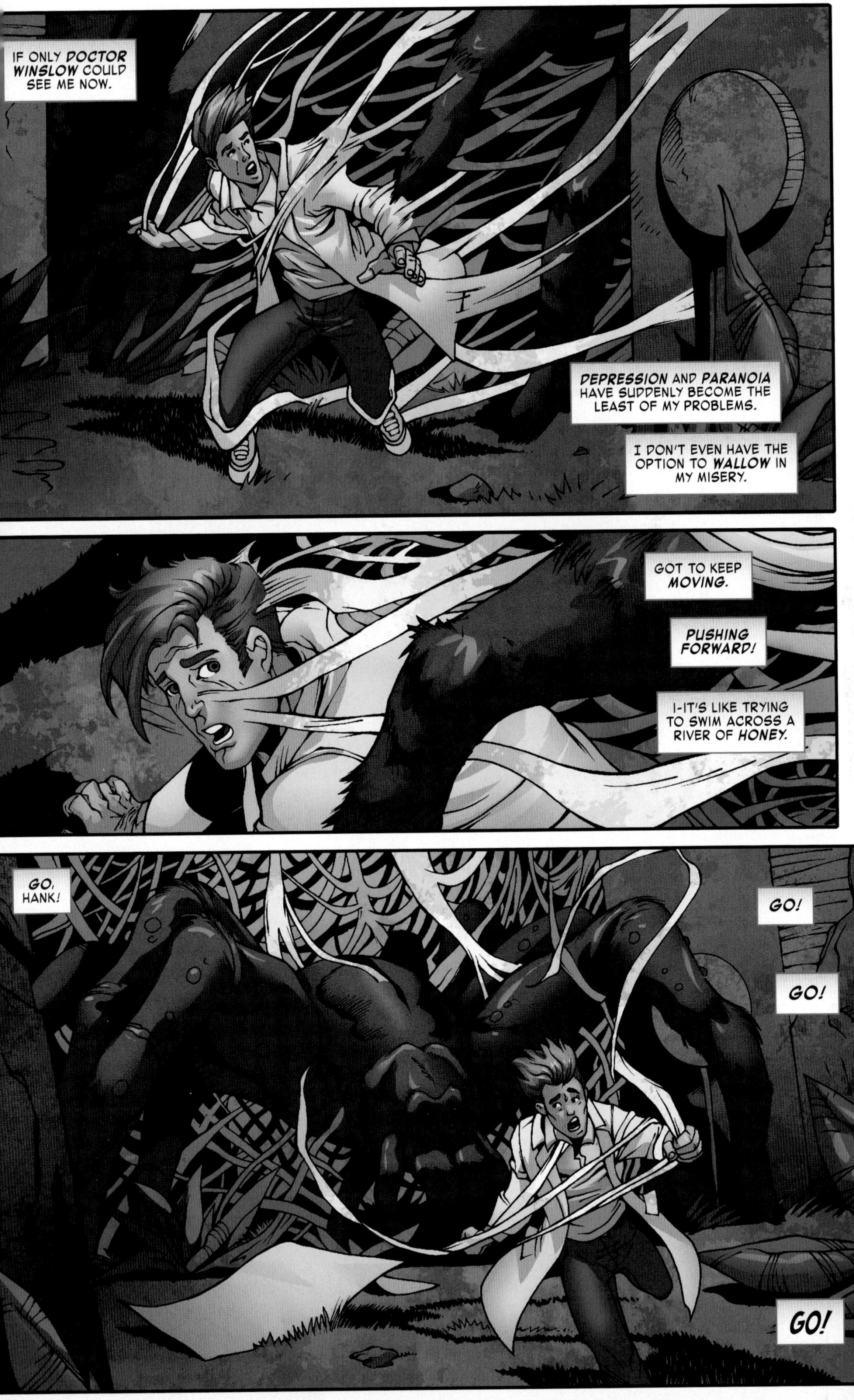
IF ONLY *DOCTOR WINSLOW* COULD SEE ME NOW.
*DEPRESSION* AND *PARANOIA* HAVE SUDDENLY BECOME THE LEAST OF MY PROBLEMS.
I DON'T EVEN HAVE THE OPTION TO *WALLOW* IN MY MISERY.
GOT TO KEEP *MOVING.*
*PUSHING FORWARD!*
I-IT'S LIKE TRYING TO SWIM ACROSS A RIVER OF *HONEY.*
GO, HANK!
*GO!*
*GO!*
*GO!*

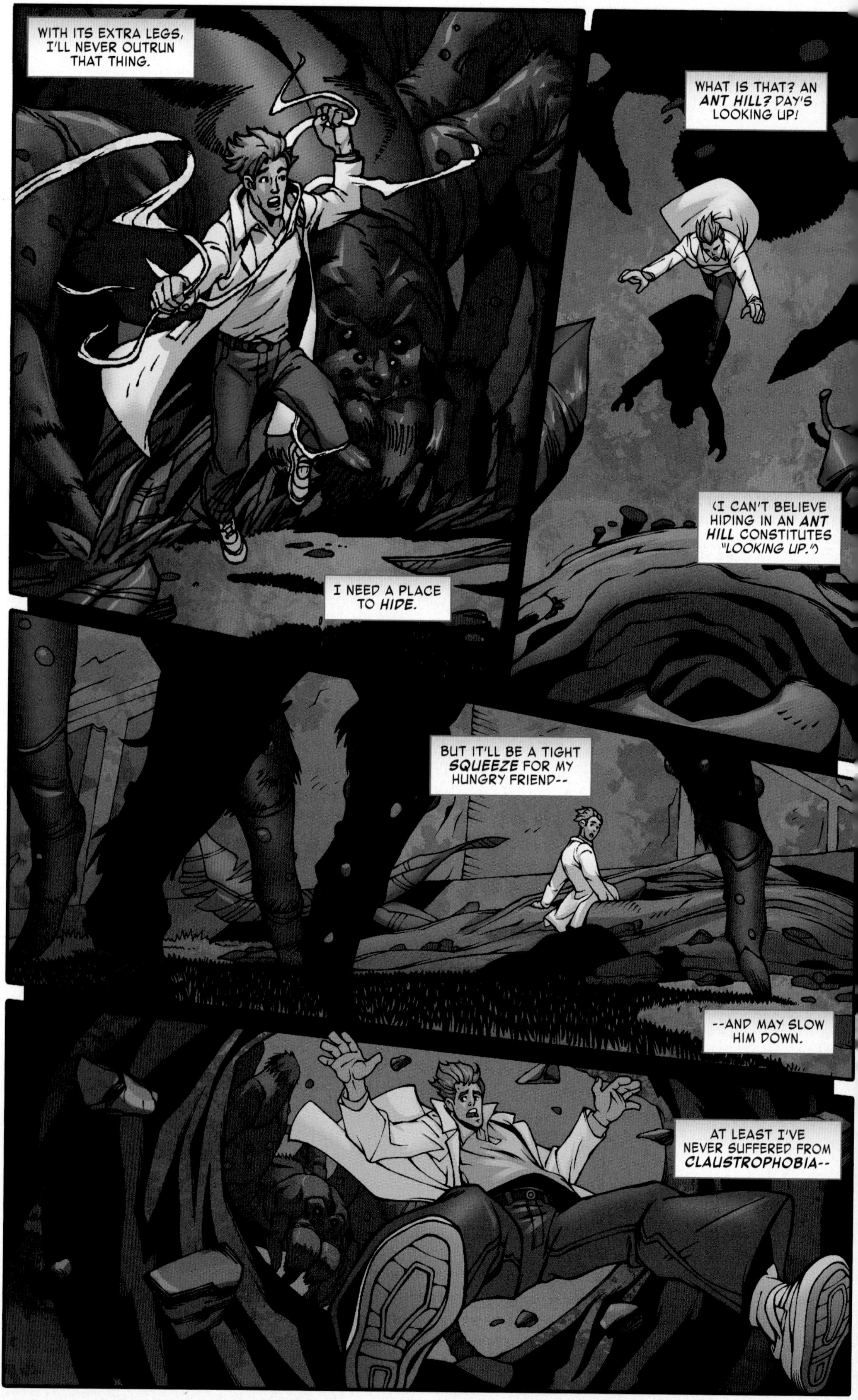
WITH ITS EXTRA LEGS, I'LL NEVER OUTRUN THAT THING.
WHAT IS THAT? AN ANT HILL? DAY'S LOOKING UP!
(I CAN'T BELIEVE HIDING IN AN ANT HILL CONSTITUTES "LOOKING UP.")
I NEED A PLACE TO HIDE.
BUT IT'LL BE A TIGHT SQUEEZE FOR MY HUNGRY FRIEND--
--AND MAY SLOW HIM DOWN.
AT LEAST I'VE NEVER SUFFERED FROM CLAUSTROPHOBIA--

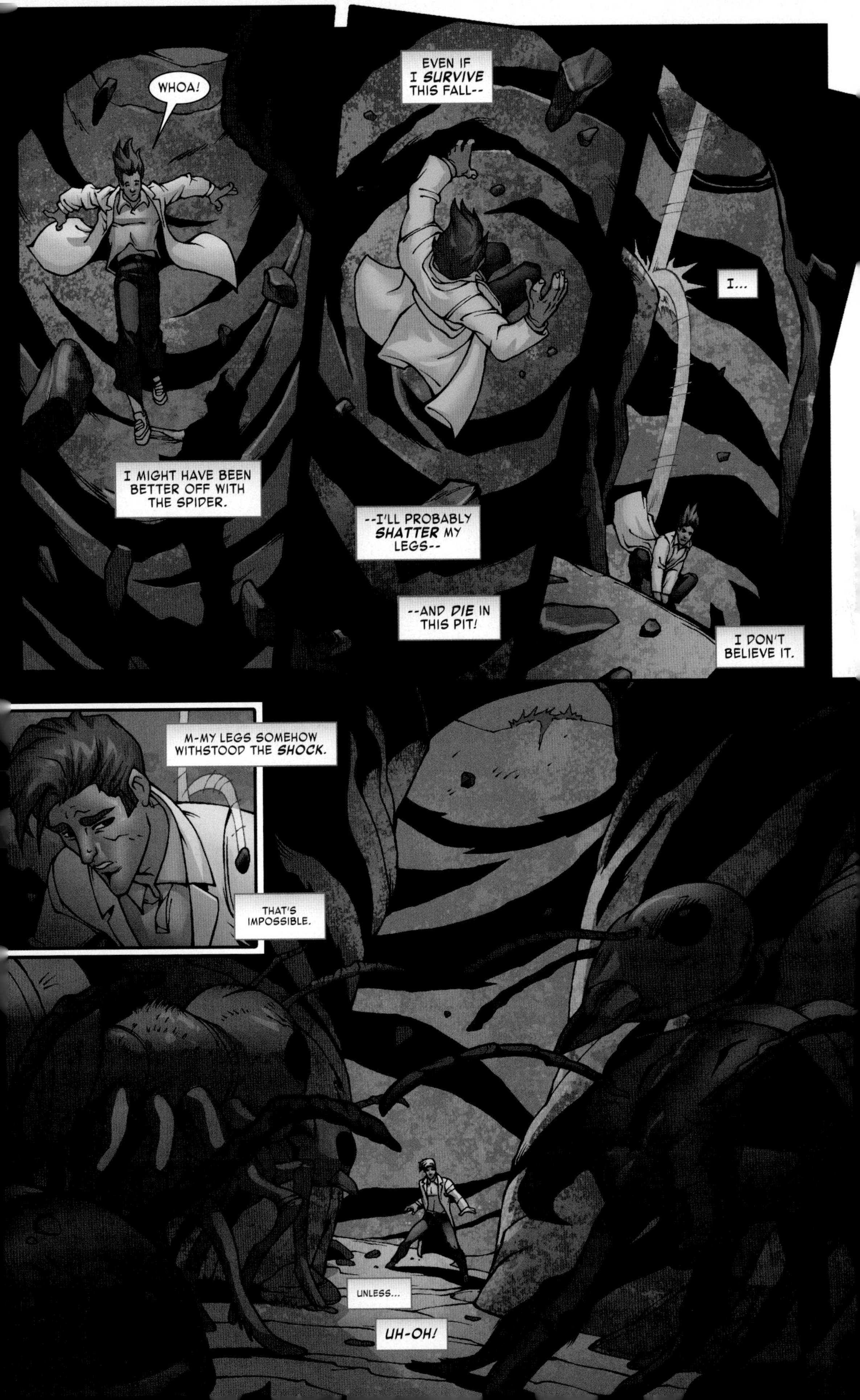
WHOA!
I MIGHT HAVE BEEN BETTER OFF WITH THE SPIDER.
EVEN IF I SURVIVE THIS FALL--
--I'LL PROBABLY SHATTER MY LEGS--
--AND DIE IN THIS PIT!
I...
I DON'T BELIEVE IT.
M-MY LEGS SOMEHOW WITHSTOOD THE SHOCK.
THAT'S IMPOSSIBLE.
UNLESS...
UH-OH!

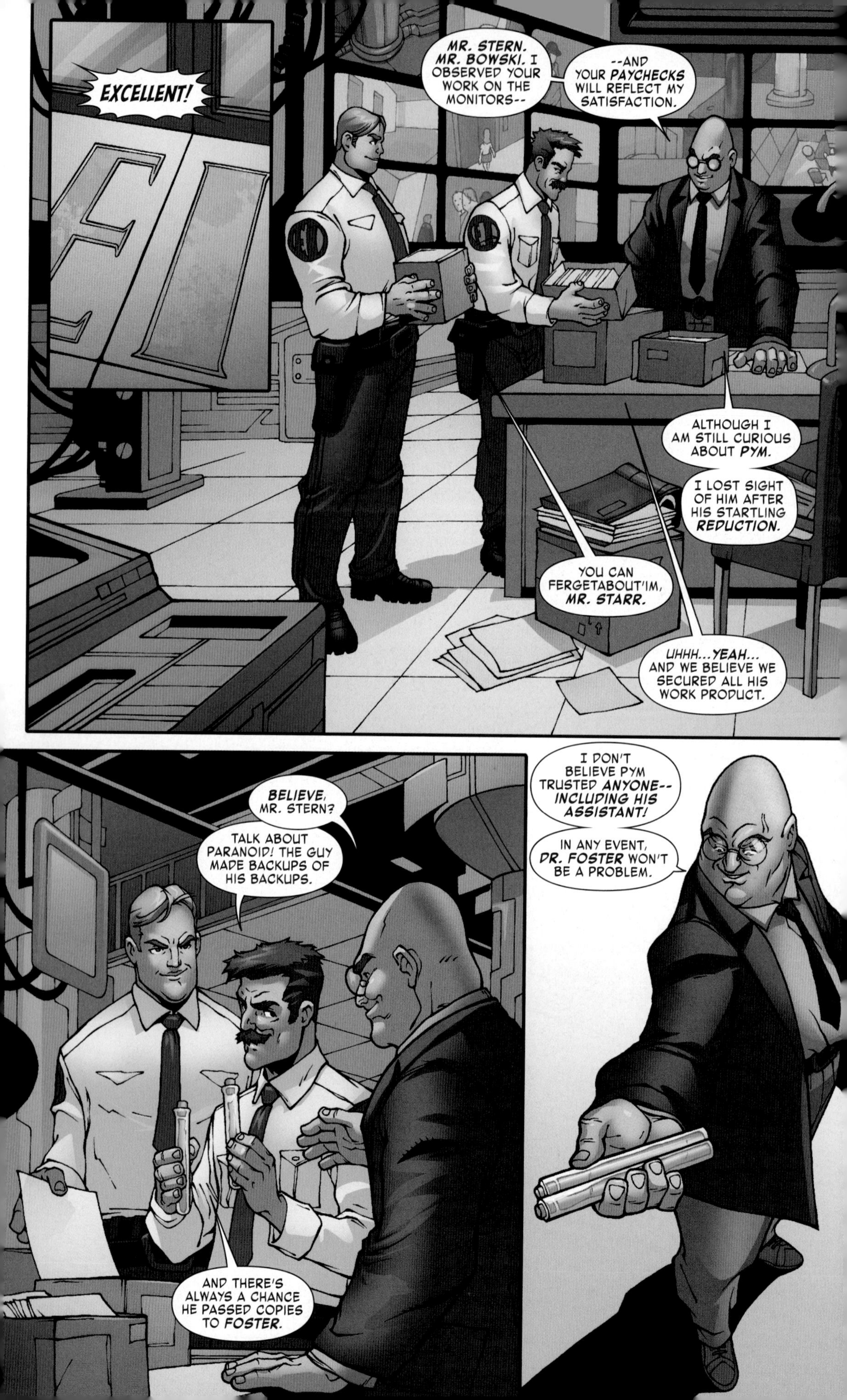
EXCELLENT!
MR. STERN. MR. BOWSKI. I OBSERVED YOUR WORK ON THE MONITORS--
--AND YOUR PAYCHECKS WILL REFLECT MY SATISFACTION.
ALTHOUGH I AM STILL CURIOUS ABOUT PYM.
I LOST SIGHT OF HIM AFTER HIS STARTLING REDUCTION.
YOU CAN FERGETABOUT'IM, MR. STARR.
UHHH...YEAH... AND WE BELIEVE WE SECURED ALL HIS WORK PRODUCT.
BELIEVE, MR. STERN?
TALK ABOUT PARANOID! THE GUY MADE BACKUPS OF HIS BACKUPS.
AND THERE'S ALWAYS A CHANCE HE PASSED COPIES TO FOSTER.
I DON'T BELIEVE PYM TRUSTED ANYONE-- INCLUDING HIS ASSISTANT!
IN ANY EVENT, DR. FOSTER WON'T BE A PROBLEM.

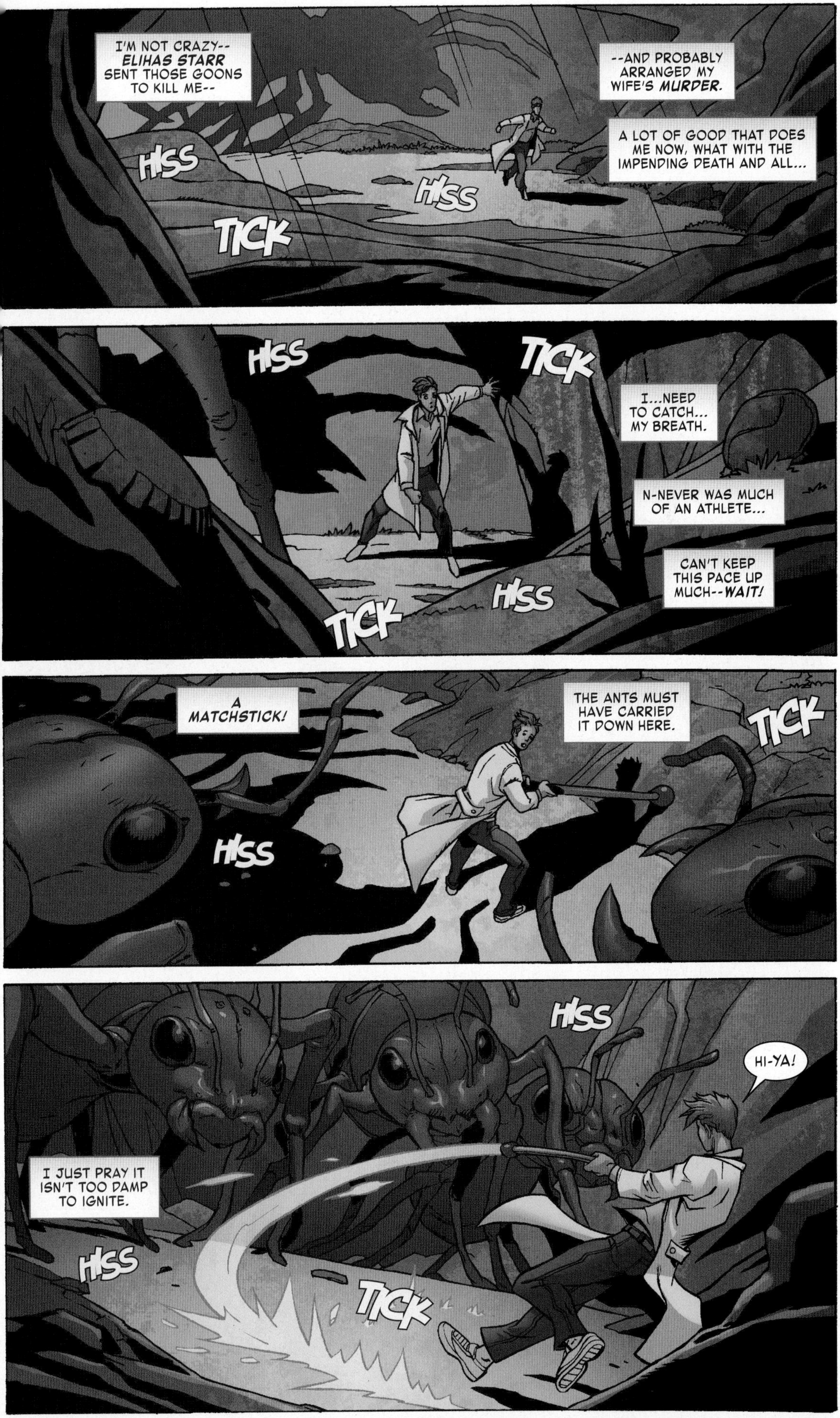
I'M NOT CRAZY-- ELIHAS STARR SENT THOSE GOONS TO KILL ME--
--AND PROBABLY ARRANGED MY WIFE'S MURDER.
A LOT OF GOOD THAT DOES ME NOW, WHAT WITH THE IMPENDING DEATH AND ALL...
HISS
HISS
TICK
HISS
TICK
I...NEED TO CATCH... MY BREATH.
N-NEVER WAS MUCH OF AN ATHLETE...
CAN'T KEEP THIS PACE UP MUCH--WAIT!
TICK
HISS
A MATCHSTICK!
THE ANTS MUST HAVE CARRIED IT DOWN HERE.
TICK
HISS
HISS
HI-YA!
I JUST PRAY IT ISN'T TOO DAMP TO IGNITE.
HISS
TICK

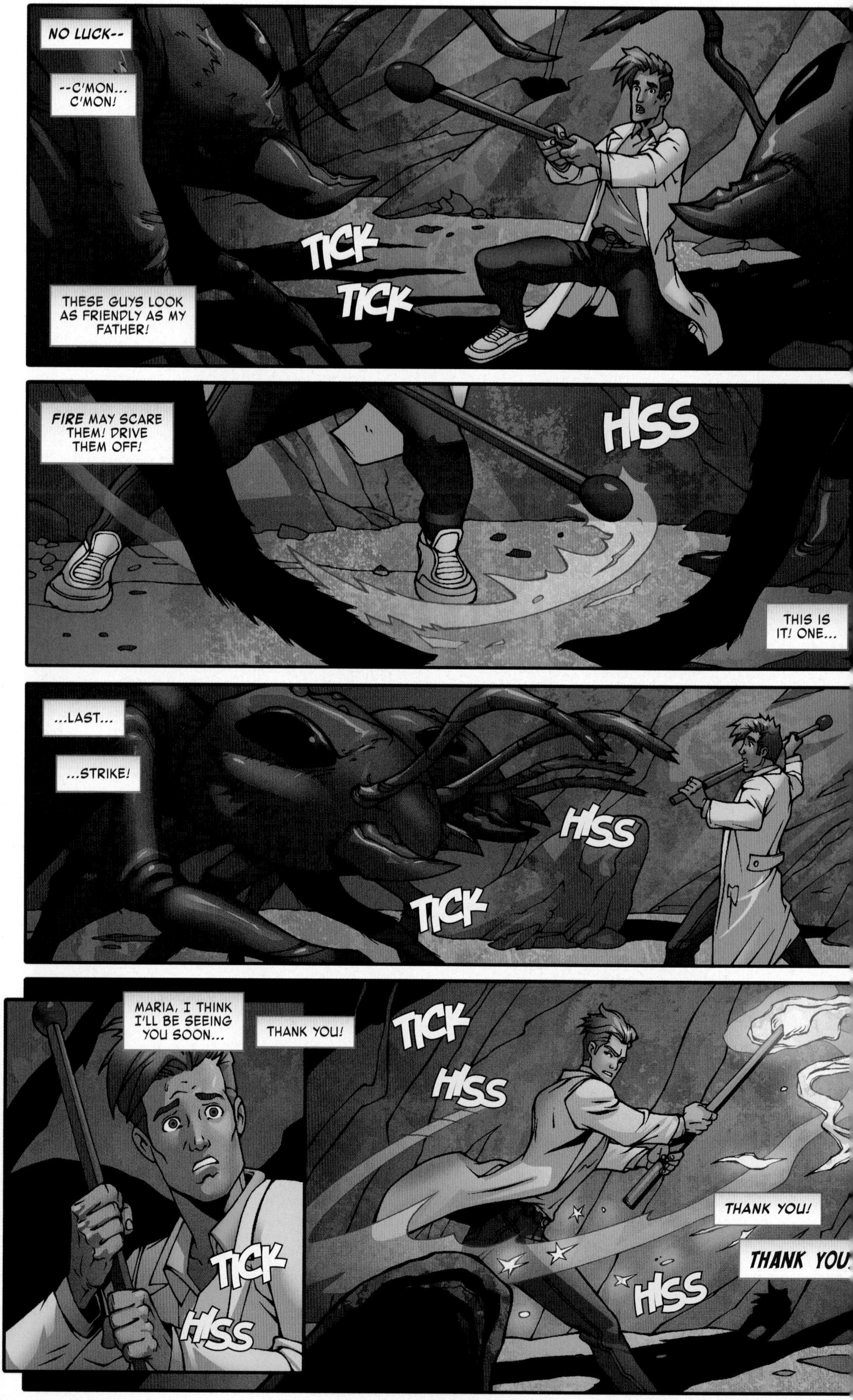

NO LUCK--
--C'MON... C'MON!
TICK
TICK
THESE GUYS LOOK AS FRIENDLY AS MY FATHER!
FIRE MAY SCARE THEM! DRIVE THEM OFF!
HISS
THIS IS IT! ONE...
...LAST...
...STRIKE!
HISS
TICK
MARIA, I THINK I'LL BE SEEING YOU SOON...
TICK
HISS
THANK YOU!
TICK
HISS
THANK YOU!
THANK YOU
HISS

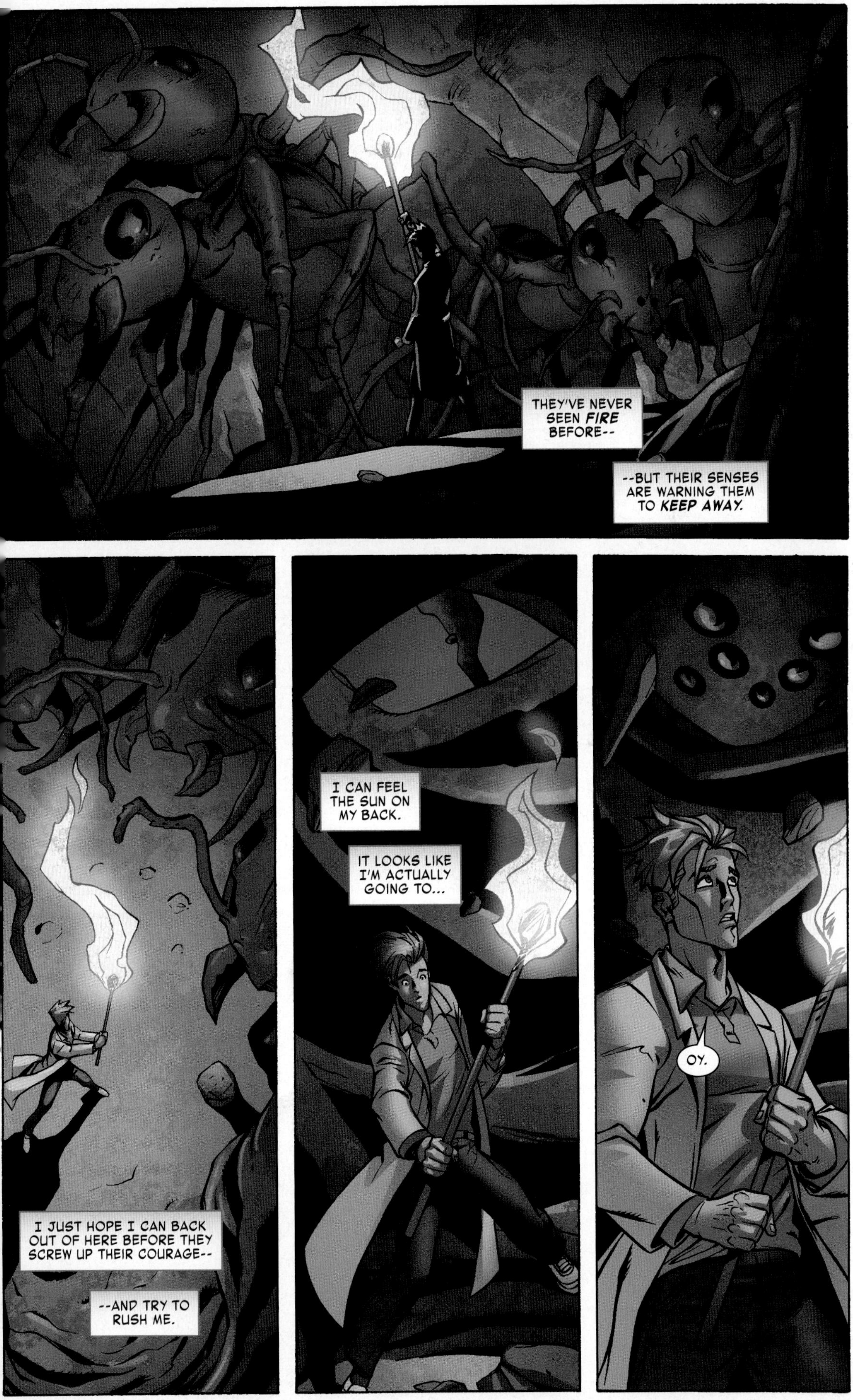
THEY'VE NEVER SEEN FIRE BEFORE--
--BUT THEIR SENSES ARE WARNING THEM TO KEEP AWAY.
I JUST HOPE I CAN BACK OUT OF HERE BEFORE THEY SCREW UP THEIR COURAGE--
--AND TRY TO RUSH ME.
I CAN FEEL THE SUN ON MY BACK.
IT LOOKS LIKE I'M ACTUALLY GOING TO...
OY.

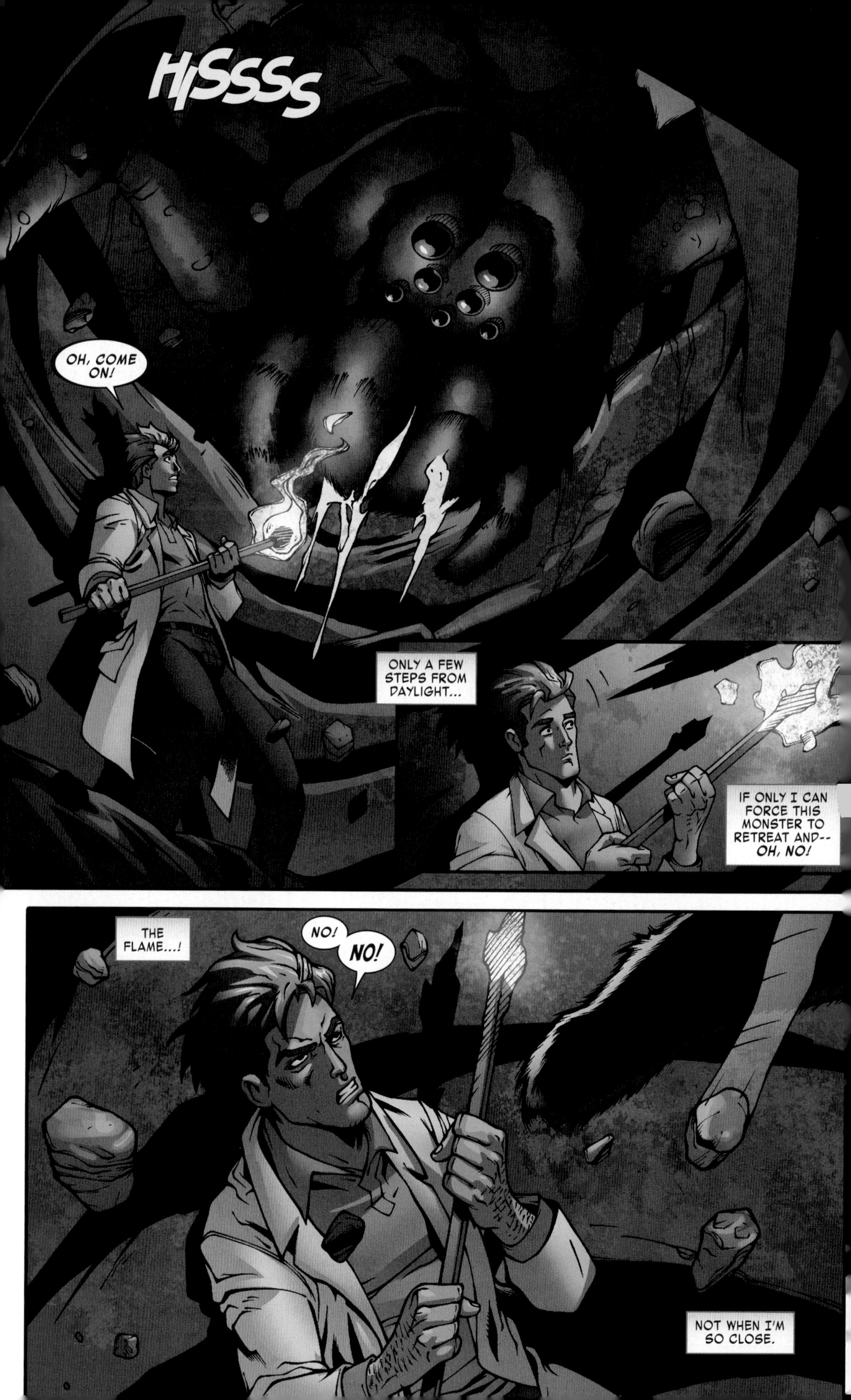
HISSSS
OH, COME ON!
ONLY A FEW STEPS FROM DAYLIGHT...
IF ONLY I CAN FORCE THIS MONSTER TO RETREAT AND-- OH, NO!
THE FLAME...!
NO!
NO!
NOT WHEN I'M SO CLOSE.

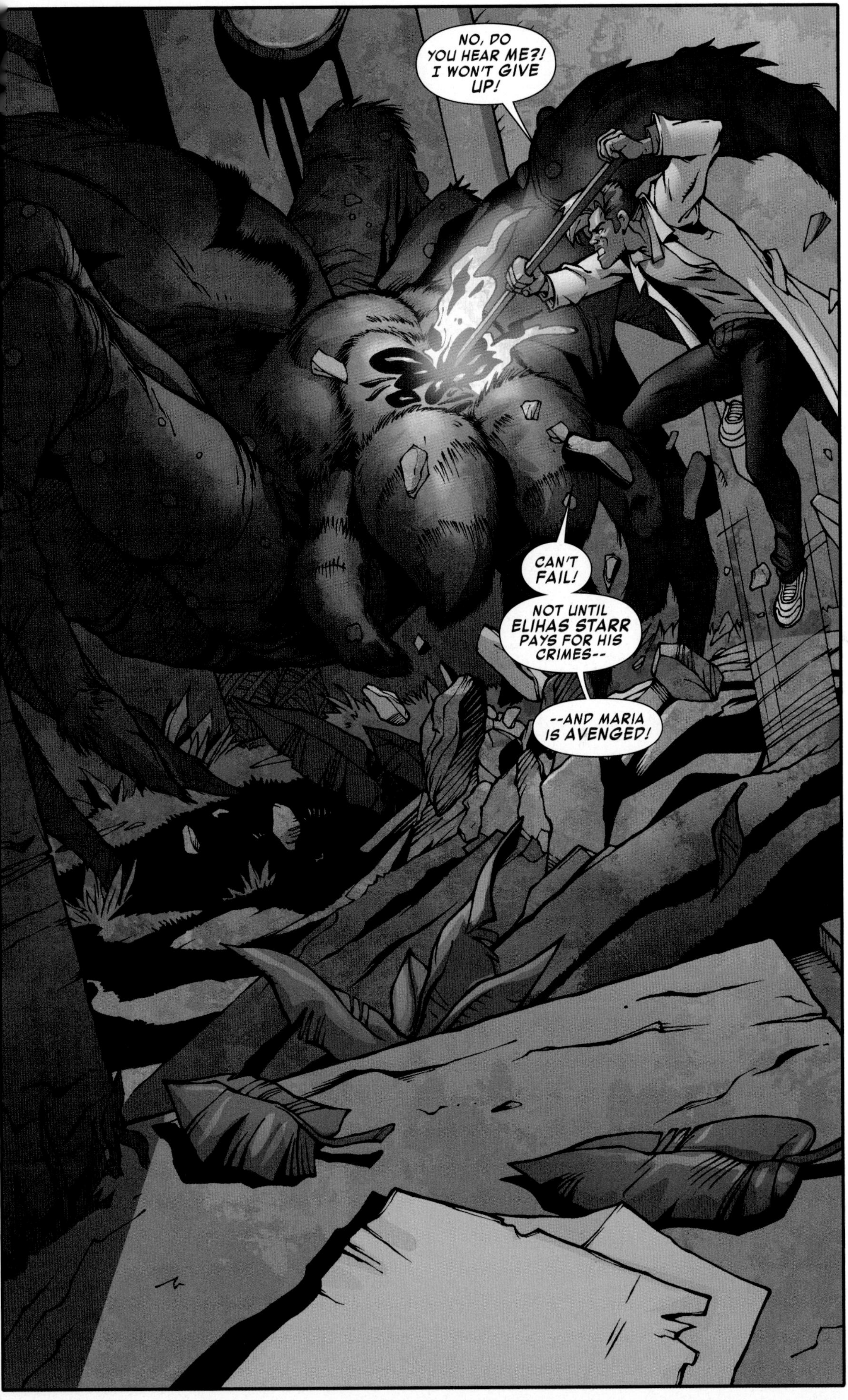
NO, DO YOU HEAR ME?! I WON'T GIVE UP!
CAN'T FAIL!
NOT UNTIL ELIHAS STARR PAYS FOR HIS CRIMES--
--AND MARIA IS AVENGED!

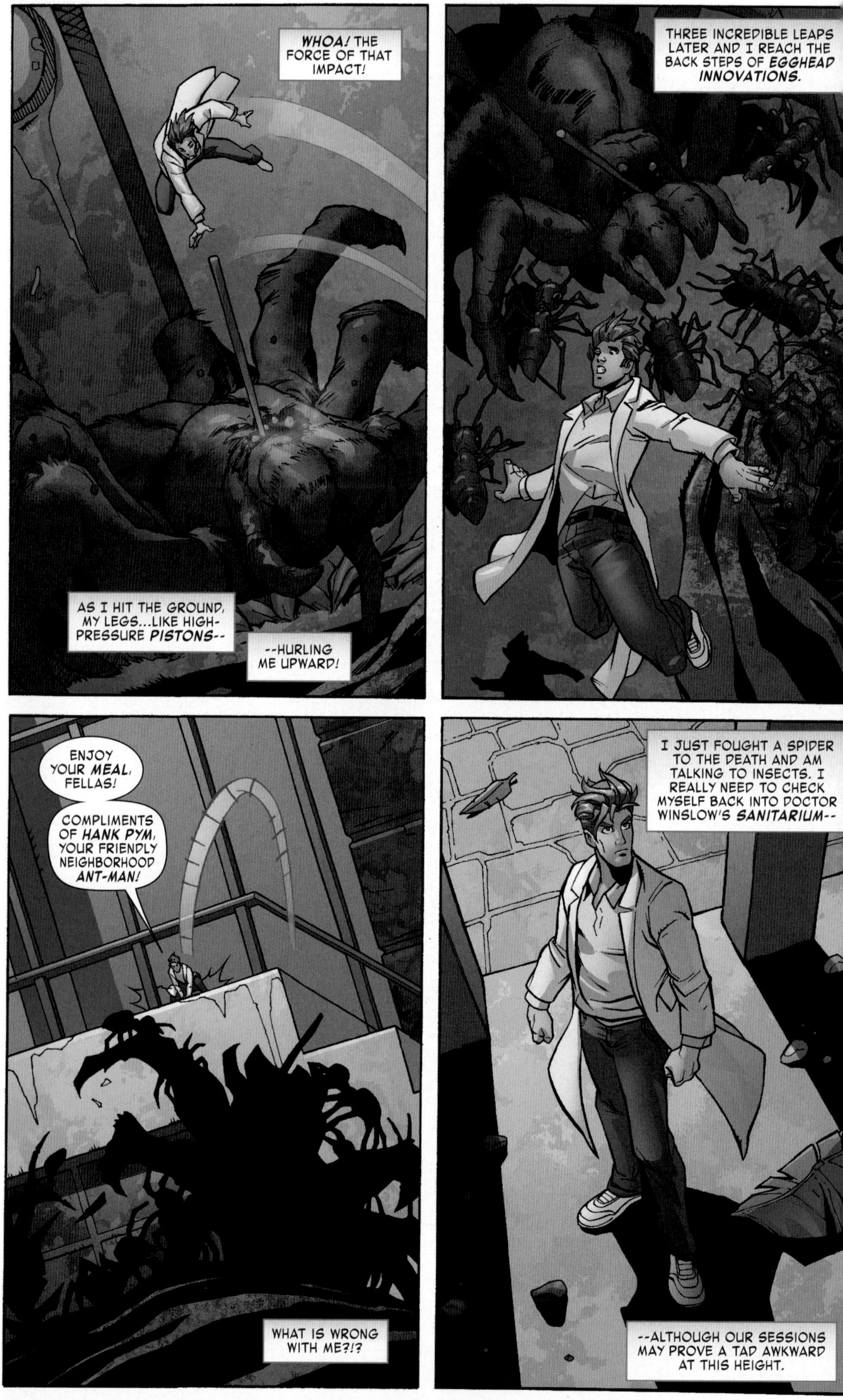
WHOA! THE FORCE OF THAT IMPACT!
AS I HIT THE GROUND, MY LEGS...LIKE HIGH-PRESSURE PISTONS--
--HURLING ME UPWARD!
THREE INCREDIBLE LEAPS LATER AND I REACH THE BACK STEPS OF EGGHEAD INNOVATIONS.
ENJOY YOUR MEAL, FELLAS!
COMPLIMENTS OF HANK PYM, YOUR FRIENDLY NEIGHBORHOOD ANT-MAN!
WHAT IS WRONG WITH ME?!?
I JUST FOUGHT A SPIDER TO THE DEATH AND AM TALKING TO INSECTS. I REALLY NEED TO CHECK MYSELF BACK INTO DOCTOR WINSLOW'S SANITARIUM--
--ALTHOUGH OUR SESSIONS MAY PROVE A TAD AWKWARD AT THIS HEIGHT.

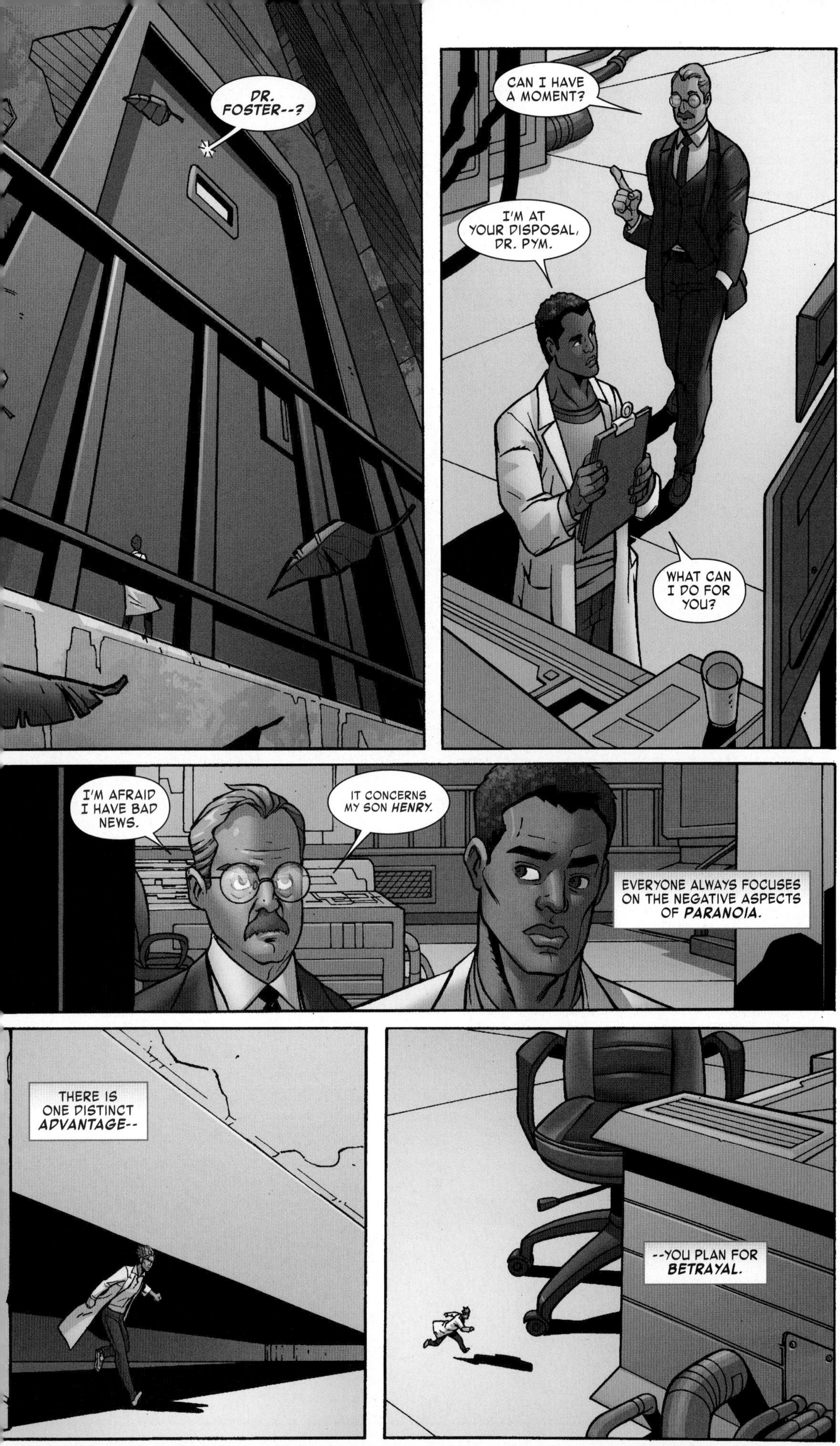
DR. FOSTER--?
CAN I HAVE A MOMENT?
I'M AT YOUR DISPOSAL, DR. PYM.
WHAT CAN I DO FOR YOU?
I'M AFRAID I HAVE BAD NEWS.
IT CONCERNS MY SON HENRY.
EVERYONE ALWAYS FOCUSES ON THE NEGATIVE ASPECTS OF PARANOIA.
THERE IS ONE DISTINCT ADVANTAGE--
--YOU PLAN FOR BETRAYAL.

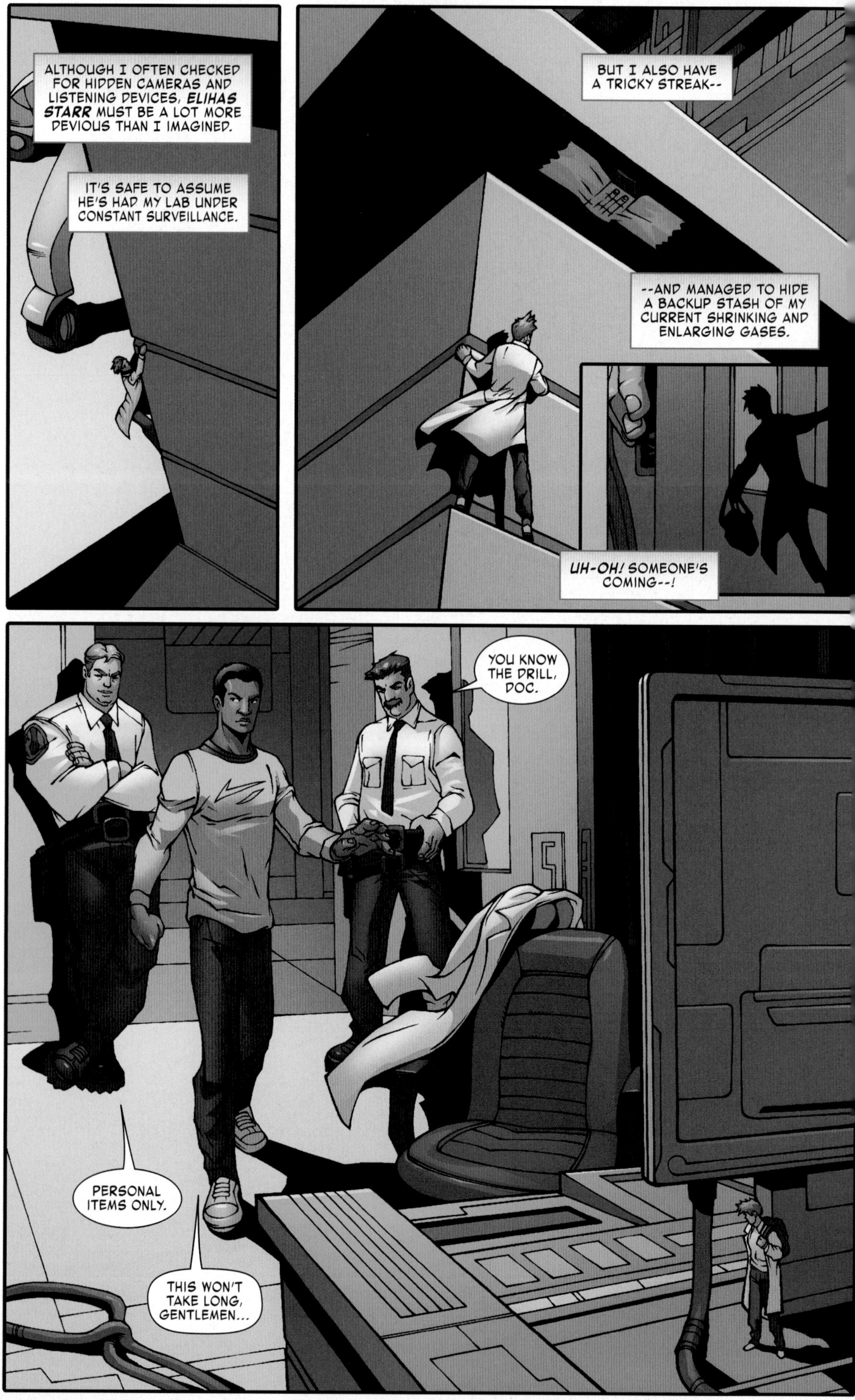
ALTHOUGH I OFTEN CHECKED FOR HIDDEN CAMERAS AND LISTENING DEVICES, *ELIHAS STARR* MUST BE A LOT MORE DEVIOUS THAN I IMAGINED.
IT'S SAFE TO ASSUME HE'S HAD MY LAB UNDER CONSTANT SURVEILLANCE.
BUT I ALSO HAVE A TRICKY STREAK--
--AND MANAGED TO HIDE A BACKUP STASH OF MY CURRENT SHRINKING AND ENLARGING GASES.
*UH-OH!* SOMEONE'S COMING--!
YOU KNOW THE DRILL, DOC.
PERSONAL ITEMS ONLY.
THIS WON'T TAKE LONG, GENTLEMEN...

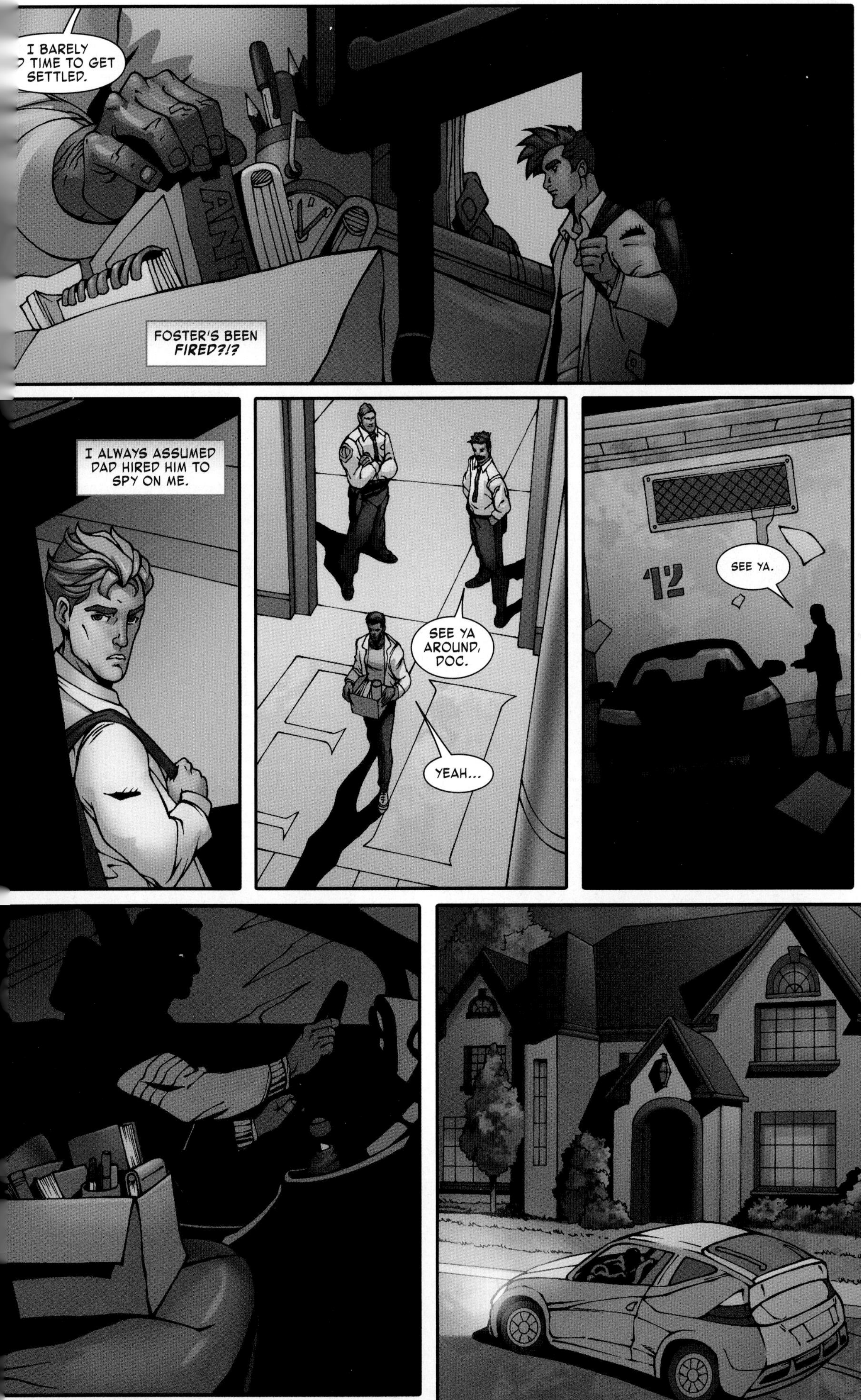
I BARELY
D TIME TO GET
SETTLED.
FOSTER'S BEEN *FIRED?!?*
I ALWAYS ASSUMED DAD HIRED HIM TO SPY ON ME.
SEE YA AROUND, DOC.
YEAH...
SEE YA.

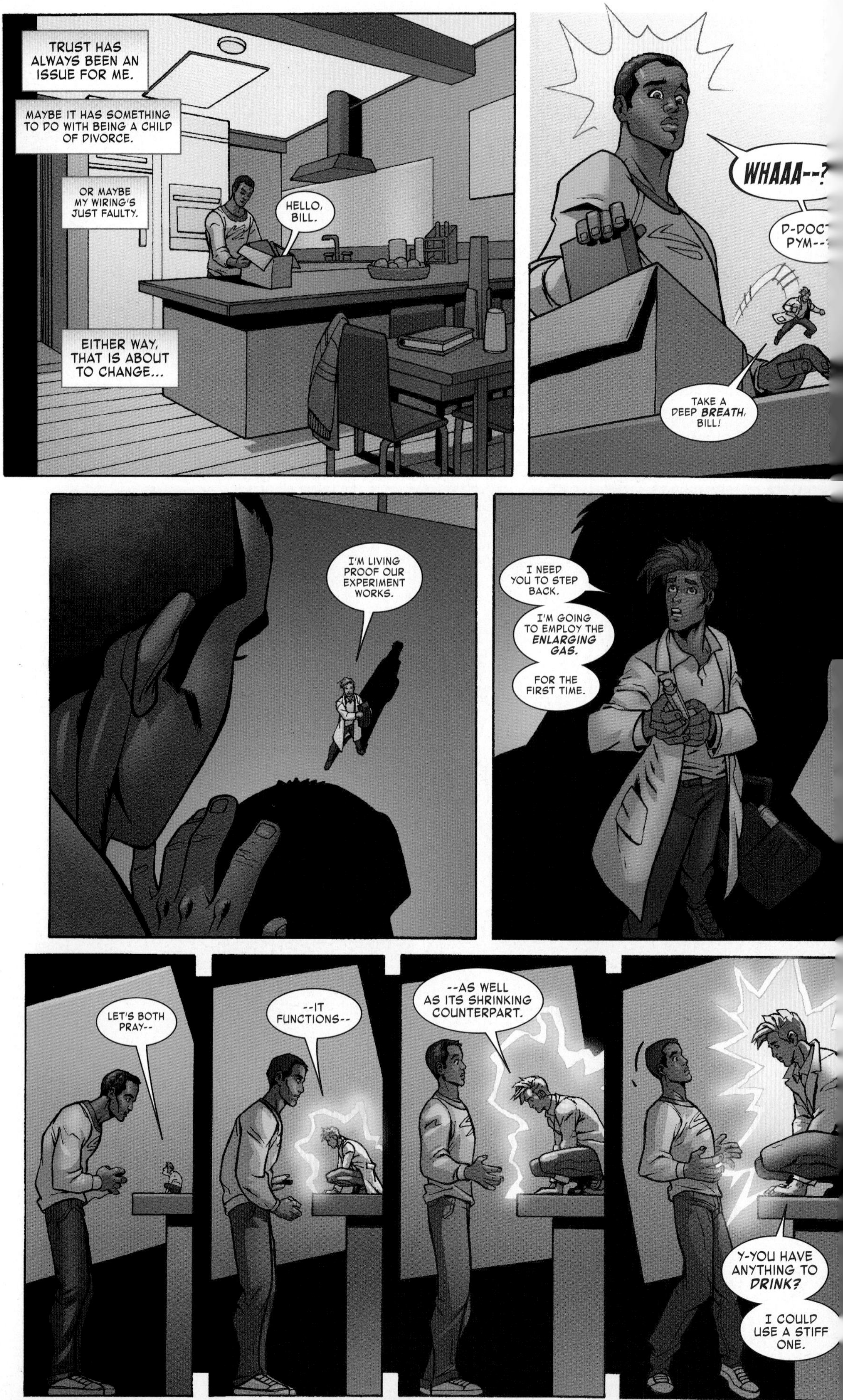

TRUST HAS ALWAYS BEEN AN ISSUE FOR ME.
MAYBE IT HAS SOMETHING TO DO WITH BEING A CHILD OF DIVORCE.
OR MAYBE MY WIRING'S JUST FAULTY.
HELLO, BILL.
EITHER WAY, THAT IS ABOUT TO CHANGE...
WHAAA--?
D-DOCT
PYM--
TAKE A DEEP BREATH, BILL!
I'M LIVING PROOF OUR EXPERIMENT WORKS.
I NEED YOU TO STEP BACK.
I'M GOING TO EMPLOY THE ENLARGING GAS.
FOR THE FIRST TIME.
LET'S BOTH PRAY--
--IT FUNCTIONS--
--AS WELL AS ITS SHRINKING COUNTERPART.
Y-YOU HAVE ANYTHING TO DRINK?
I COULD USE A STIFF ONE.

ELIHAS STARR IS ONE OF THE MOST RESPECTED SCIENTISTS IN THE WORLD.

HARD TO BELIEVE HE'D ORCHESTRATE A CONSPIRACY AGAINST YOU AND YOUR WIFE.

I WAS TOLD YOU HAD SUFFERED ANOTHER MENTAL...

BY WHOM?

YOUR FATHER.

FIGURES.

HE'S ALWAYS BEEN STARR'S TOADY.

ALWAYS CHOSEN HIM OVER ME.

I HATE TO PUT YOU ON THE SPOT, BILL, BUT I NEED HELP TO RECOVER MY RESEARCH FROM STARR.

WHY DON'T YOU JUST GO TO THE POLICE?

WHO DO YOU THINK THEY'LL BELIEVE? THE LOCAL CELEBRITY WHO EMPLOYS THOUSANDS OR ME--

--WITH MY HISTORY OF MENTAL ILLNESS?!

I CAN ALMOST TASTE THE TENSION AS BILL FOSTER STARES OUT THE WINDOW AND THEN...

OKAY, I'M IN.

TERRIFIC! I NEED TO BORROW YOUR LAPTOP.

I HID COPIES OF ALL MY NOTES ON A SECURE SITE AND HAVE TO DOWNLOAD THEM.

MY EXPERIENCE WITH THE ANTS HAS INSPIRED ME TO COMPLETE MARIA'S WORK.

THESE SCHEMATICS ARE INCREDIBLE.

A DEVICE TO COMMUNICATE WITH ANTS THROUGH THEIR *ANTENNAE?!?*

THAT'S RIGHT, BILL. WE'RE ABOUT TO TRANSFORM MY WIFE'S THEORIES--

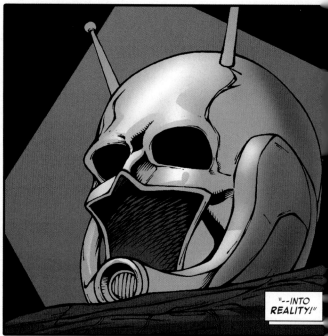

"*--INTO REALITY!*"

IT TOOK LONG ENOUGH, AND THAT DOESN'T COUNT THE TIME WE SPENT CONVERTING MY GARAGE INTO A MAKESHIFT LAB, BUT THE PROTOTYPE'S LOOKING GOOD.

I KNOW THIS IS COMPLETELY OFF-TOPIC, BUT DO THEY REALLY CALL STARR *"EGGHEAD"* BEHIND HIS BACK?

ABSOLUTELY... FOR ALL THE OBVIOUS REASONS.

WHAT DO THEY CALL ME?

MR. PARANOID.

HOW DO YOU PROPOSE WE TEST THIS PROTOTYPE?

ONLY ONE WAY TO DO IT PROPERLY--*IN THE FIELD!*

YOU'RE NOT SERIOUSLY SUGGESTING--

I AM.

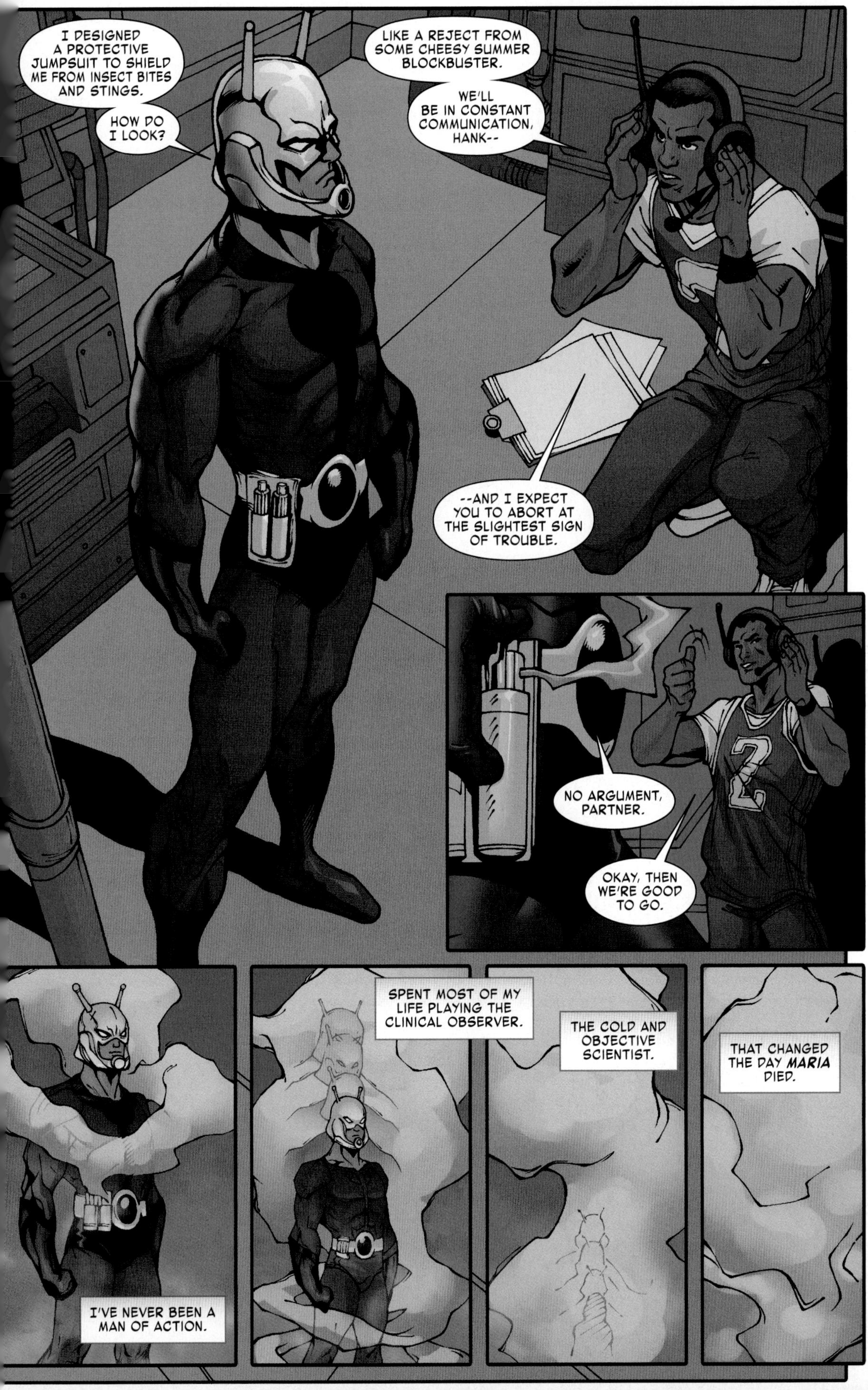

I DESIGNED A PROTECTIVE JUMPSUIT TO SHIELD ME FROM INSECT BITES AND STINGS.
HOW DO I LOOK?
LIKE A REJECT FROM SOME CHEESY SUMMER BLOCKBUSTER.
WE'LL BE IN CONSTANT COMMUNICATION, HANK--
--AND I EXPECT YOU TO ABORT AT THE SLIGHTEST SIGN OF TROUBLE.
NO ARGUMENT, PARTNER.
OKAY, THEN WE'RE GOOD TO GO.
I'VE NEVER BEEN A MAN OF ACTION.
SPENT MOST OF MY LIFE PLAYING THE CLINICAL OBSERVER.
THE COLD AND OBJECTIVE SCIENTIST.
THAT CHANGED THE DAY MARIA DIED.

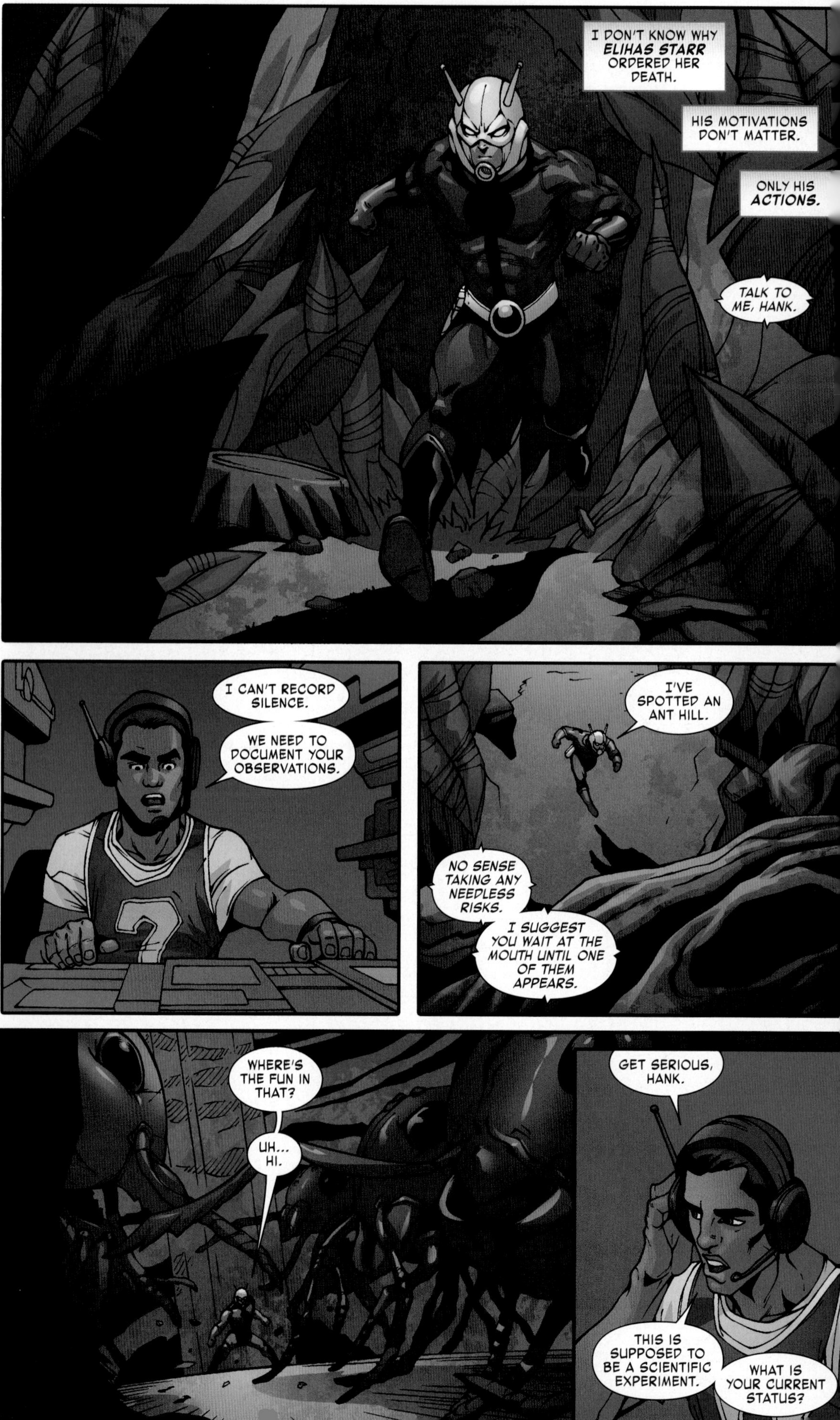
I DON'T KNOW WHY ELIHAS STARR ORDERED HER DEATH.
HIS MOTIVATIONS DON'T MATTER.
ONLY HIS ACTIONS.
TALK TO ME, HANK.
I CAN'T RECORD SILENCE.
WE NEED TO DOCUMENT YOUR OBSERVATIONS.
I'VE SPOTTED AN ANT HILL.
NO SENSE TAKING ANY NEEDLESS RISKS.
I SUGGEST YOU WAIT AT THE MOUTH UNTIL ONE OF THEM APPEARS.
WHERE'S THE FUN IN THAT?
UH... HI.
GET SERIOUS, HANK.
THIS IS SUPPOSED TO BE A SCIENTIFIC EXPERIMENT.
WHAT IS YOUR CURRENT STATUS?

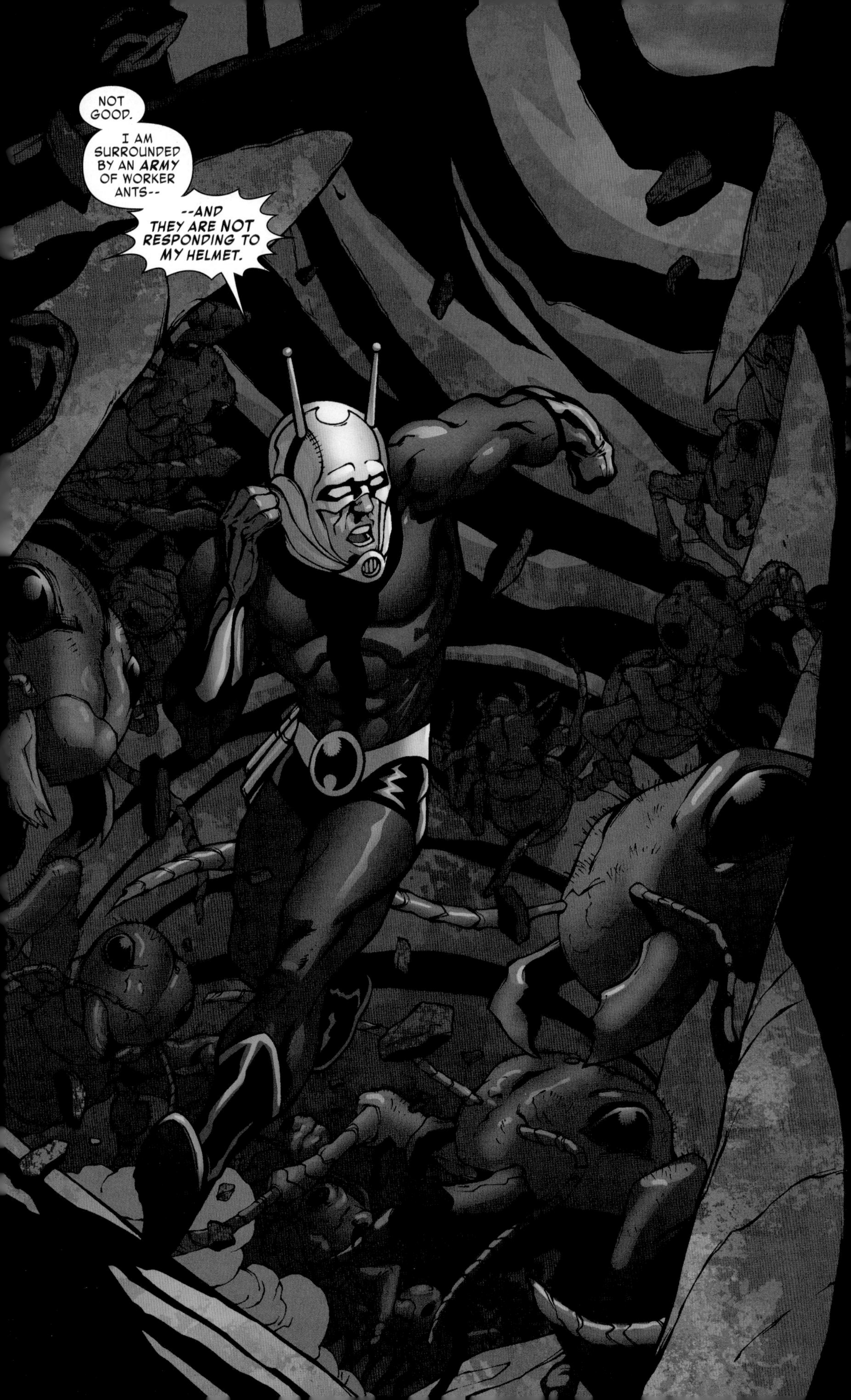
NOT GOOD.
I AM SURROUNDED BY AN ARMY OF WORKER ANTS--
--AND THEY ARE NOT RESPONDING TO MY HELMET.

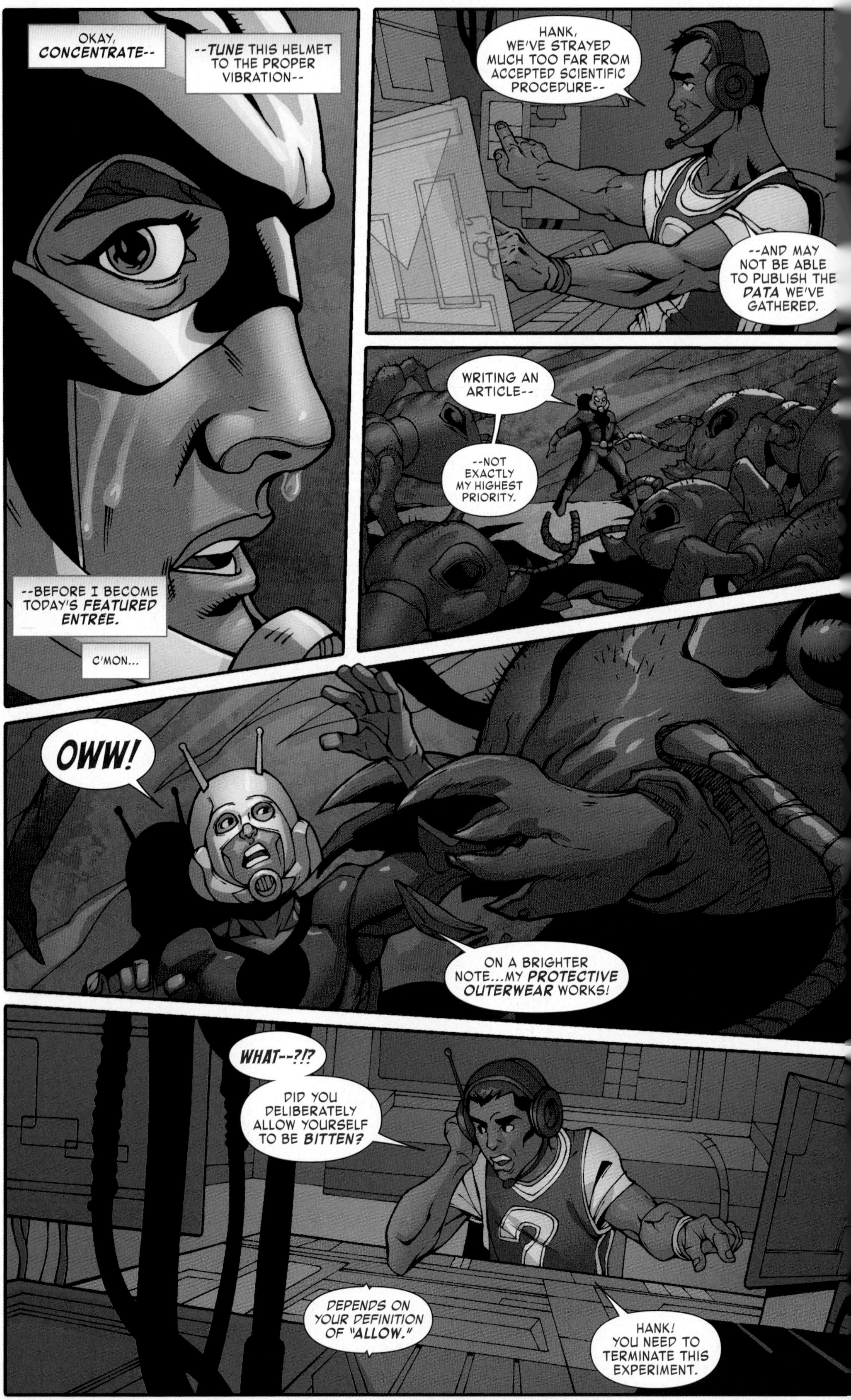

OKAY, CONCENTRATE--
--TUNE THIS HELMET TO THE PROPER VIBRATION--
--BEFORE I BECOME TODAY'S FEATURED ENTRÉE.
C'MON...
HANK, WE'VE STRAYED MUCH TOO FAR FROM ACCEPTED SCIENTIFIC PROCEDURE--
--AND MAY NOT BE ABLE TO PUBLISH THE DATA WE'VE GATHERED.
WRITING AN ARTICLE--
--NOT EXACTLY MY HIGHEST PRIORITY.
OWW!
ON A BRIGHTER NOTE...MY PROTECTIVE OUTERWEAR WORKS!
WHAT--?!?
DID YOU DELIBERATELY ALLOW YOURSELF TO BE BITTEN?
DEPENDS ON YOUR DEFINITION OF "ALLOW."
HANK! YOU NEED TO TERMINATE THIS EXPERIMENT.

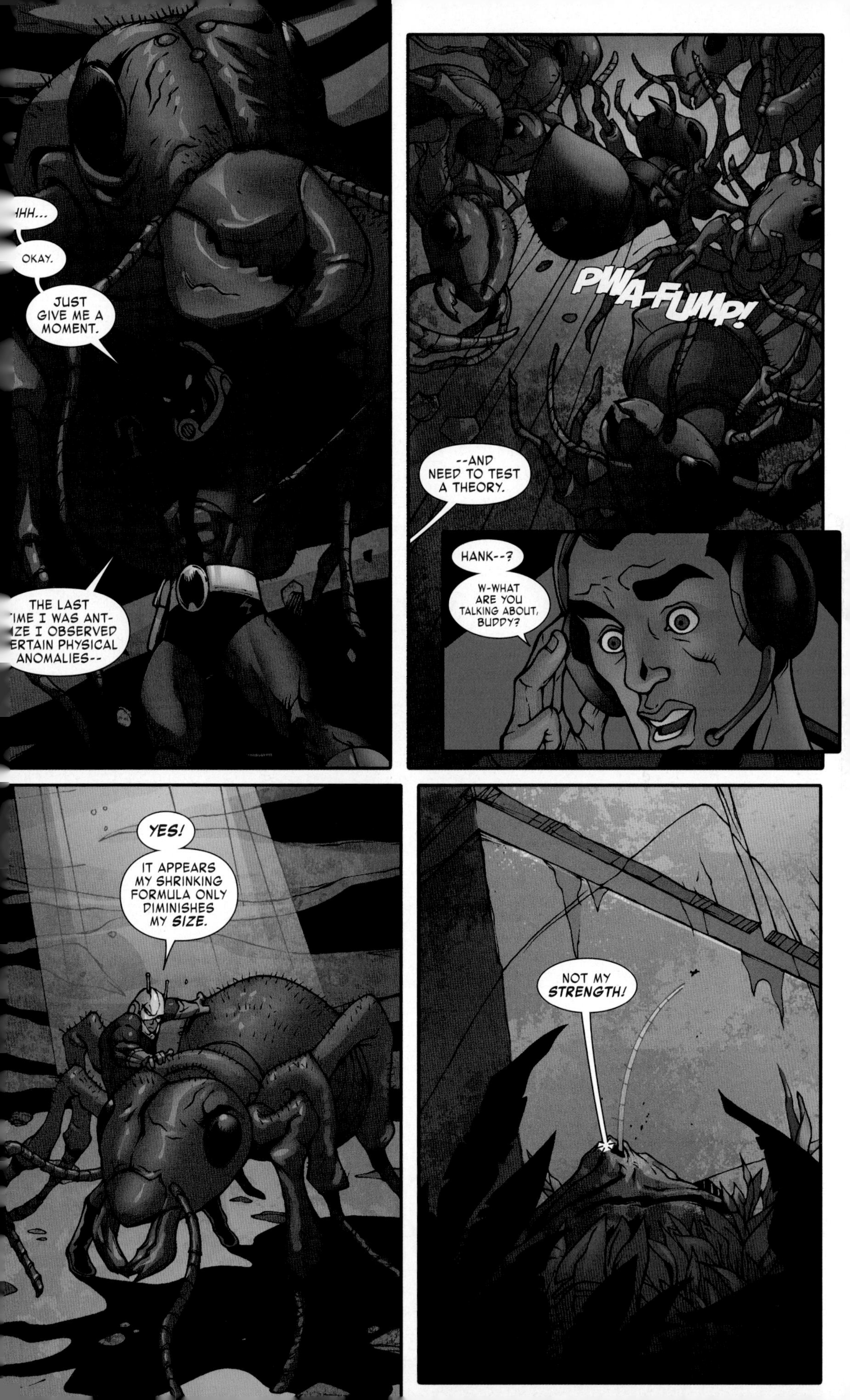
HHH...
OKAY.
JUST GIVE ME A MOMENT.
THE LAST IME I WAS ANT-ZE I OBSERVED ERTAIN PHYSICAL ANOMALIES--
PWA-FUMP!
--AND NEED TO TEST A THEORY.
HANK--?
W-WHAT ARE YOU TALKING ABOUT, BUDDY?
YES!
IT APPEARS MY SHRINKING FORMULA ONLY DIMINISHES MY SIZE.
NOT MY STRENGTH!

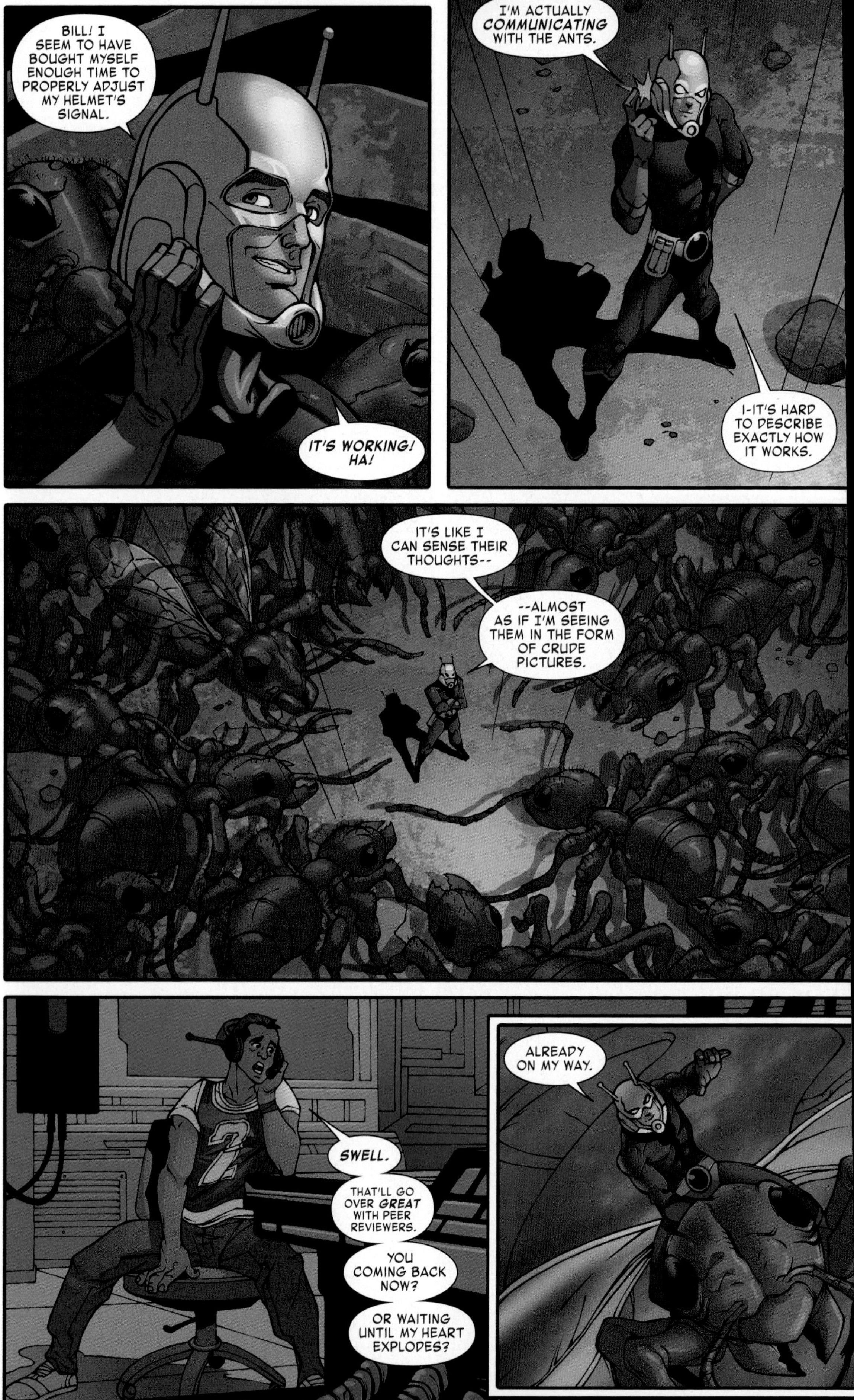
BILL! I SEEM TO HAVE BOUGHT MYSELF ENOUGH TIME TO PROPERLY ADJUST MY HELMET'S SIGNAL.
IT'S WORKING! HA!
I'M ACTUALLY COMMUNICATING WITH THE ANTS.
I-IT'S HARD TO DESCRIBE EXACTLY HOW IT WORKS.
IT'S LIKE I CAN SENSE THEIR THOUGHTS--
--ALMOST AS IF I'M SEEING THEM IN THE FORM OF CRUDE PICTURES.
SWELL.
THAT'LL GO OVER GREAT WITH PEER REVIEWERS.
YOU COMING BACK NOW?
OR WAITING UNTIL MY HEART EXPLODES?
ALREADY ON MY WAY.

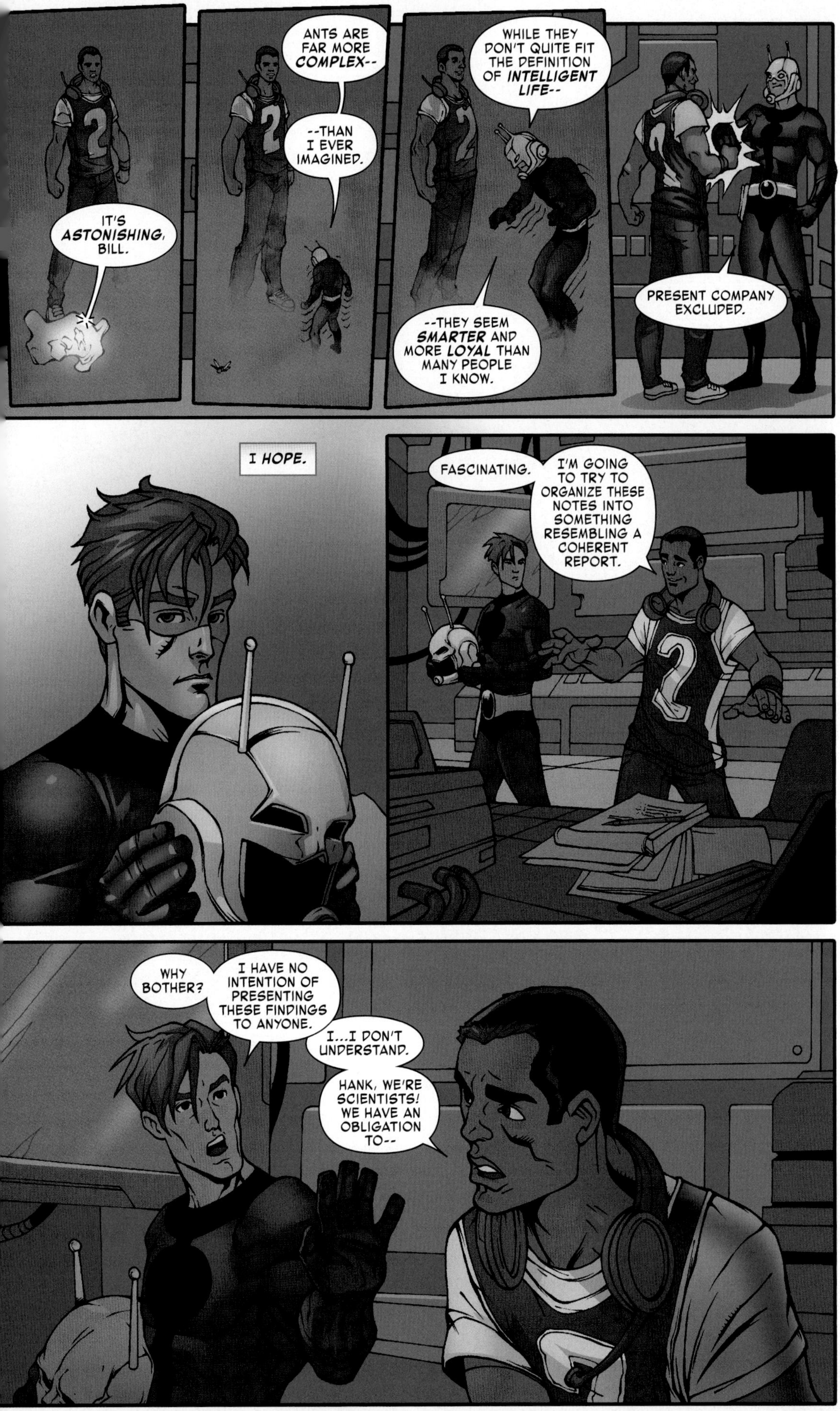
IT'S ASTONISHING, BILL.
ANTS ARE FAR MORE COMPLEX--
--THAN I EVER IMAGINED.
WHILE THEY DON'T QUITE FIT THE DEFINITION OF INTELLIGENT LIFE--
--THEY SEEM SMARTER AND MORE LOYAL THAN MANY PEOPLE I KNOW.
PRESENT COMPANY EXCLUDED.
I HOPE.
FASCINATING.
I'M GOING TO TRY TO ORGANIZE THESE NOTES INTO SOMETHING RESEMBLING A COHERENT REPORT.
WHY BOTHER?
I HAVE NO INTENTION OF PRESENTING THESE FINDINGS TO ANYONE.
I...I DON'T UNDERSTAND.
HANK, WE'RE SCIENTISTS! WE HAVE AN OBLIGATION TO--

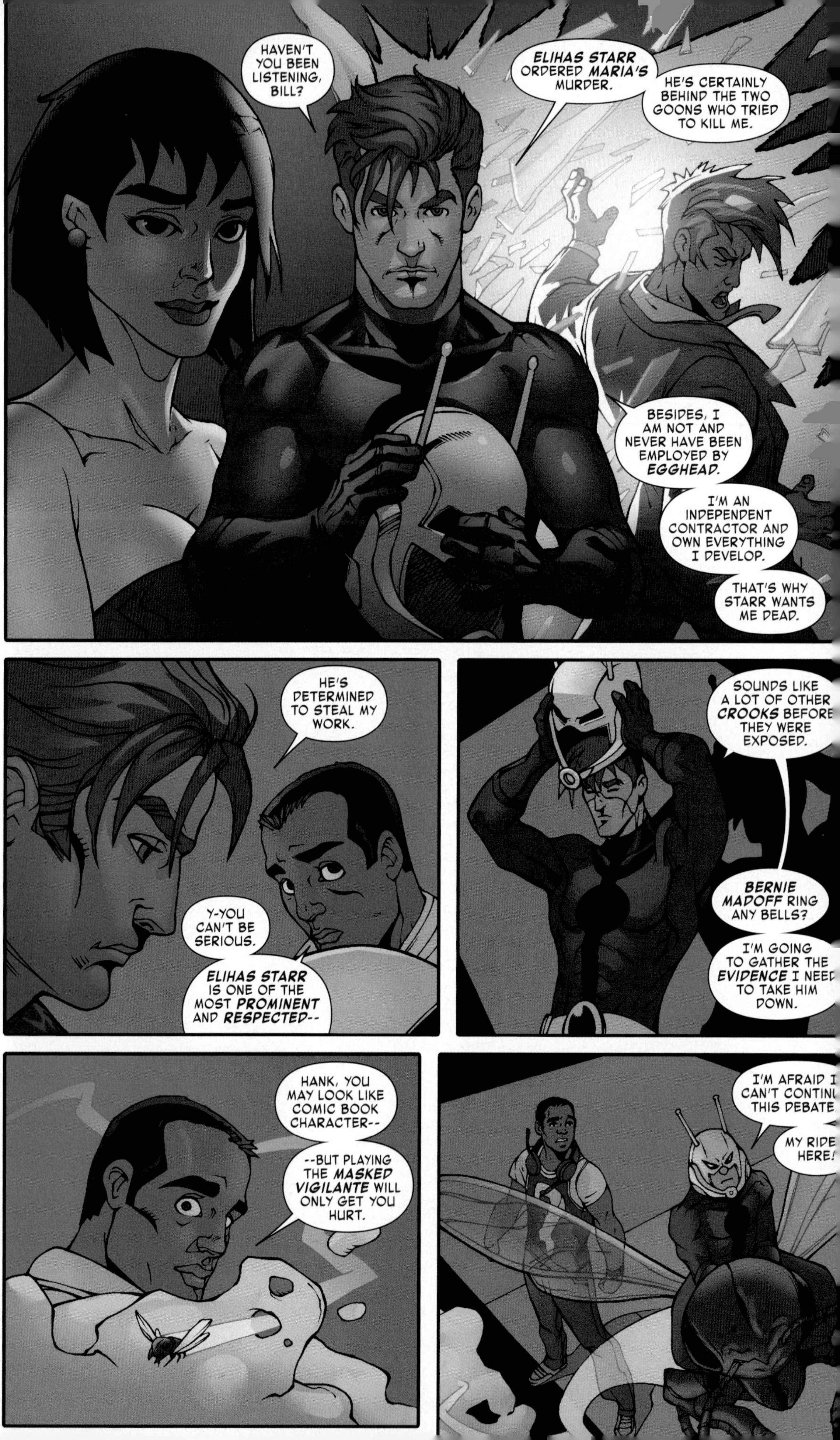
HAVEN'T YOU BEEN LISTENING, BILL?
ELIHAS STARR ORDERED MARIA'S MURDER.
HE'S CERTAINLY BEHIND THE TWO GOONS WHO TRIED TO KILL ME.
BESIDES, I AM NOT AND NEVER HAVE BEEN EMPLOYED BY EGGHEAD.
I'M AN INDEPENDENT CONTRACTOR AND OWN EVERYTHING I DEVELOP.
THAT'S WHY STARR WANTS ME DEAD.
HE'S DETERMINED TO STEAL MY WORK.
Y-YOU CAN'T BE SERIOUS.
ELIHAS STARR IS ONE OF THE MOST PROMINENT AND RESPECTED--
SOUNDS LIKE A LOT OF OTHER CROOKS BEFORE THEY WERE EXPOSED.
BERNIE MADOFF RING ANY BELLS?
I'M GOING TO GATHER THE EVIDENCE I NEE TO TAKE HIM DOWN.
HANK, YOU MAY LOOK LIKE COMIC BOOK CHARACTER--
--BUT PLAYING THE MASKED VIGILANTE WILL ONLY GET YOU HURT.
I'M AFRAID I CAN'T CONTINU THIS DEBATE
MY RIDE HERE!

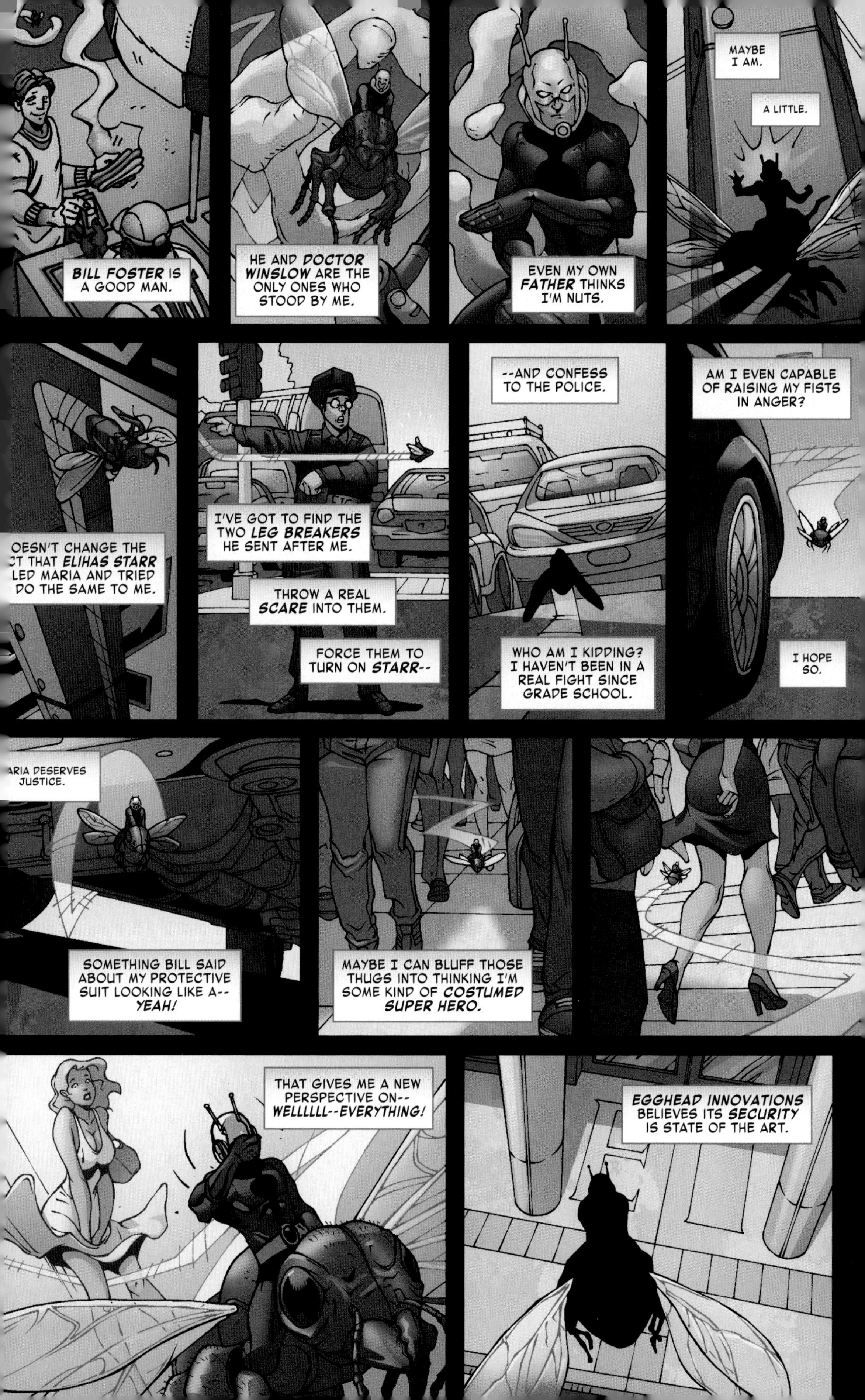
BILL FOSTER IS A GOOD MAN.
HE AND DOCTOR WINSLOW ARE THE ONLY ONES WHO STOOD BY ME.
EVEN MY OWN FATHER THINKS I'M NUTS.
MAYBE I AM.
A LITTLE.
OESN'T CHANGE THE CT THAT ELIHAS STARR LED MARIA AND TRIED DO THE SAME TO ME.
I'VE GOT TO FIND THE TWO LEG BREAKERS HE SENT AFTER ME.
THROW A REAL SCARE INTO THEM.
FORCE THEM TO TURN ON STARR--
--AND CONFESS TO THE POLICE.
WHO AM I KIDDING? I HAVEN'T BEEN IN A REAL FIGHT SINCE GRADE SCHOOL.
AM I EVEN CAPABLE OF RAISING MY FISTS IN ANGER?
I HOPE SO.
ARIA DESERVES JUSTICE.
SOMETHING BILL SAID ABOUT MY PROTECTIVE SUIT LOOKING LIKE A-- YEAH!
MAYBE I CAN BLUFF THOSE THUGS INTO THINKING I'M SOME KIND OF COSTUMED SUPER HERO.
THAT GIVES ME A NEW PERSPECTIVE ON-- WELLLLLL--EVERYTHING!
EGGHEAD INNOVATIONS BELIEVES ITS SECURITY IS STATE OF THE ART.

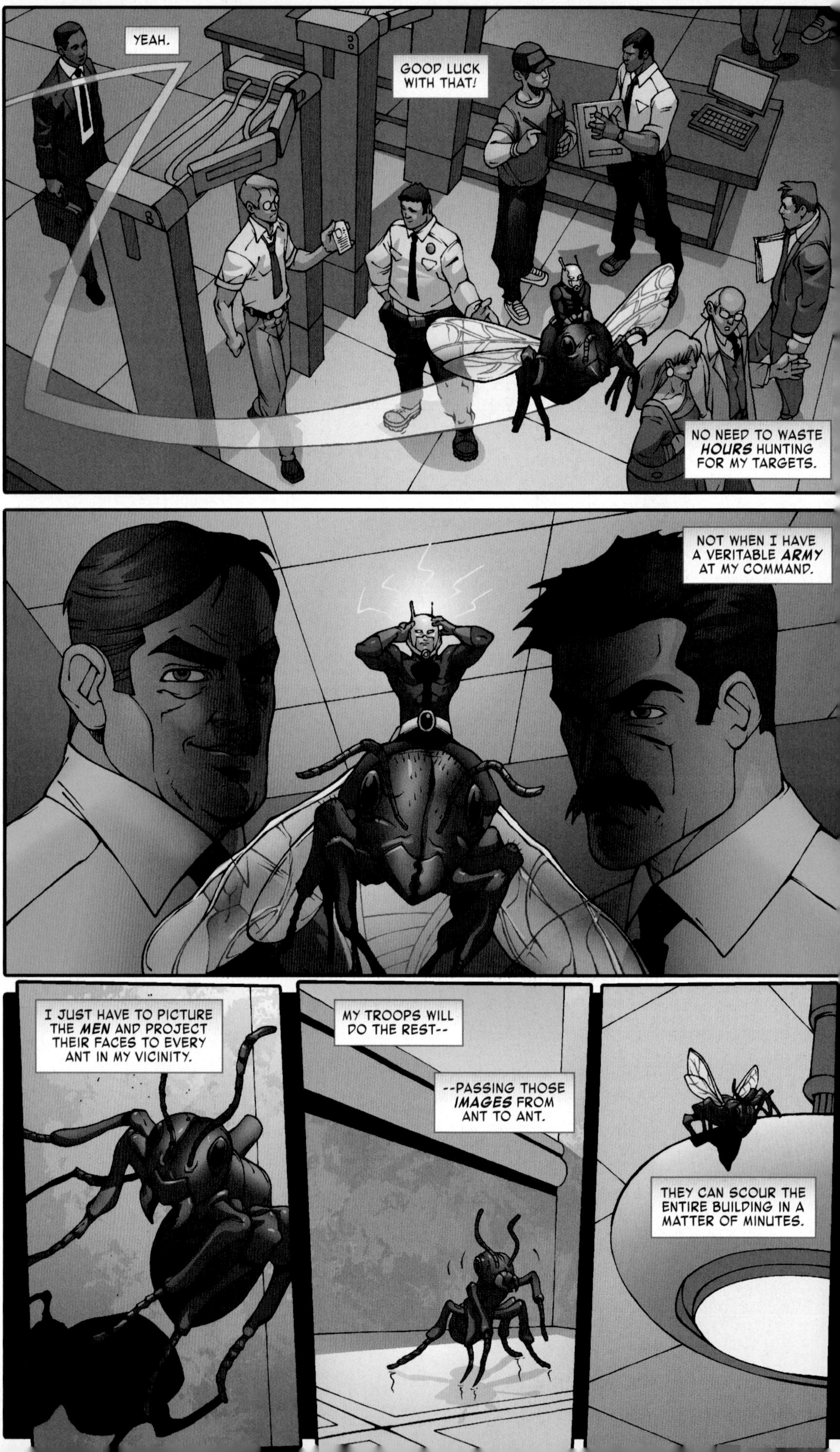
YEAH.
GOOD LUCK WITH THAT!
NO NEED TO WASTE HOURS HUNTING FOR MY TARGETS.
NOT WHEN I HAVE A VERITABLE ARMY AT MY COMMAND.
I JUST HAVE TO PICTURE THE MEN AND PROJECT THEIR FACES TO EVERY ANT IN MY VICINITY.
MY TROOPS WILL DO THE REST--
--PASSING THOSE IMAGES FROM ANT TO ANT.
THEY CAN SCOUR THE ENTIRE BUILDING IN A MATTER OF MINUTES.

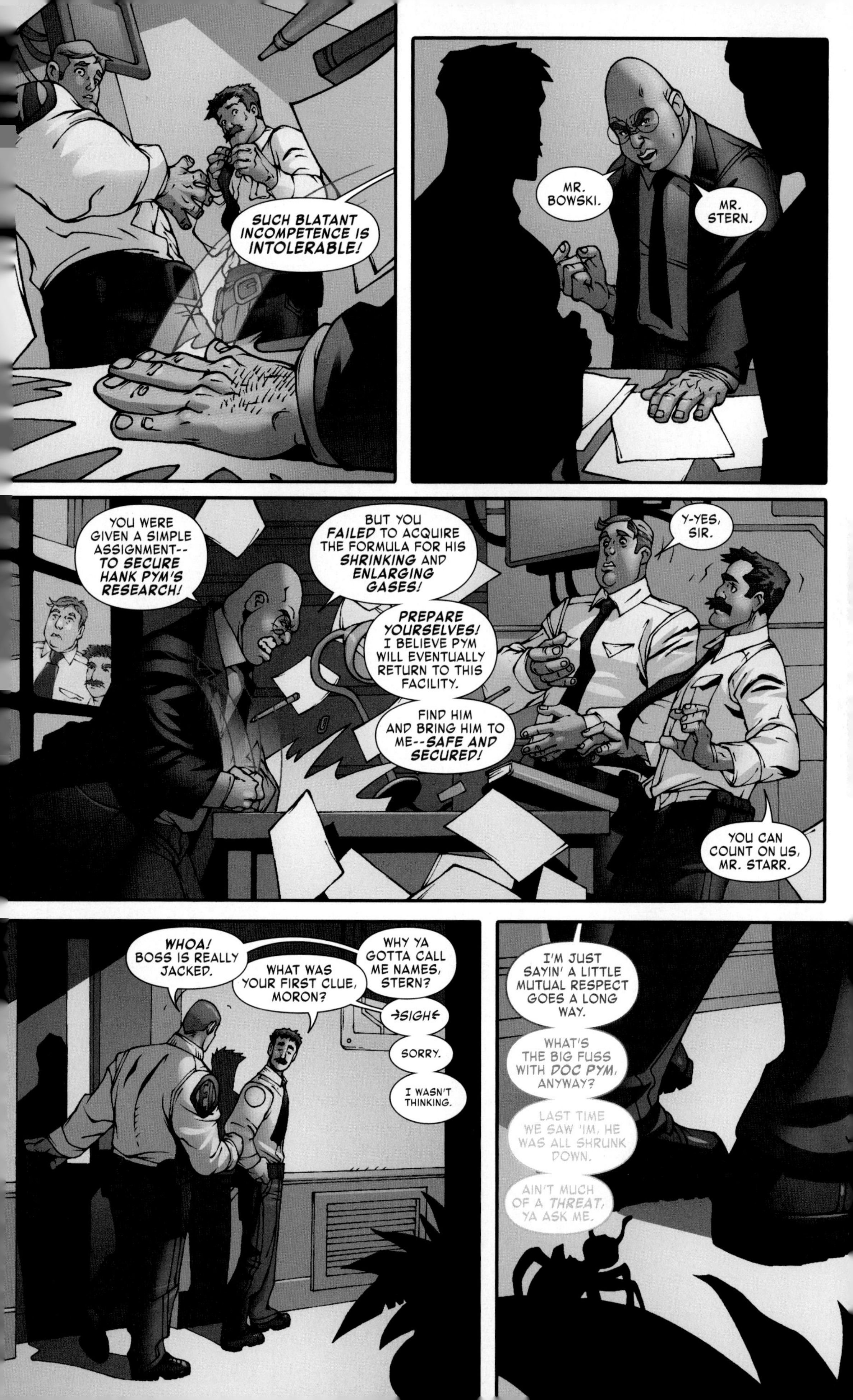
SUCH BLATANT INCOMPETENCE IS INTOLERABLE!
MR. BOWSKI.
MR. STERN.
YOU WERE GIVEN A SIMPLE ASSIGNMENT-- TO SECURE HANK PYM'S RESEARCH!
BUT YOU FAILED TO ACQUIRE THE FORMULA FOR HIS SHRINKING AND ENLARGING GASES!
Y-YES, SIR.
PREPARE YOURSELVES! I BELIEVE PYM WILL EVENTUALLY RETURN TO THIS FACILITY.
FIND HIM AND BRING HIM TO ME--SAFE AND SECURED!
YOU CAN COUNT ON US, MR. STARR.
WHOA! BOSS IS REALLY JACKED.
WHAT WAS YOUR FIRST CLUE, MORON?
WHY YA GOTTA CALL ME NAMES, STERN?
SIGH
SORRY.
I WASN'T THINKING.
I'M JUST SAYIN' A LITTLE MUTUAL RESPECT GOES A LONG WAY.
WHAT'S THE BIG FUSS WITH DOC PYM, ANYWAY?
LAST TIME WE SAW 'IM, HE WAS ALL SHRUNK DOWN.
AIN'T MUCH OF A THREAT, YA ASK ME.

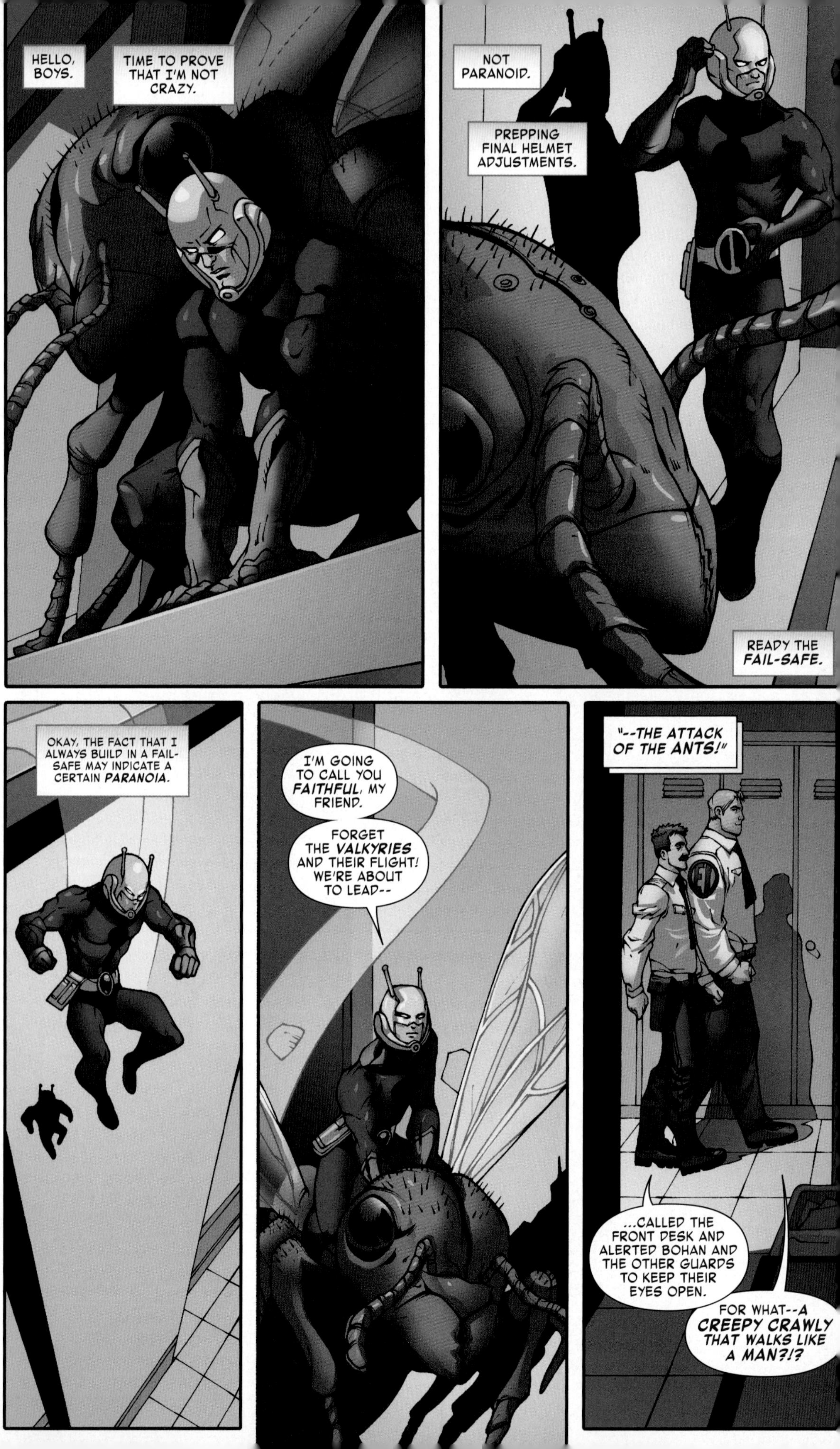
HELLO, BOYS.
TIME TO PROVE THAT I'M NOT CRAZY.
NOT PARANOID.
PREPPING FINAL HELMET ADJUSTMENTS.
READY THE FAIL-SAFE.
OKAY, THE FACT THAT I ALWAYS BUILD IN A FAIL-SAFE MAY INDICATE A CERTAIN PARANOIA.
I'M GOING TO CALL YOU FAITHFUL, MY FRIEND.
FORGET THE VALKYRIES AND THEIR FLIGHT! WE'RE ABOUT TO LEAD--
"--THE ATTACK OF THE ANTS!"
...CALLED THE FRONT DESK AND ALERTED BOHAN AND THE OTHER GUARDS TO KEEP THEIR EYES OPEN.
FOR WHAT--A CREEPY CRAWLY THAT WALKS LIKE A MAN?!?

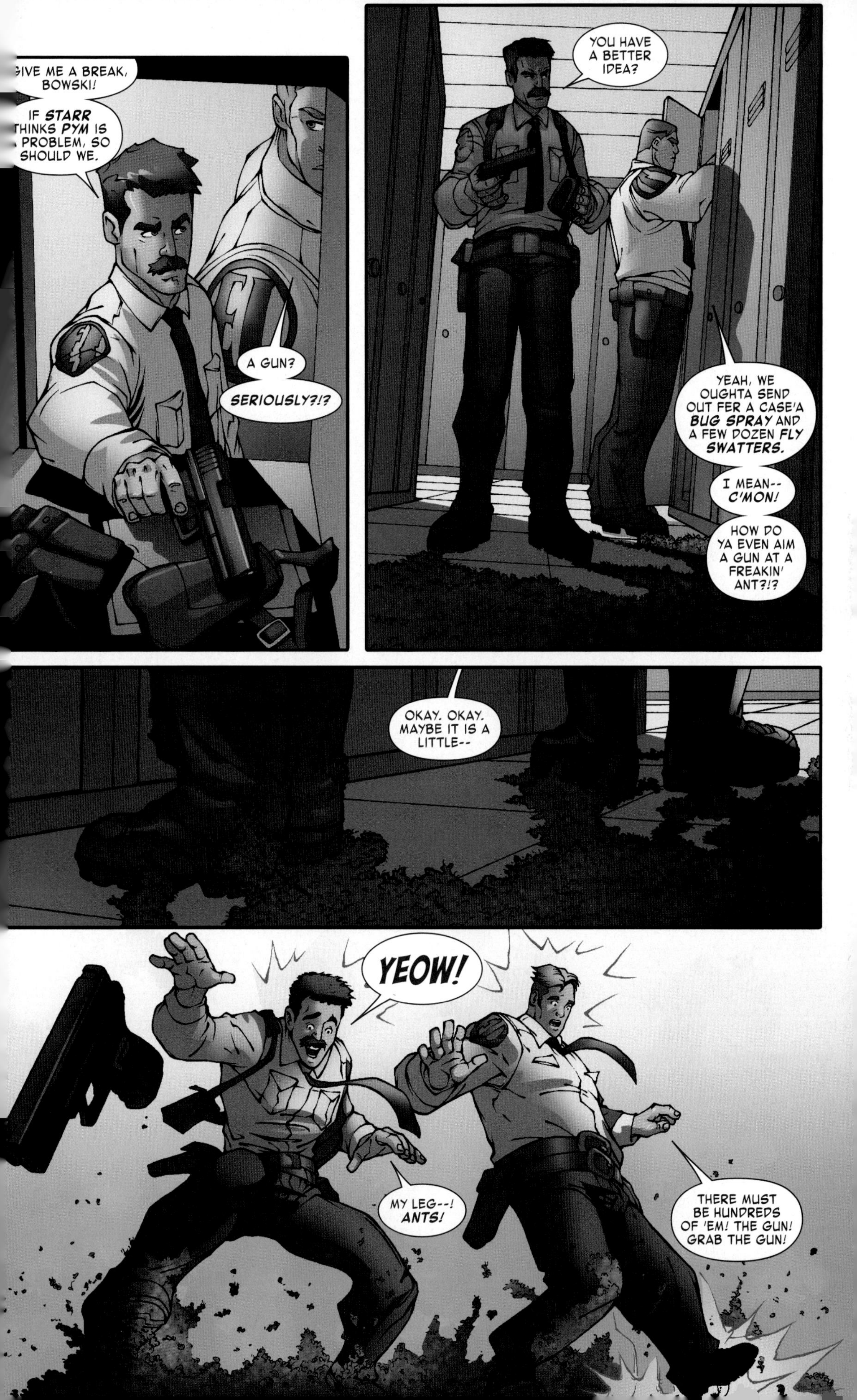
GIVE ME A BREAK, BOWSKI!
IF STARR THINKS PYM IS A PROBLEM, SO SHOULD WE.
A GUN?
SERIOUSLY?!?
YOU HAVE A BETTER IDEA?
YEAH, WE OUGHTA SEND OUT FER A CASE'A BUG SPRAY AND A FEW DOZEN FLY SWATTERS.
I MEAN-- C'MON!
HOW DO YA EVEN AIM A GUN AT A FREAKIN' ANT?!?
OKAY. OKAY. MAYBE IT IS A LITTLE--
YEOW!
MY LEG--! ANTS!
THERE MUST BE HUNDREDS OF 'EM! THE GUN! GRAB THE GUN!

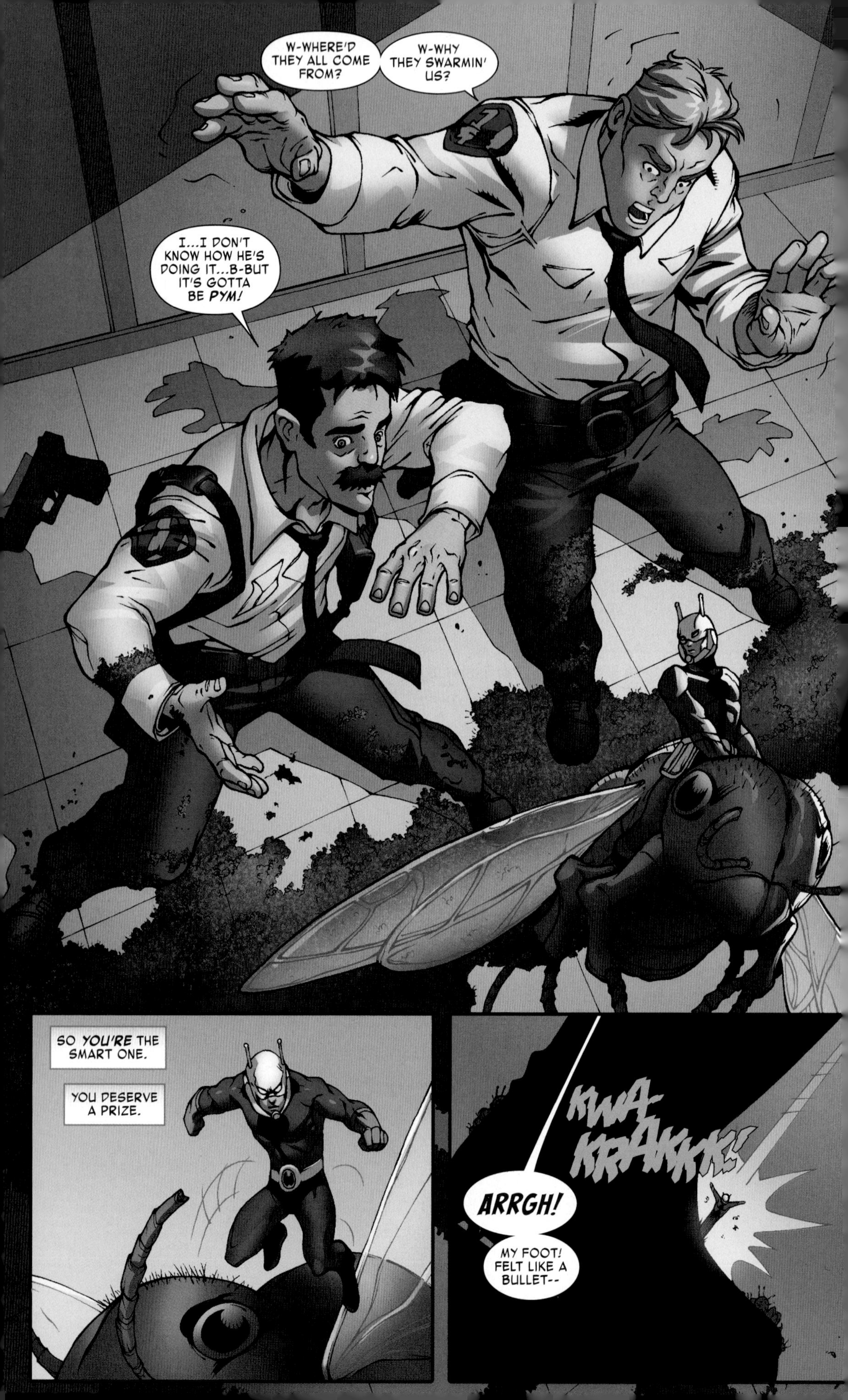
W-WHERE'D THEY ALL COME FROM?
W-WHY THEY SWARMIN' US?
I...I DON'T KNOW HOW HE'S DOING IT...B-BUT IT'S GOTTA BE *PYM!*
SO *YOU'RE* THE SMART ONE.
YOU DESERVE A PRIZE.
KWA-KRAKKK!
ARRGH!
MY FOOT! FELT LIKE A BULLET--

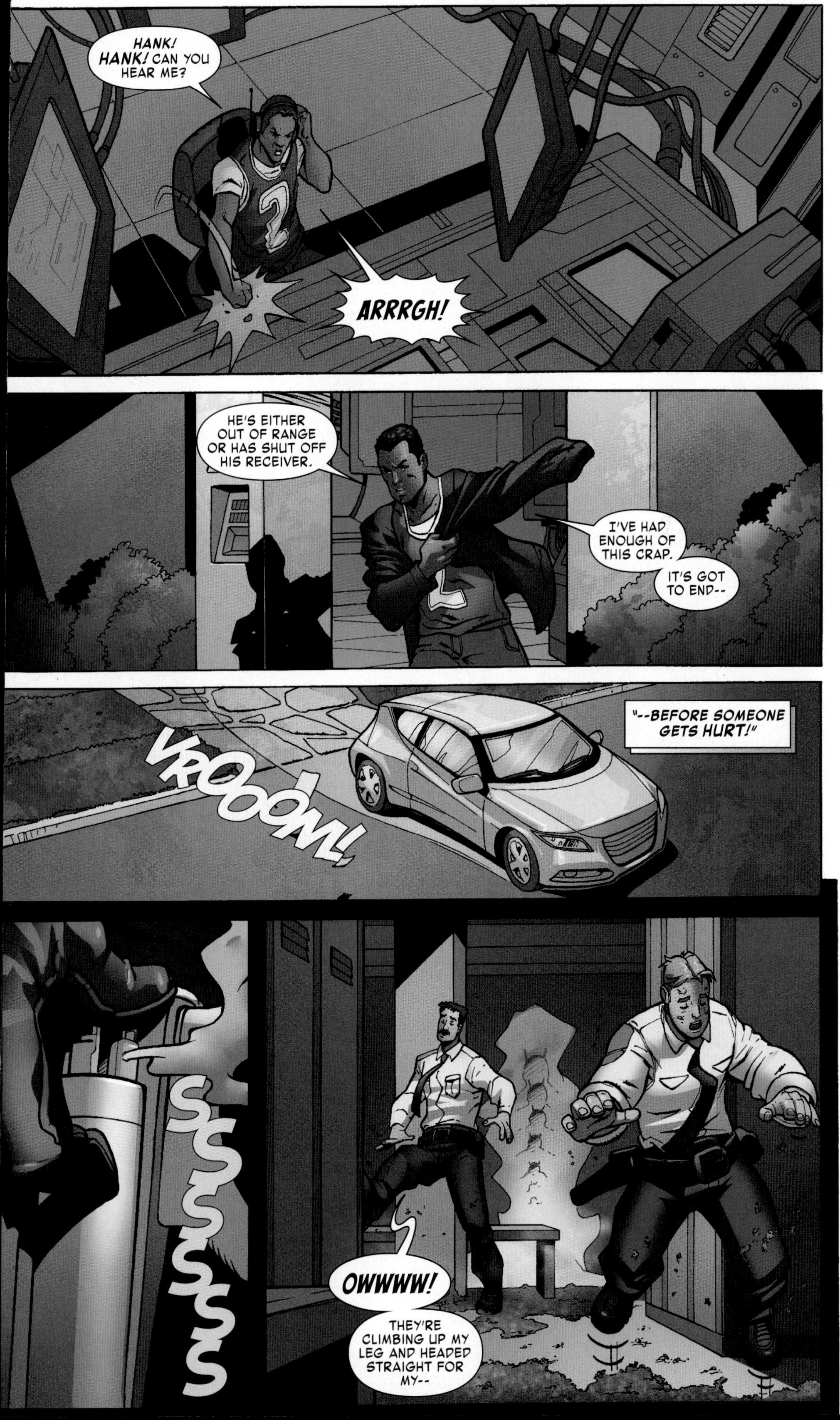
HANK! HANK! CAN YOU HEAR ME?
ARRRGH!
HE'S EITHER OUT OF RANGE OR HAS SHUT OFF HIS RECEIVER.
I'VE HAD ENOUGH OF THIS CRAP.
IT'S GOT TO END--
VROOOOM!
"--BEFORE SOMEONE GETS HURT!"
SSSSSS
OWWWW!
THEY'RE CLIMBING UP MY LEG AND HEADED STRAIGHT FOR MY--

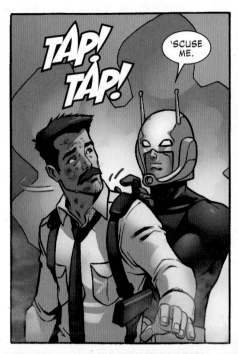

TAP! TAP!

'SCUSE ME.

THWAK!

STERN!

Y-YOU OKAY, MAN?

WHO WAS THAT *LUNATIC* IN THE FREAKY *STAR WARS* GETUP?

I...I THINK IT WAS PYM.

YOU KIDDIN'?

W-WISH I WAS.

W-WE GOTTA GET, MAN.

IF HE'S RUNNING AROUND LIKE THAT, DUDE'S OBVIOUSLY CROSSED INTO TOTAL *PSYCHO-VILLE!*

SSSSSSS

I *LIKE* THE GET-UP!

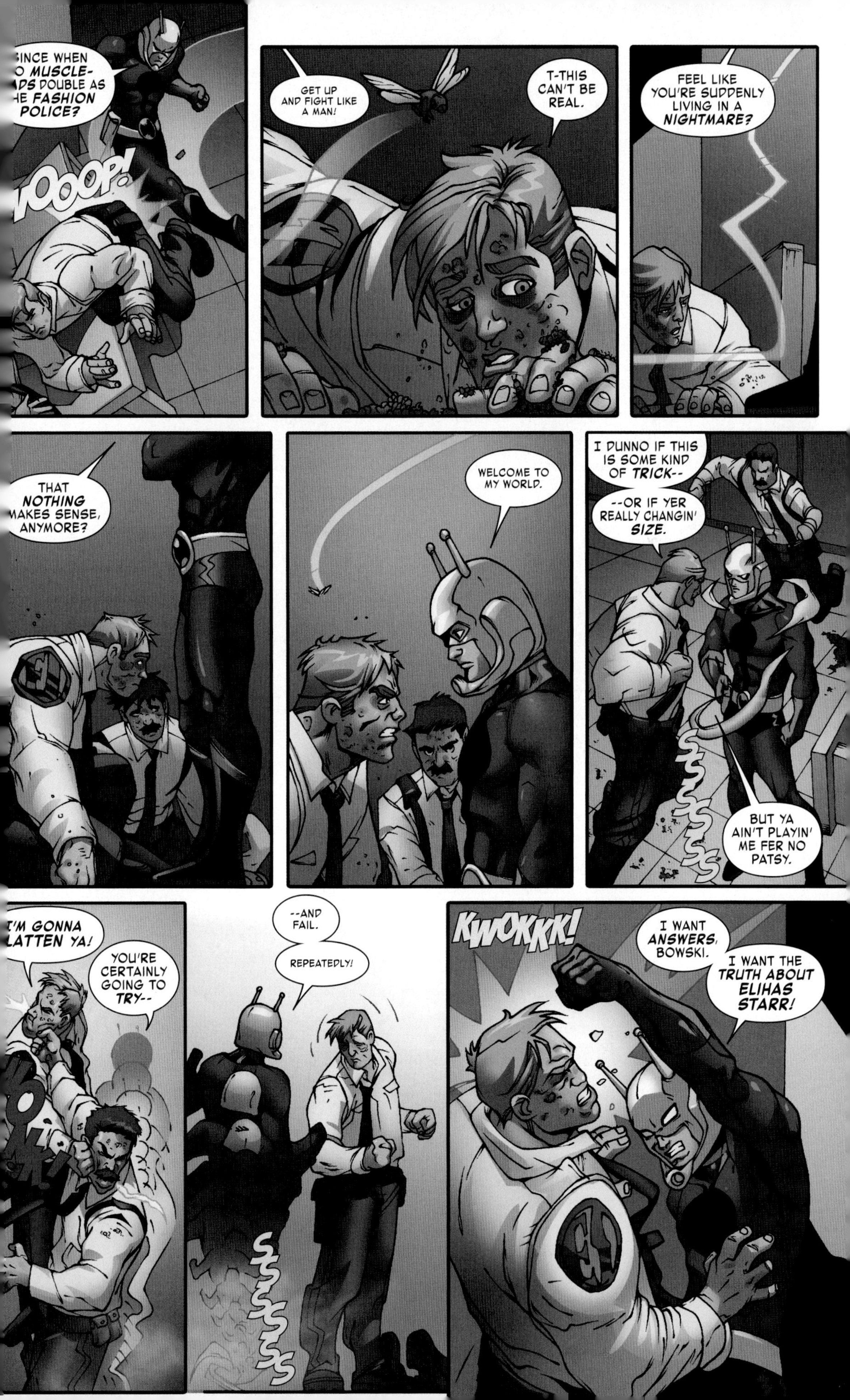
SINCE WHEN
DO MUSCLE-
HEADS DOUBLE AS
THE FASHION
POLICE?
WOOOP!
GET UP AND FIGHT LIKE A MAN!
T-THIS CAN'T BE REAL.
FEEL LIKE YOU'RE SUDDENLY LIVING IN A NIGHTMARE?
THAT NOTHING MAKES SENSE, ANYMORE?
WELCOME TO MY WORLD.
I DUNNO IF THIS IS SOME KIND OF TRICK--
--OR IF YER REALLY CHANGIN' SIZE.
SSSSSS
BUT YA AIN'T PLAYIN' ME FER NO PATSY.
I'M GONNA FLATTEN YA!
YOU'RE CERTAINLY GOING TO TRY--
--AND FAIL.
REPEATEDLY!
SSSSSS
KWOKKK!
I WANT ANSWERS, BOWSKI.
I WANT THE TRUTH ABOUT ELIHAS STARR!

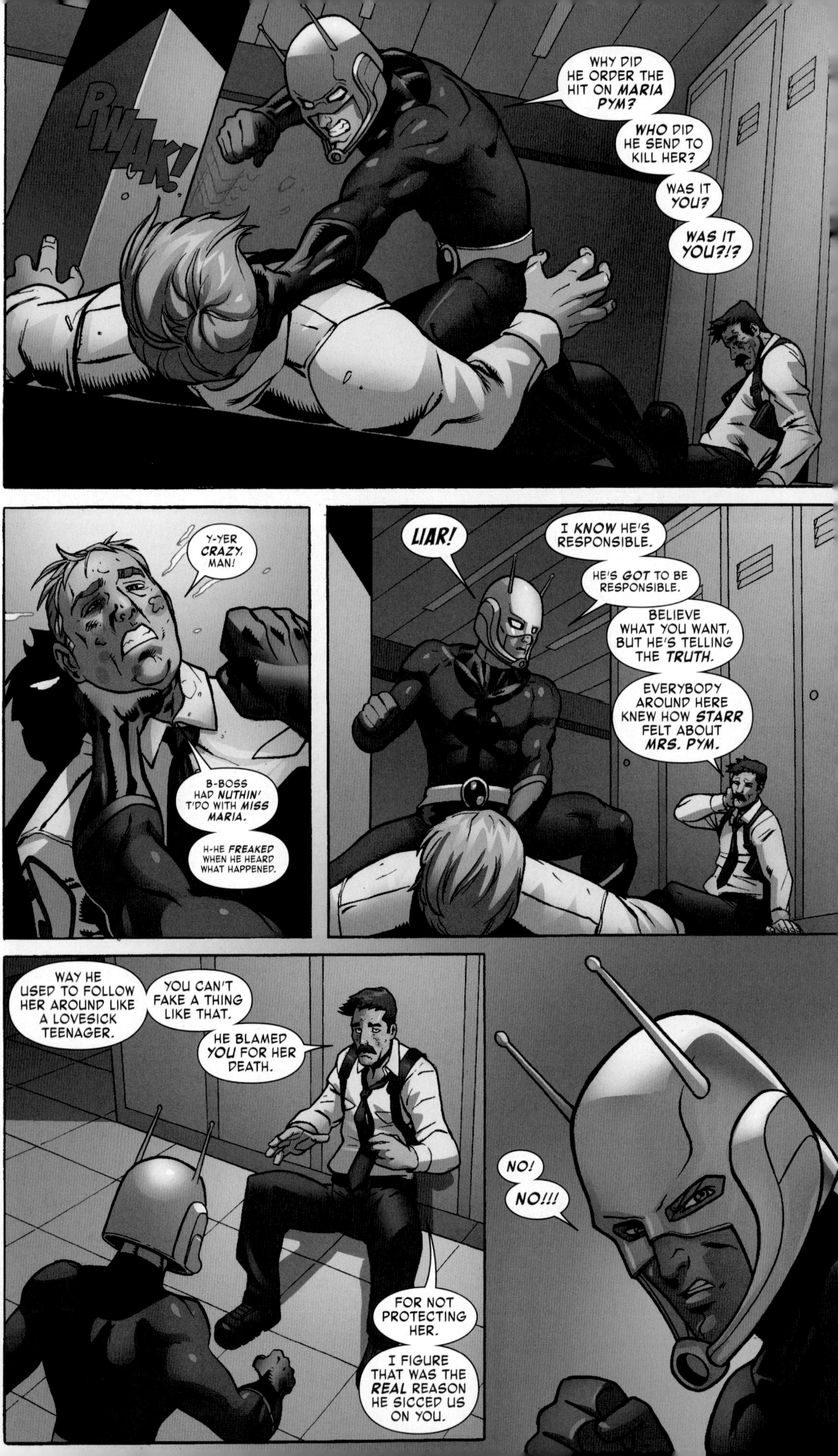
PWAK!
WHY DID HE ORDER THE HIT ON MARIA PYM?
WHO DID HE SEND TO KILL HER?
WAS IT YOU?
WAS IT YOU?!?
Y-YER CRAZY, MAN!
B-BOSS HAD NUTHIN' T'DO WITH MISS MARIA.
H-HE FREAKED WHEN HE HEARD WHAT HAPPENED.
LIAR!
I KNOW HE'S RESPONSIBLE.
HE'S GOT TO BE RESPONSIBLE.
BELIEVE WHAT YOU WANT, BUT HE'S TELLING THE TRUTH.
EVERYBODY AROUND HERE KNEW HOW STARR FELT ABOUT MRS. PYM.
WAY HE USED TO FOLLOW HER AROUND LIKE A LOVESICK TEENAGER.
YOU CAN'T FAKE A THING LIKE THAT.
HE BLAMED YOU FOR HER DEATH.
FOR NOT PROTECTING HER.
I FIGURE THAT WAS THE REAL REASON HE SICCED US ON YOU.
NO!
NO!!!

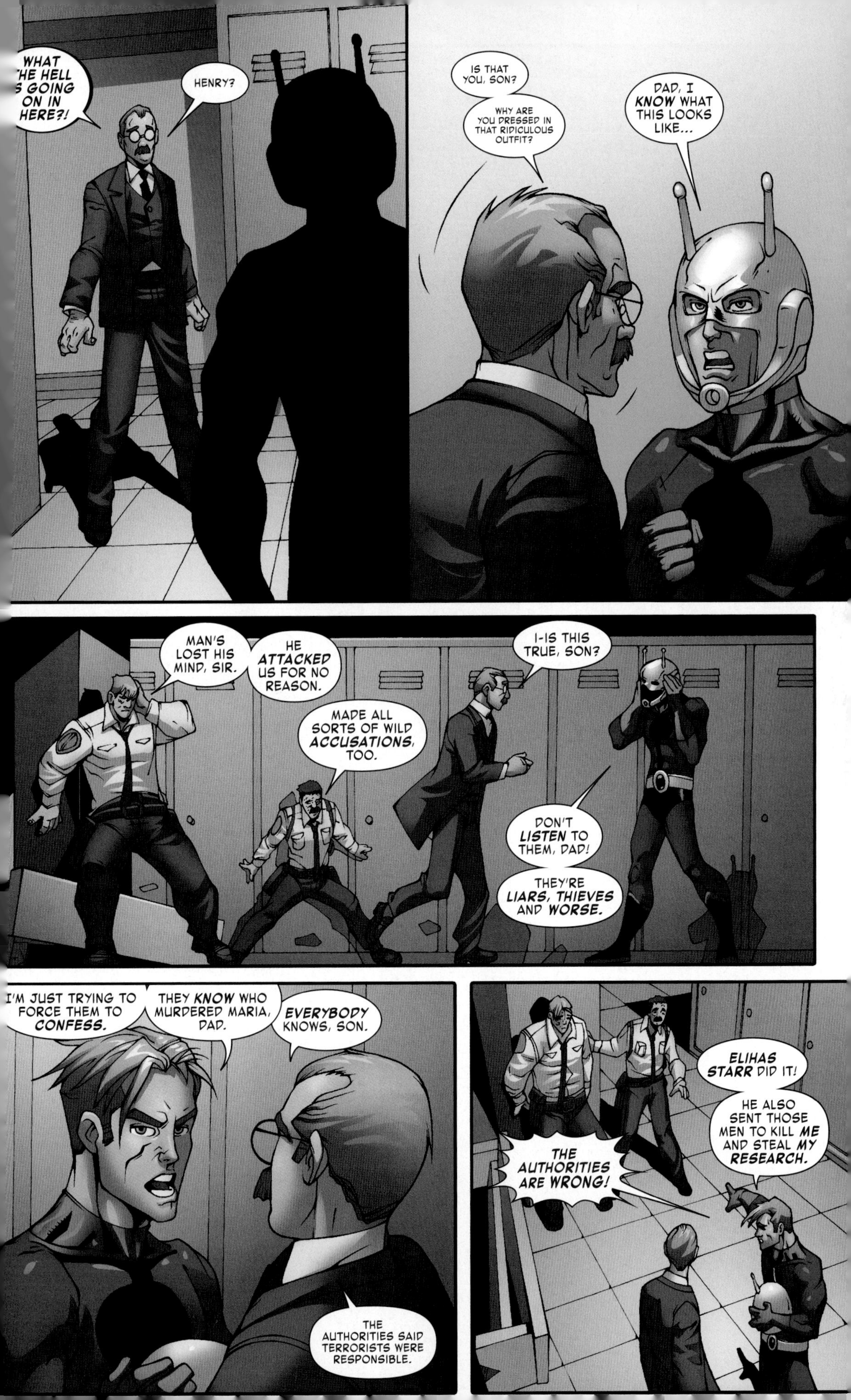

WHAT THE HELL IS GOING ON IN HERE?!
HENRY?
IS THAT YOU, SON?
WHY ARE YOU DRESSED IN THAT RIDICULOUS OUTFIT?
DAD, I KNOW WHAT THIS LOOKS LIKE...
MAN'S LOST HIS MIND, SIR.
HE ATTACKED US FOR NO REASON.
MADE ALL SORTS OF WILD ACCUSATIONS, TOO.
I-IS THIS TRUE, SON?
DON'T LISTEN TO THEM, DAD!
THEY'RE LIARS, THIEVES AND WORSE.
I'M JUST TRYING TO FORCE THEM TO CONFESS.
THEY KNOW WHO MURDERED MARIA, DAD.
EVERYBODY KNOWS, SON.
THE AUTHORITIES SAID TERRORISTS WERE RESPONSIBLE.
THE AUTHORITIES ARE WRONG!
ELIHAS STARR DID IT!
HE ALSO SENT THOSE MEN TO KILL ME AND STEAL MY RESEARCH.

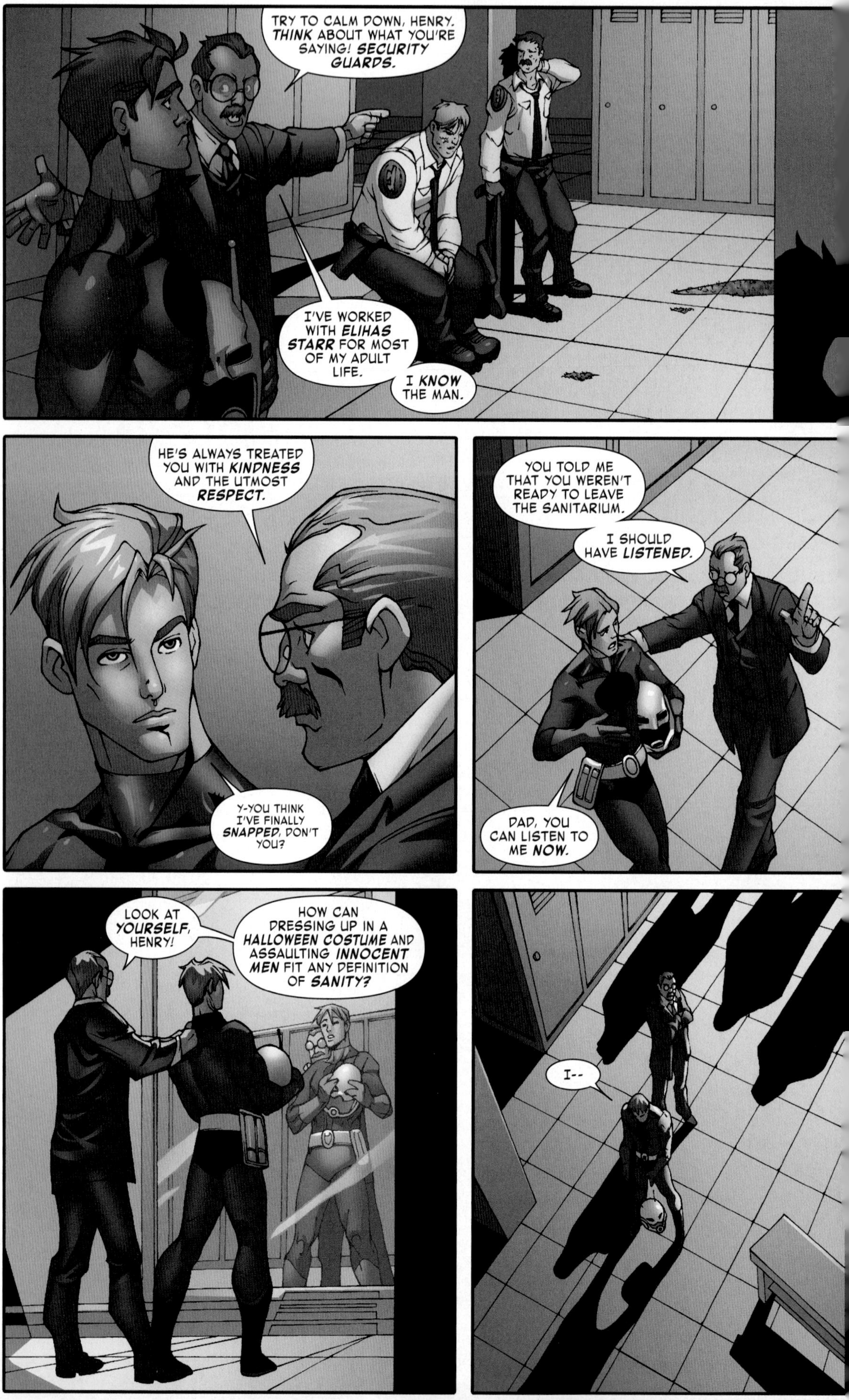
TRY TO CALM DOWN, HENRY. THINK ABOUT WHAT YOU'RE SAYING! SECURITY GUARDS.
I'VE WORKED WITH ELIHAS STARR FOR MOST OF MY ADULT LIFE.
I KNOW THE MAN.
HE'S ALWAYS TREATED YOU WITH KINDNESS AND THE UTMOST RESPECT.
Y-YOU THINK I'VE FINALLY SNAPPED, DON'T YOU?
YOU TOLD ME THAT YOU WEREN'T READY TO LEAVE THE SANITARIUM.
I SHOULD HAVE LISTENED.
DAD, YOU CAN LISTEN TO ME NOW.
LOOK AT YOURSELF, HENRY!
HOW CAN DRESSING UP IN A HALLOWEEN COSTUME AND ASSAULTING INNOCENT MEN FIT ANY DEFINITION OF SANITY?
I--

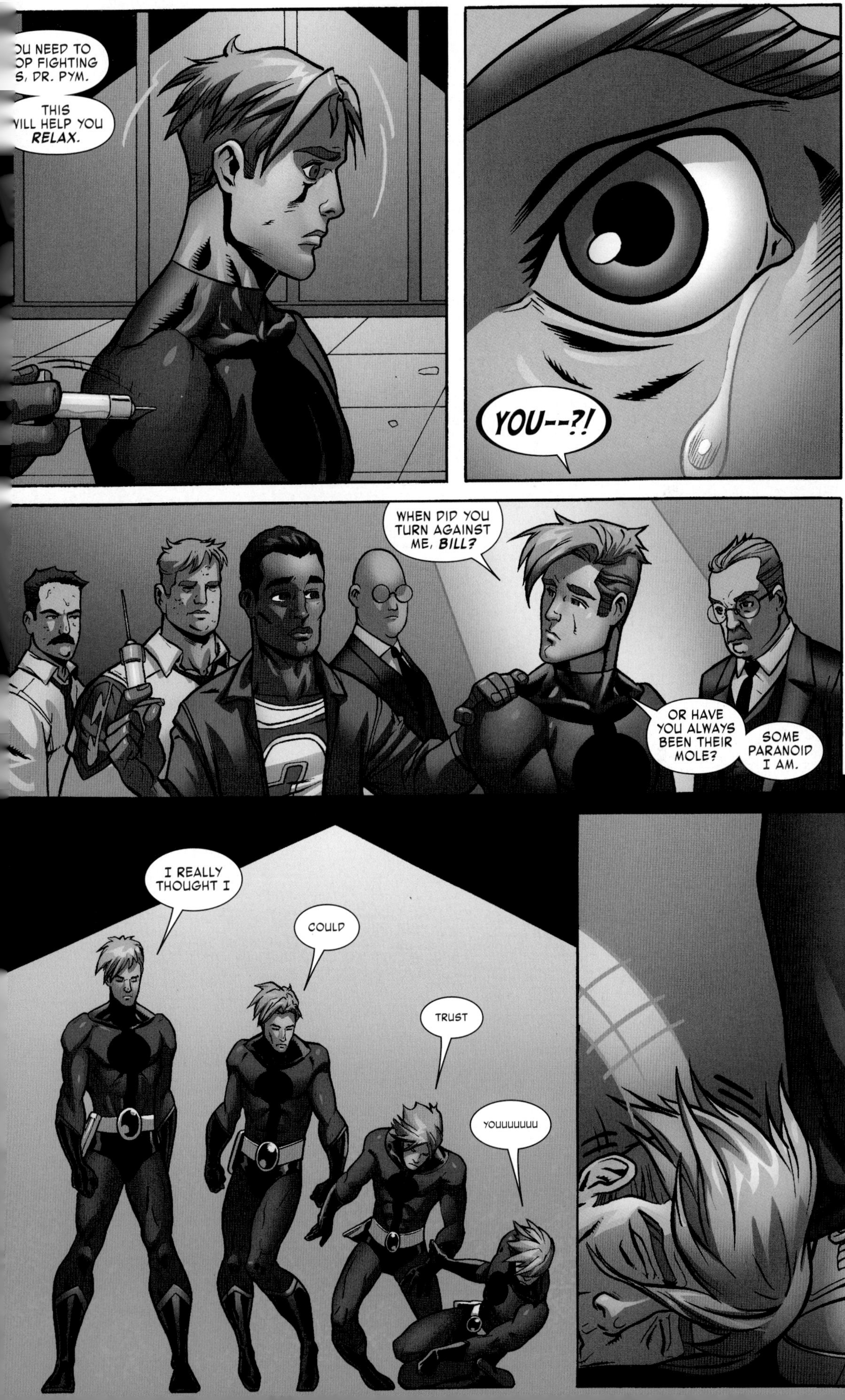
OU NEED TO
OP FIGHTING
S, DR. PYM.
THIS
WILL HELP YOU
RELAX.
YOU--?!
WHEN DID YOU
TURN AGAINST
ME, BILL?
OR HAVE
YOU ALWAYS
BEEN THEIR
MOLE?
SOME
PARANOID
I AM.
I REALLY
THOUGHT I
COULD
TRUST
YOUUUUUUU

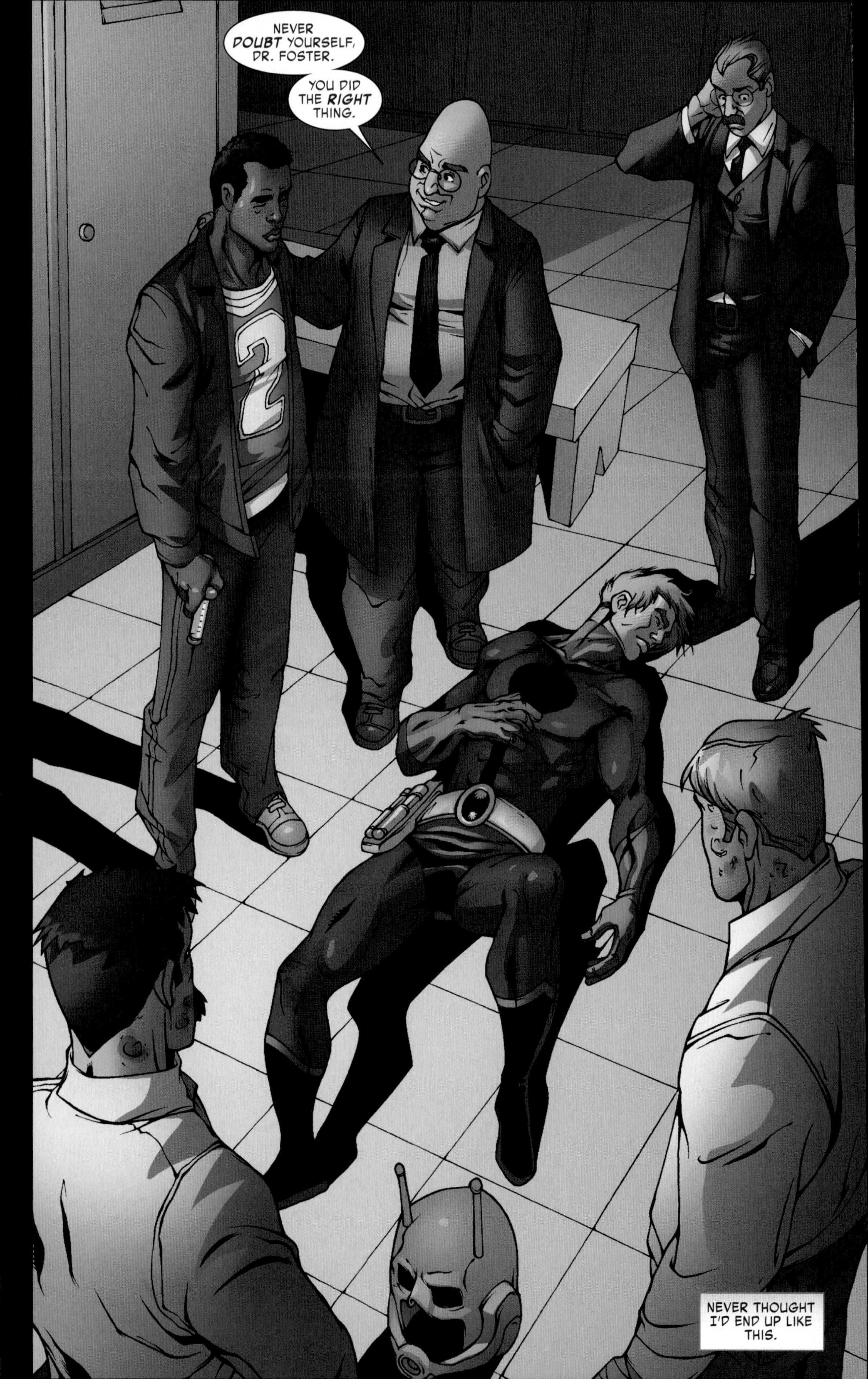
NEVER DOUBT YOURSELF, DR. FOSTER.
YOU DID THE RIGHT THING.
NEVER THOUGHT I'D END UP LIKE THIS.

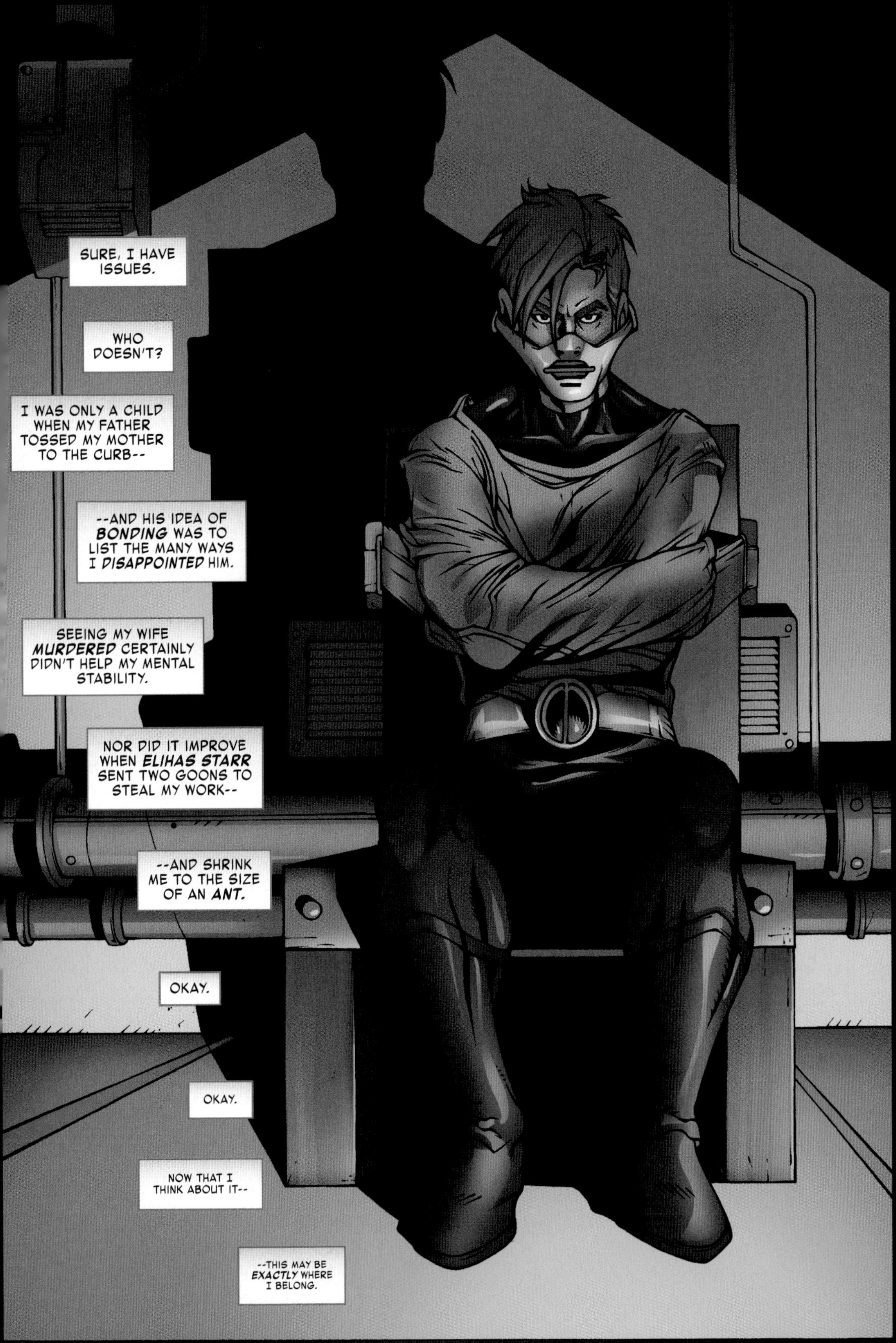
SURE, I HAVE ISSUES.
WHO DOESN'T?
I WAS ONLY A CHILD WHEN MY FATHER TOSSED MY MOTHER TO THE CURB--
--AND HIS IDEA OF *BONDING* WAS TO LIST THE MANY WAYS I *DISAPPOINTED* HIM.
SEEING MY WIFE *MURDERED* CERTAINLY DIDN'T HELP MY MENTAL STABILITY.
NOR DID IT IMPROVE WHEN *ELIHAS STARR* SENT TWO GOONS TO STEAL MY WORK--
--AND SHRINK ME TO THE SIZE OF AN *ANT.*
OKAY.
OKAY.
NOW THAT I THINK ABOUT IT--
--THIS MAY BE *EXACTLY* WHERE I BELONG.

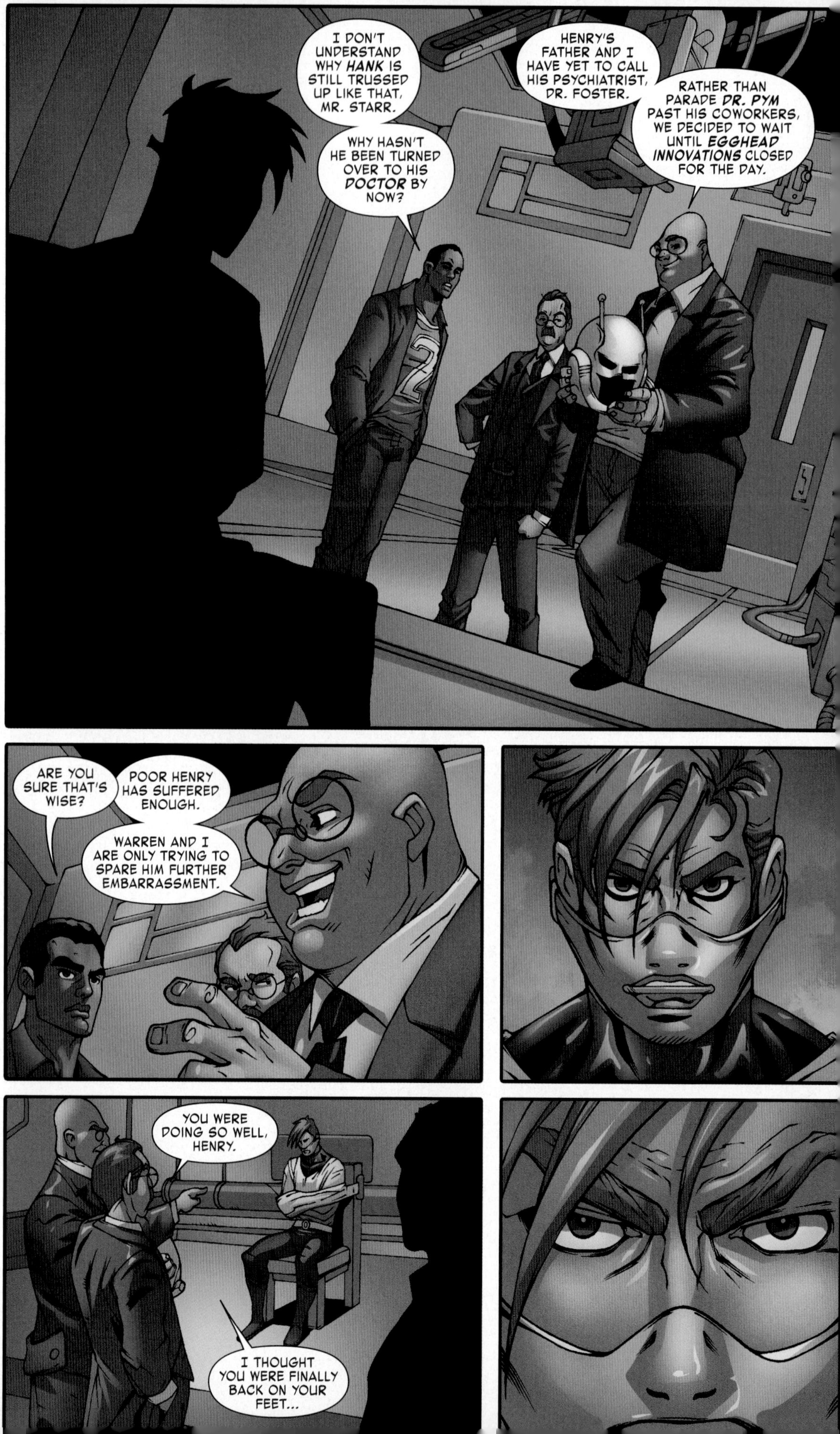
I DON'T UNDERSTAND WHY HANK IS STILL TRUSSED UP LIKE THAT, MR. STARR.
WHY HASN'T HE BEEN TURNED OVER TO HIS DOCTOR BY NOW?
HENRY'S FATHER AND I HAVE YET TO CALL HIS PSYCHIATRIST, DR. FOSTER.
RATHER THAN PARADE DR. PYM PAST HIS COWORKERS, WE DECIDED TO WAIT UNTIL EGGHEAD INNOVATIONS CLOSED FOR THE DAY.
ARE YOU SURE THAT'S WISE?
POOR HENRY HAS SUFFERED ENOUGH.
WARREN AND I ARE ONLY TRYING TO SPARE HIM FURTHER EMBARRASSMENT.
YOU WERE DOING SO WELL, HENRY.
I THOUGHT YOU WERE FINALLY BACK ON YOUR FEET...

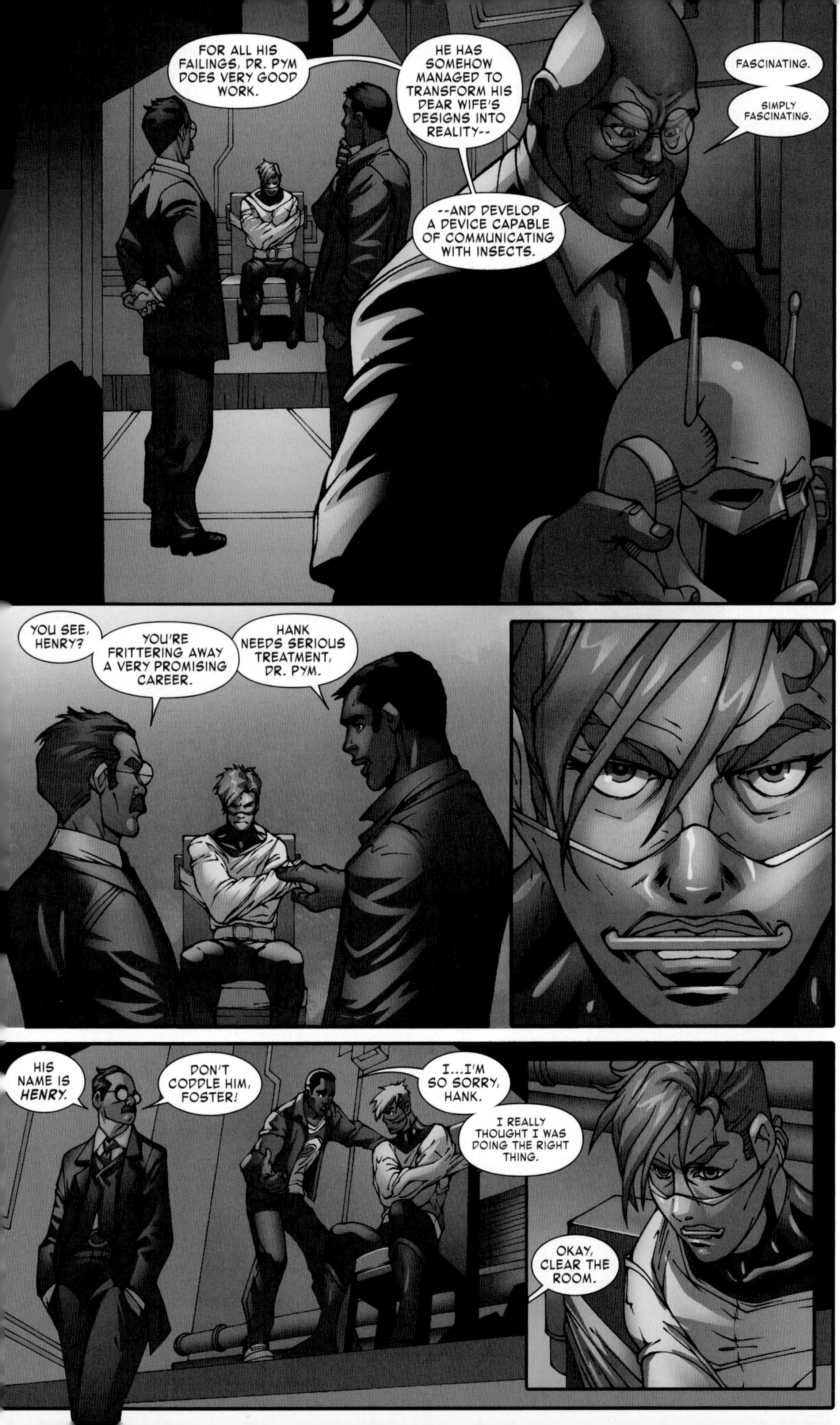
FOR ALL HIS FAILINGS, DR. PYM DOES VERY GOOD WORK.
HE HAS SOMEHOW MANAGED TO TRANSFORM HIS DEAR WIFE'S DESIGNS INTO REALITY--
--AND DEVELOP A DEVICE CAPABLE OF COMMUNICATING WITH INSECTS.
FASCINATING.
SIMPLY FASCINATING.
YOU SEE, HENRY?
YOU'RE FRITTERING AWAY A VERY PROMISING CAREER.
HANK NEEDS SERIOUS TREATMENT, DR. PYM.
HIS NAME IS *HENRY*.
DON'T CODDLE HIM, FOSTER!
I...I'M SO SORRY, HANK.
I REALLY THOUGHT I WAS DOING THE RIGHT THING.
OKAY, CLEAR THE ROOM.

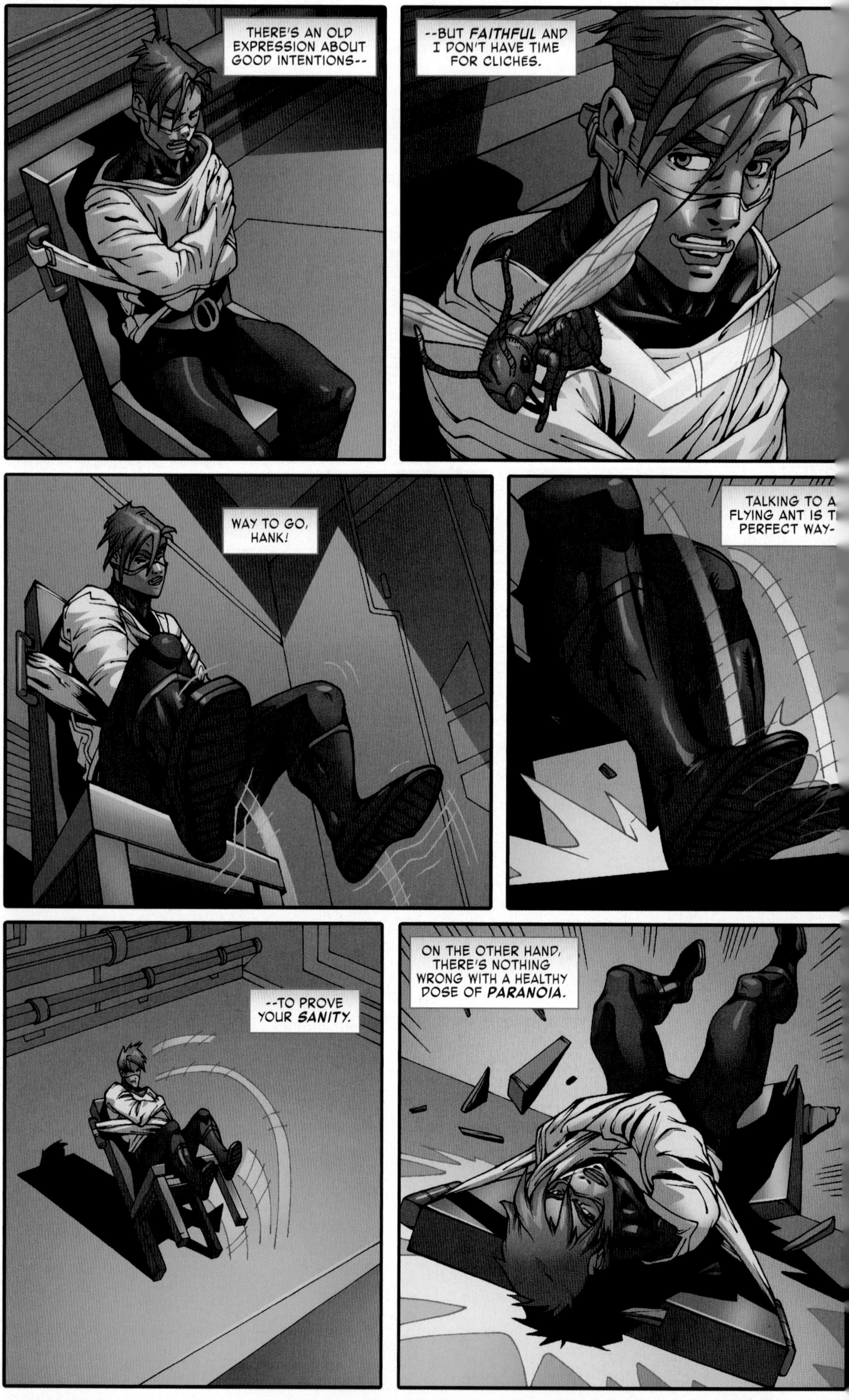
THERE'S AN OLD EXPRESSION ABOUT GOOD INTENTIONS--
--BUT FAITHFUL AND I DON'T HAVE TIME FOR CLICHES.
WAY TO GO, HANK!
TALKING TO A FLYING ANT IS T PERFECT WAY-
--TO PROVE YOUR SANITY.
ON THE OTHER HAND, THERE'S NOTHING WRONG WITH A HEALTHY DOSE OF PARANOIA.

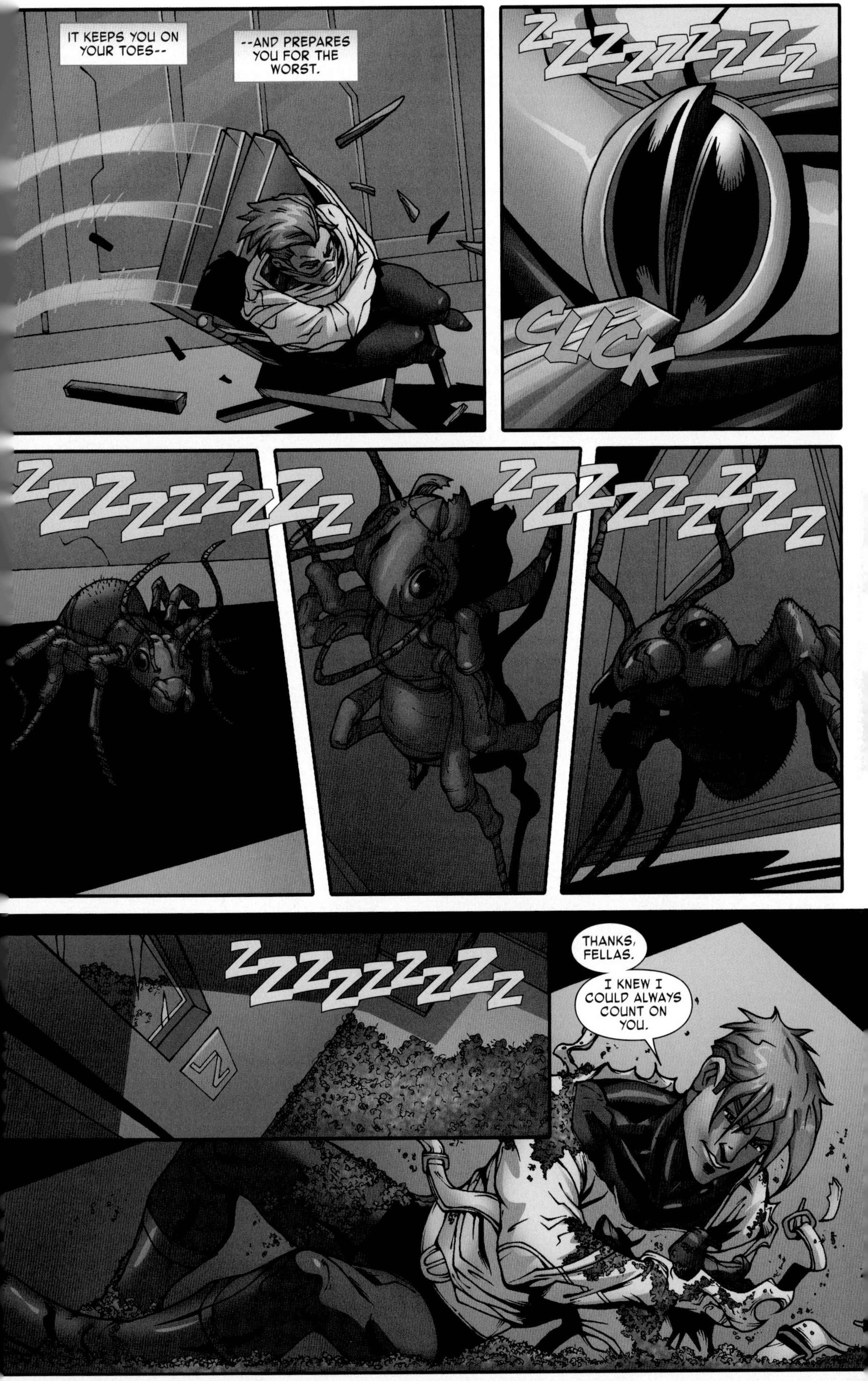
IT KEEPS YOU ON YOUR TOES--
--AND PREPARES YOU FOR THE WORST.
ZZZZZZZZZZZ
CLICK
ZZZZZZZZZZ
ZZZZZZZZZZZ
ZZZZZZZZZZZ
THANKS, FELLAS.
I KNEW I COULD ALWAYS COUNT ON YOU.

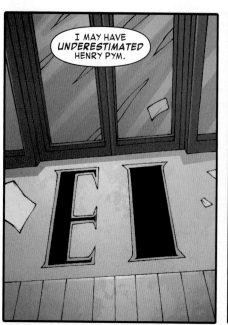

I MAY HAVE *UNDERESTIMATED* HENRY PYM.

THIS HELMET IS PURE GENIUS.

MY OWN VERSION IS, OF COURSE, FAR SUPERIOR.

STILL, IT AMAZES ME HOW MUCH HE ACCOMPLISHED.

MY DEAR, SWEET MARIA MAY HAVE CONCEIVED THIS DEVICE, BUT HENRY'S CONTRIBUTIONS CANNOT BE MINIMIZED.

UHHH... MR. STARR?

WHAT IS IT, MR. STERN?

I REMEMBER CORRECTLY, *MRS. PYM* SPECIALIZED IN *ANTS*.

SO WHY THE *HORNETS?!?*

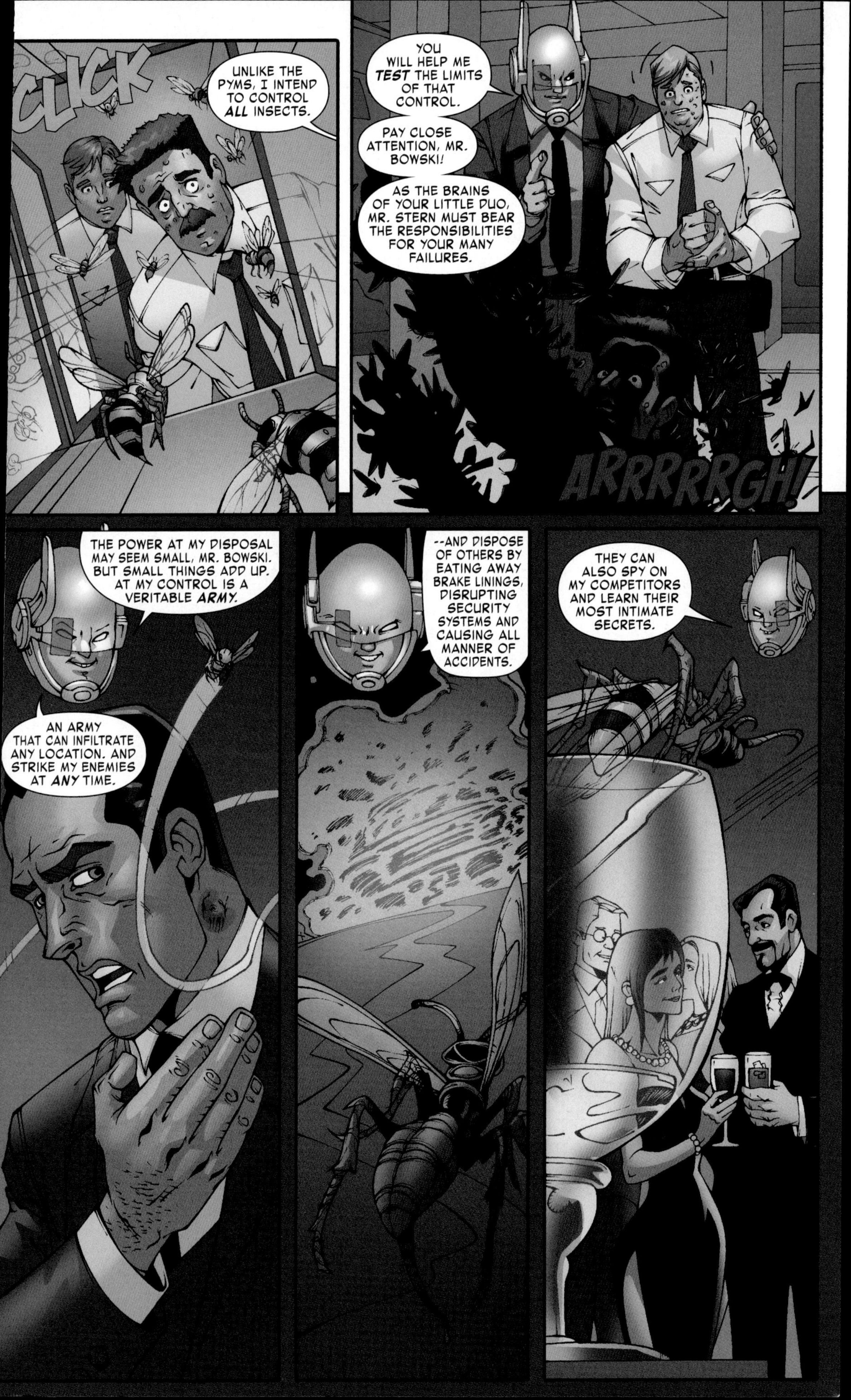
CLICK
UNLIKE THE PYMS, I INTEND TO CONTROL ALL INSECTS.
YOU WILL HELP ME TEST THE LIMITS OF THAT CONTROL.
PAY CLOSE ATTENTION, MR. BOWSKI!
AS THE BRAINS OF YOUR LITTLE DUO, MR. STERN MUST BEAR THE RESPONSIBILITIES FOR YOUR MANY FAILURES.
ARRRRRGH!
THE POWER AT MY DISPOSAL MAY SEEM SMALL, MR. BOWSKI. BUT SMALL THINGS ADD UP. AT MY CONTROL IS A VERITABLE ARMY.
AN ARMY THAT CAN INFILTRATE ANY LOCATION. AND STRIKE MY ENEMIES AT ANY TIME.
--AND DISPOSE OF OTHERS BY EATING AWAY BRAKE LININGS, DISRUPTING SECURITY SYSTEMS AND CAUSING ALL MANNER OF ACCIDENTS.
THEY CAN ALSO SPY ON MY COMPETITORS AND LEARN THEIR MOST INTIMATE SECRETS.

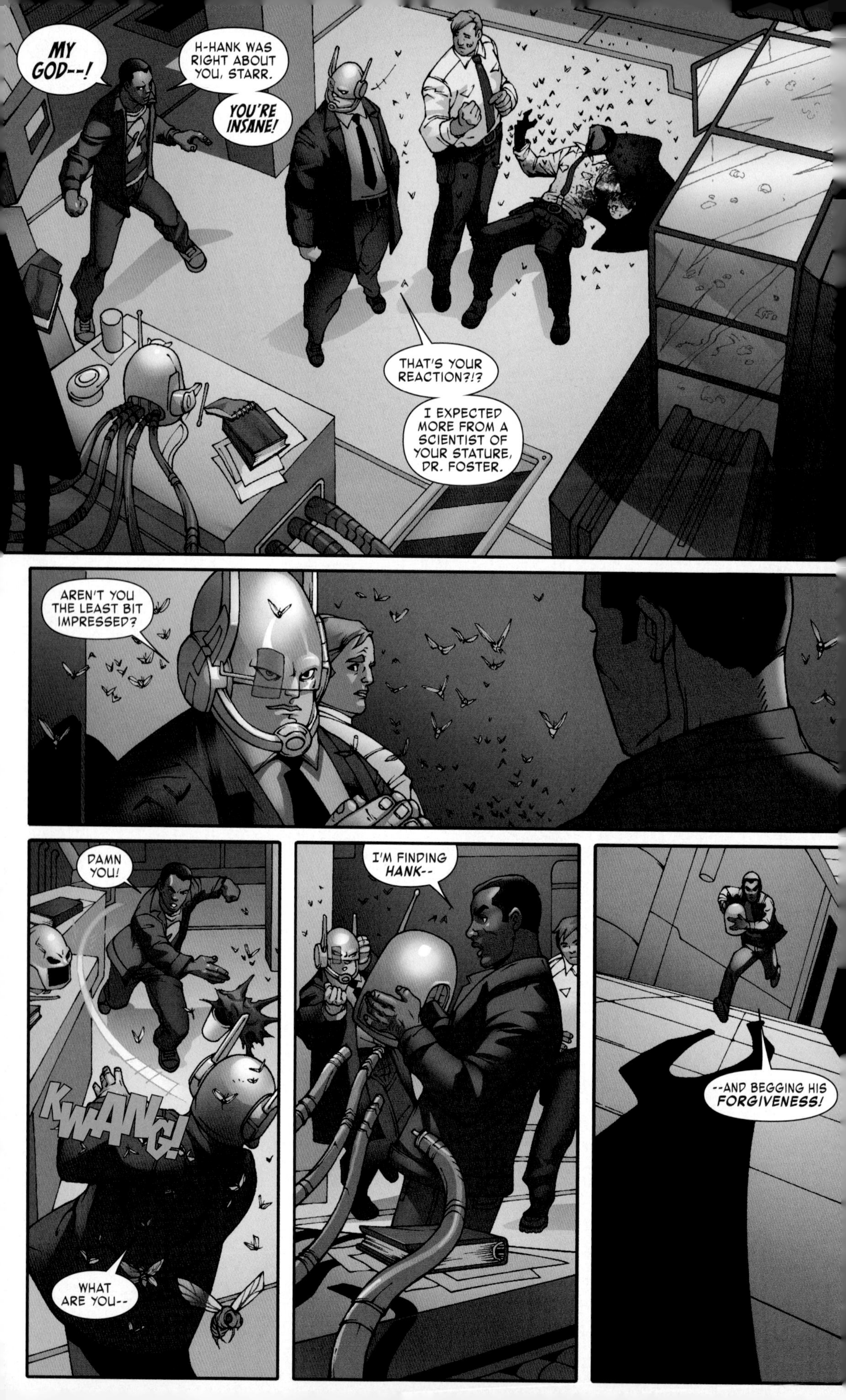

MY GOD--!
H-HANK WAS RIGHT ABOUT YOU, STARR.
YOU'RE INSANE!
THAT'S YOUR REACTION?!?
I EXPECTED MORE FROM A SCIENTIST OF YOUR STATURE, DR. FOSTER.
AREN'T YOU THE LEAST BIT IMPRESSED?
DAMN YOU!
KWANG!
WHAT ARE YOU--
I'M FINDING HANK--
--AND BEGGING HIS FORGIVENESS!

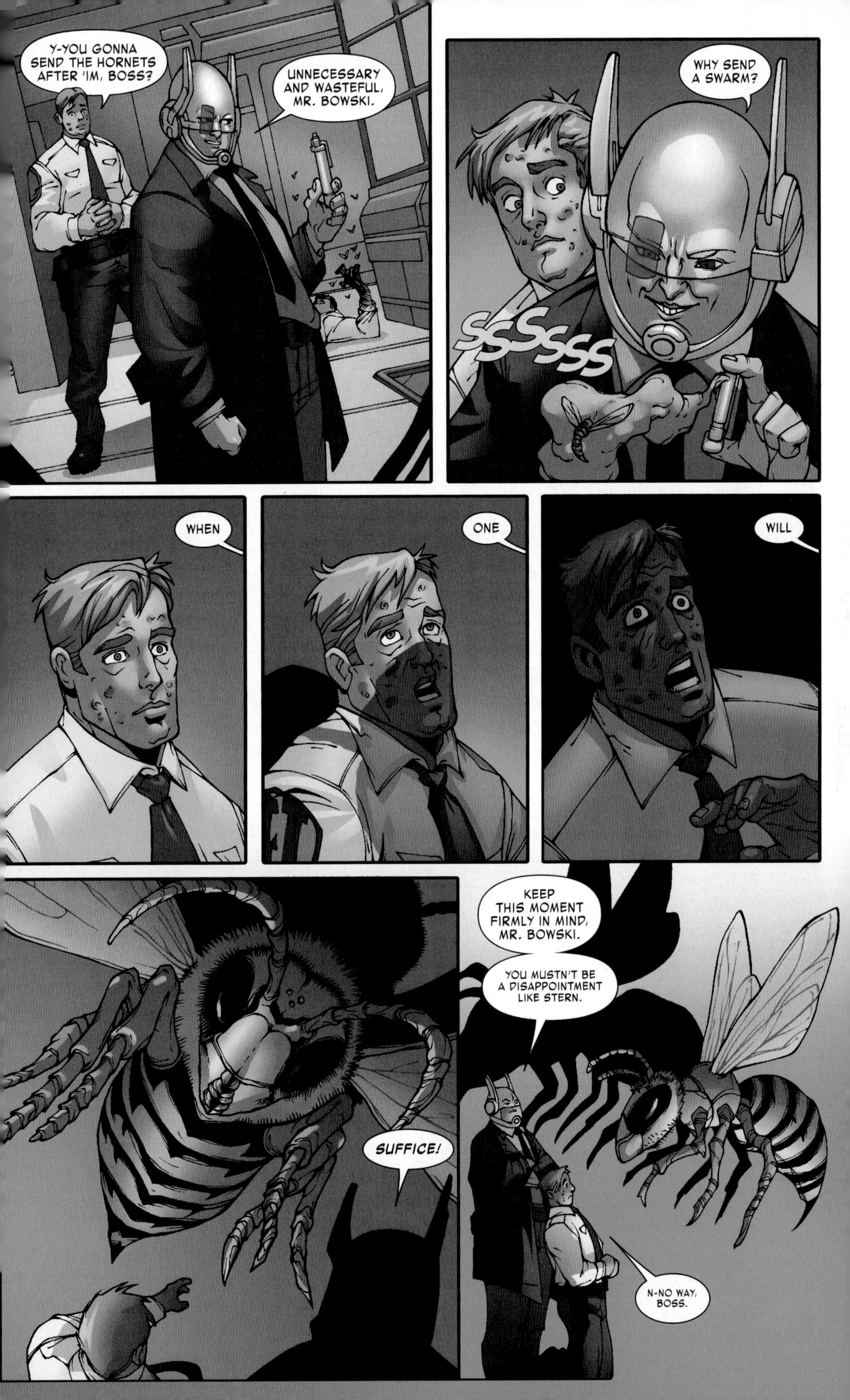
Y-YOU GONNA SEND THE HORNETS AFTER 'IM, BOSS?
UNNECESSARY AND WASTEFUL, MR. BOWSKI.
WHY SEND A SWARM?
SSSSSSS
WHEN
ONE
WILL
SUFFICE!
KEEP THIS MOMENT FIRMLY IN MIND, MR. BOWSKI.
YOU MUSTN'T BE A DISAPPOINTMENT LIKE STERN.
N-NO WAY, BOSS.

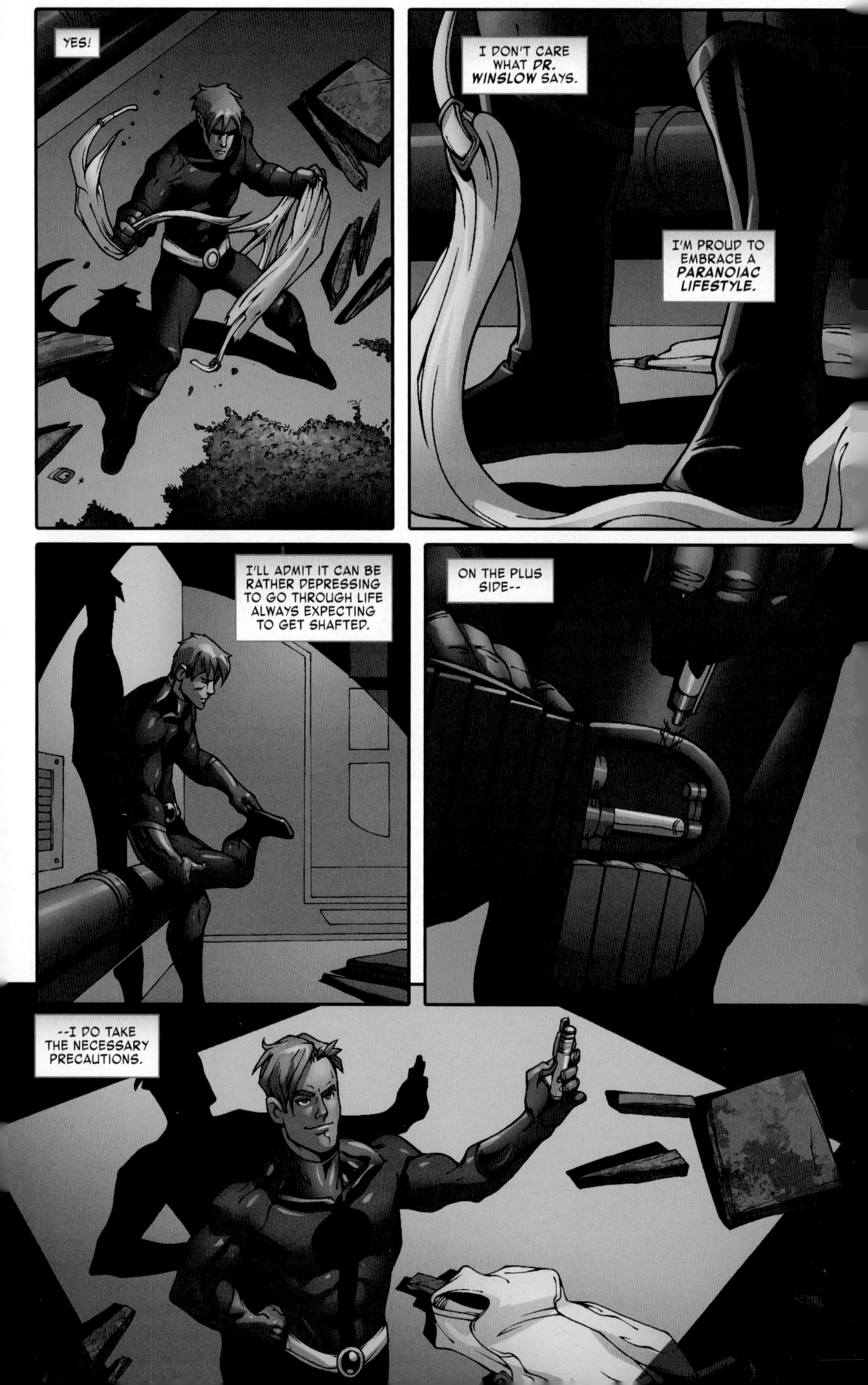
YES!
I DON'T CARE WHAT DR. WINSLOW SAYS.
I'M PROUD TO EMBRACE A PARANOIAC LIFESTYLE.
I'LL ADMIT IT CAN BE RATHER DEPRESSING TO GO THROUGH LIFE ALWAYS EXPECTING TO GET SHAFTED.
ON THE PLUS SIDE--
--I DO TAKE THE NECESSARY PRECAUTIONS.

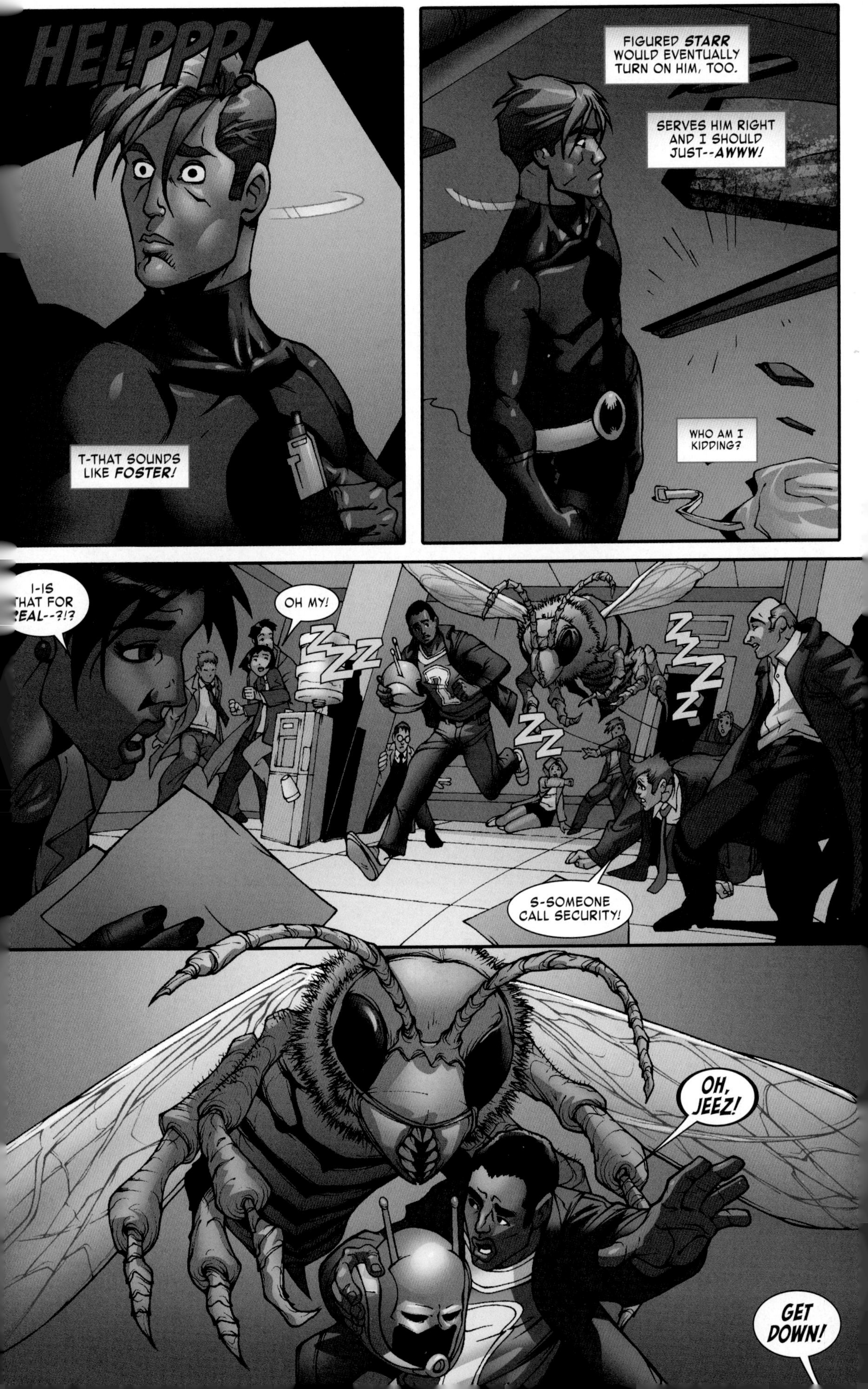
HELPPP!
T-THAT SOUNDS LIKE FOSTER!
FIGURED STARR WOULD EVENTUALLY TURN ON HIM, TOO.
SERVES HIM RIGHT AND I SHOULD JUST--AWWW!
WHO AM I KIDDING?
I-IS THAT FOR REAL--?!?
OH MY!
ZZZ
ZZ
ZZZZ
S-SOMEONE CALL SECURITY!
OH, JEEZ!
GET DOWN!

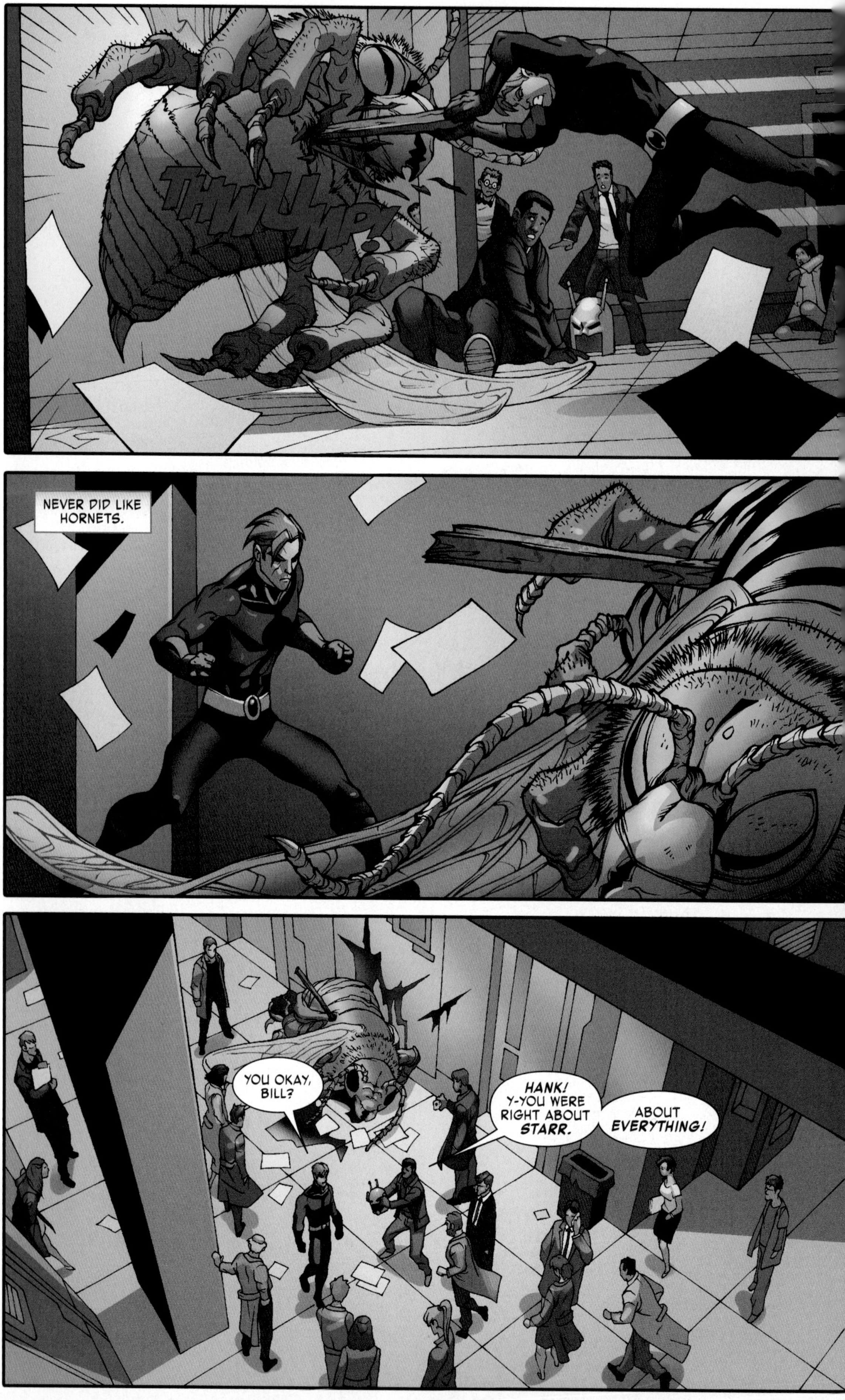
THWUMP!
NEVER DID LIKE HORNETS.
YOU OKAY, BILL?
HANK! Y-YOU WERE RIGHT ABOUT STARR.
ABOUT EVERYTHING!

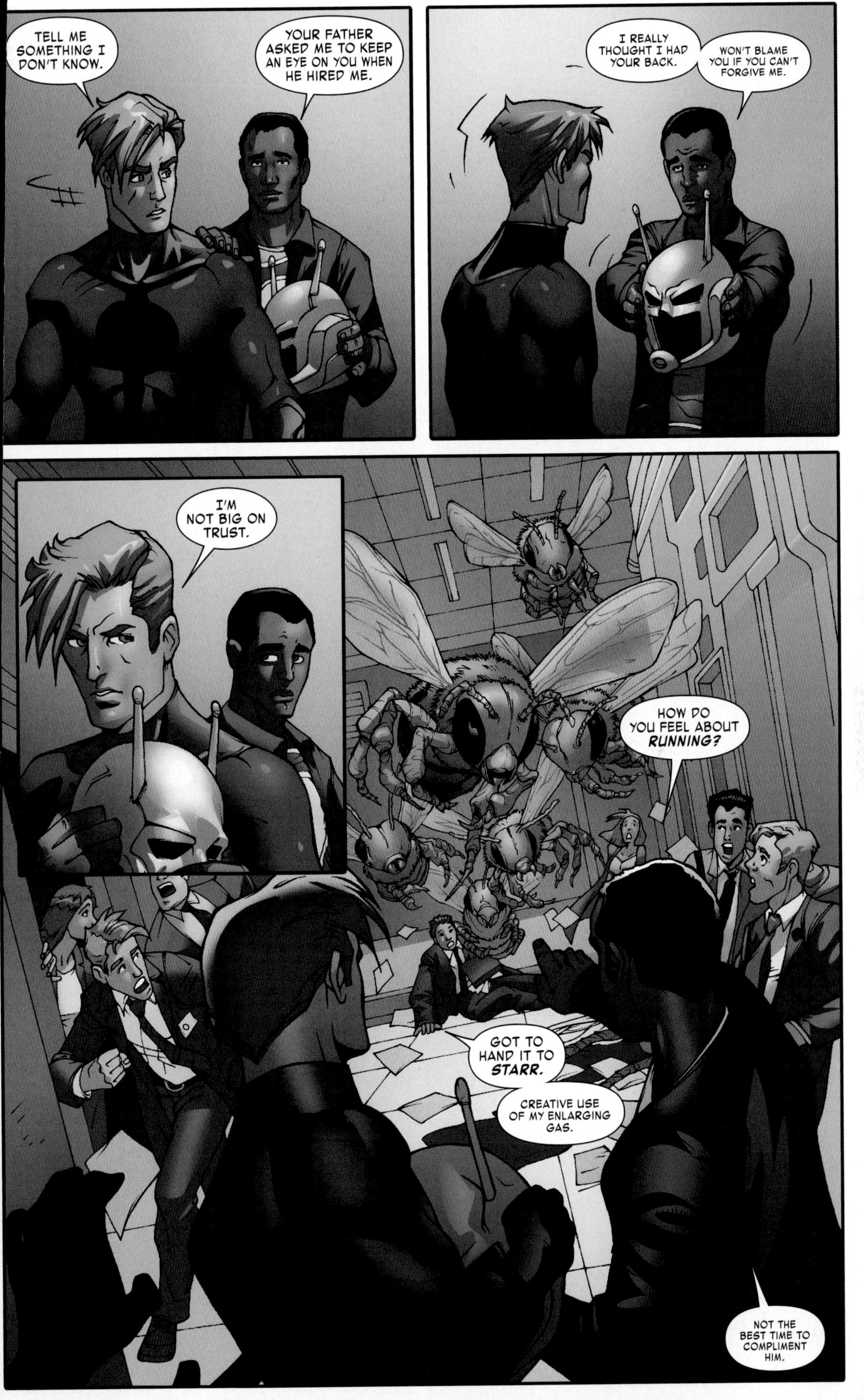
TELL ME SOMETHING I DON'T KNOW.
YOUR FATHER ASKED ME TO KEEP AN EYE ON YOU WHEN HE HIRED ME.
I REALLY THOUGHT I HAD YOUR BACK.
WON'T BLAME YOU IF YOU CAN'T FORGIVE ME.
I'M NOT BIG ON TRUST.
HOW DO YOU FEEL ABOUT *RUNNING?*
GOT TO HAND IT TO *STARR.*
CREATIVE USE OF MY ENLARGING GAS.
NOT THE BEST TIME TO COMPLIMENT HIM.

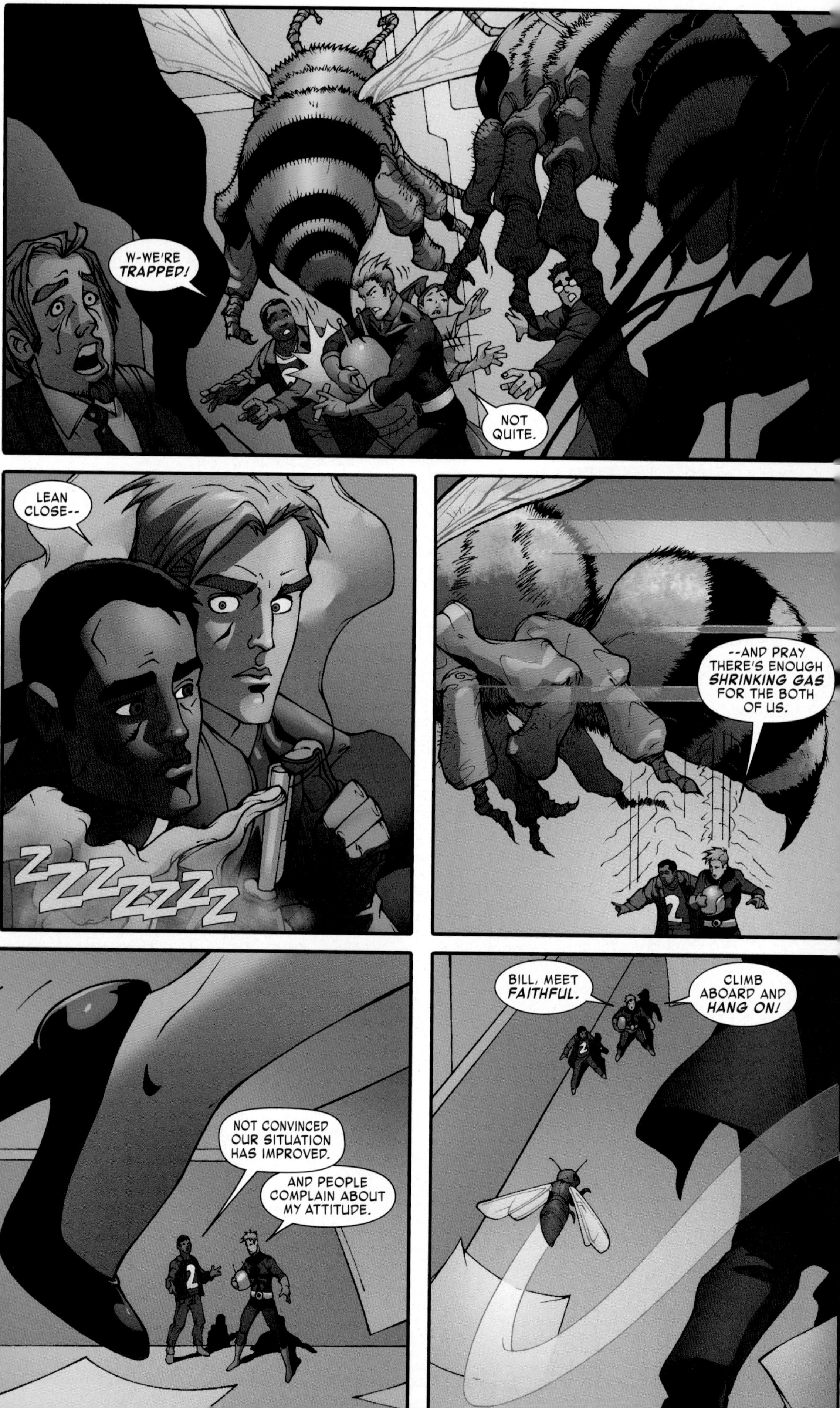
W-WE'RE TRAPPED!
NOT QUITE.
LEAN CLOSE--
ZZZZZZZZ
--AND PRAY THERE'S ENOUGH SHRINKING GAS FOR THE BOTH OF US.
NOT CONVINCED OUR SITUATION HAS IMPROVED.
AND PEOPLE COMPLAIN ABOUT MY ATTITUDE.
BILL, MEET FAITHFUL.
CLIMB ABOARD AND HANG ON!

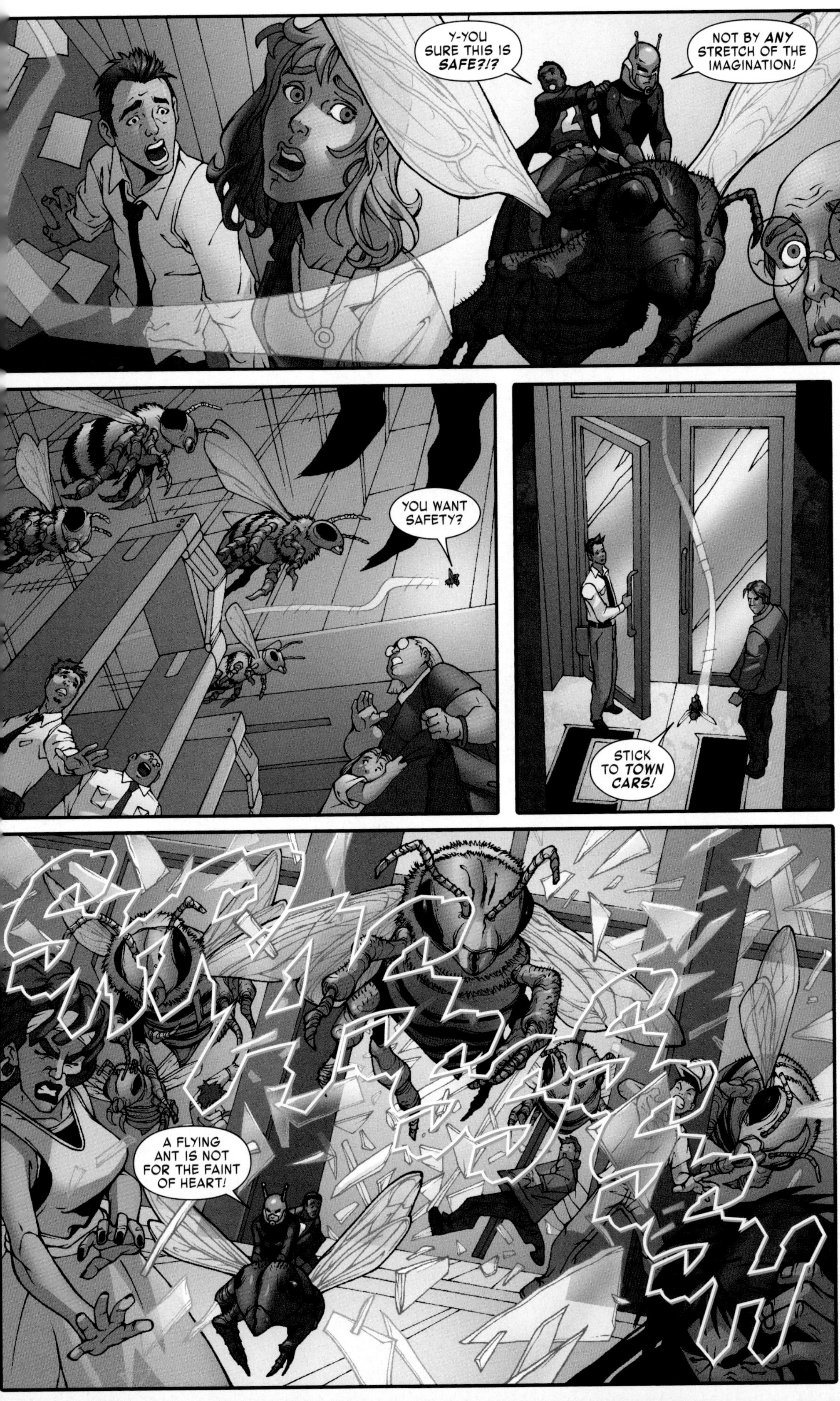
Y-YOU SURE THIS IS SAFE?!?
NOT BY ANY STRETCH OF THE IMAGINATION!
YOU WANT SAFETY?
STICK TO TOWN CARS!
A FLYING ANT IS NOT FOR THE FAINT OF HEART!

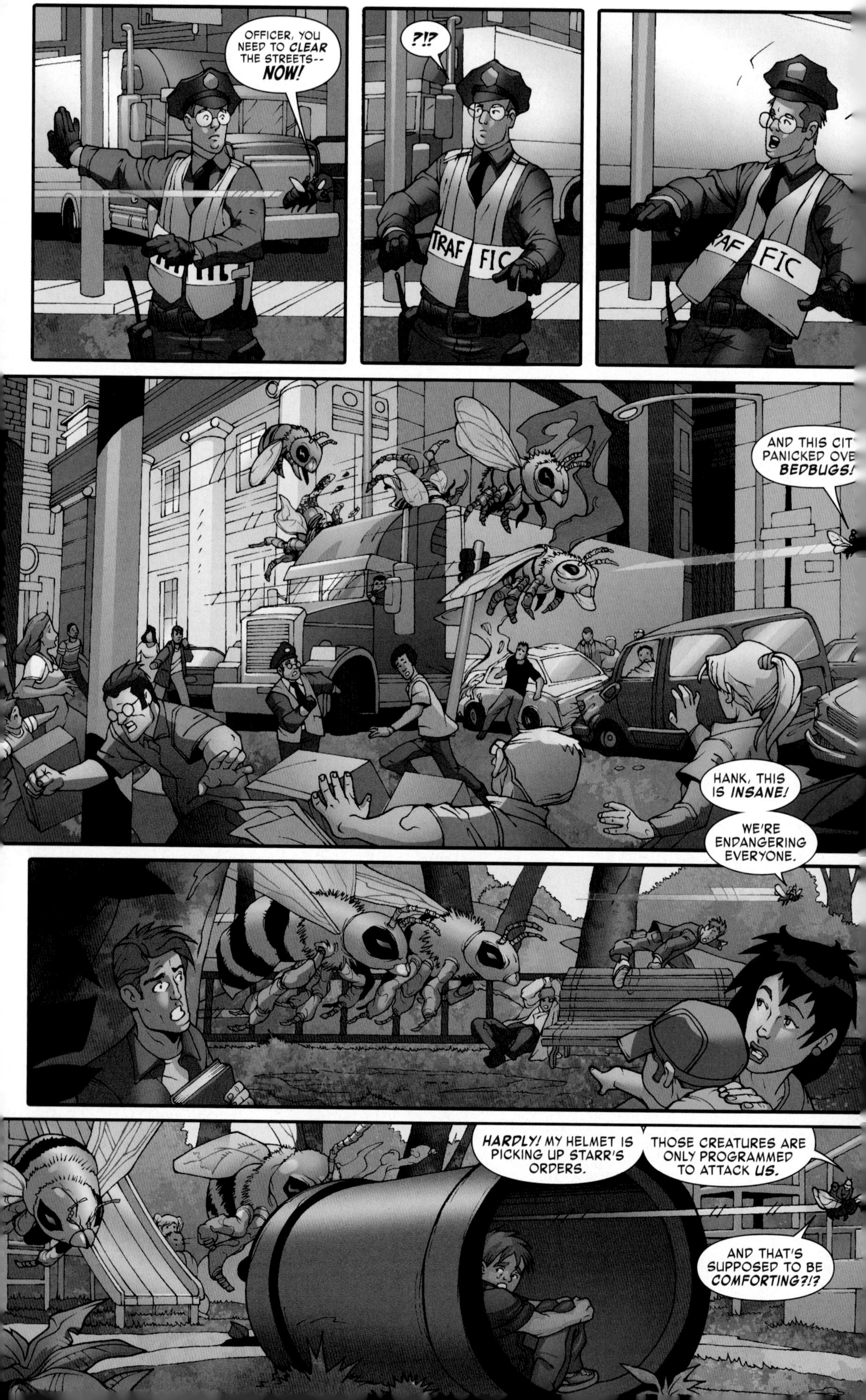

OFFICER, YOU NEED TO *CLEAR* THE STREETS-- ***NOW!***
?!?
TRAF FIC
AND THIS CIT PANICKED OVE ***BEDBUGS!***
HANK, THIS IS ***INSANE!***
WE'RE ENDANGERING EVERYONE.
***HARDLY!*** MY HELMET IS PICKING UP STARR'S ORDERS.
THOSE CREATURES ARE ONLY PROGRAMMED TO ATTACK ***US.***
AND THAT'S SUPPOSED TO BE ***COMFORTING?!?***

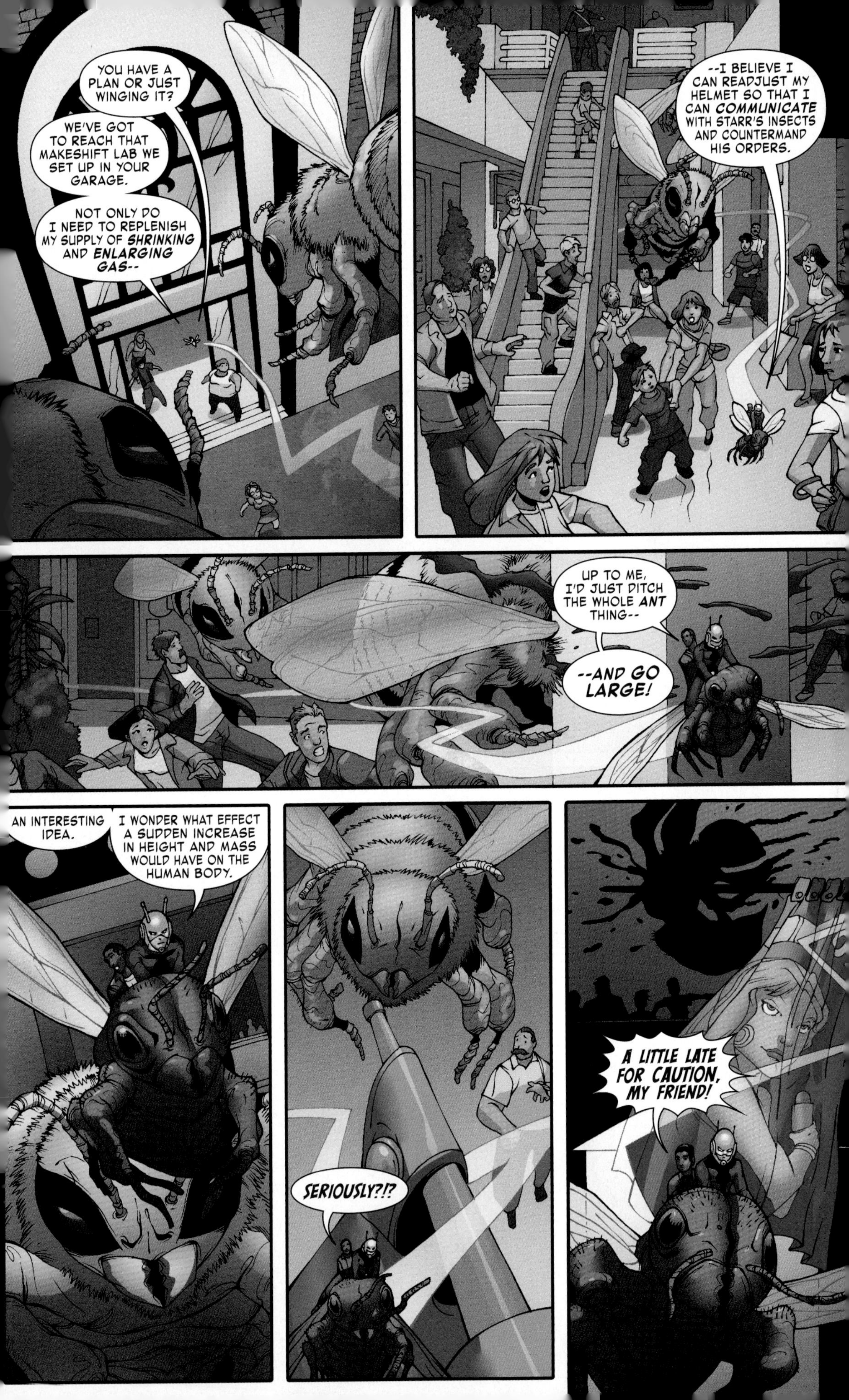
YOU HAVE A PLAN OR JUST WINGING IT?
WE'VE GOT TO REACH THAT MAKESHIFT LAB WE SET UP IN YOUR GARAGE.
NOT ONLY DO I NEED TO REPLENISH MY SUPPLY OF SHRINKING AND ENLARGING GAS--
--I BELIEVE I CAN READJUST MY HELMET SO THAT I CAN COMMUNICATE WITH STARR'S INSECTS AND COUNTERMAND HIS ORDERS.
UP TO ME, I'D JUST DITCH THE WHOLE ANT THING--
--AND GO LARGE!
AN INTERESTING IDEA.
I WONDER WHAT EFFECT A SUDDEN INCREASE IN HEIGHT AND MASS WOULD HAVE ON THE HUMAN BODY.
SERIOUSLY?!?
A LITTLE LATE FOR CAUTION, MY FRIEND!

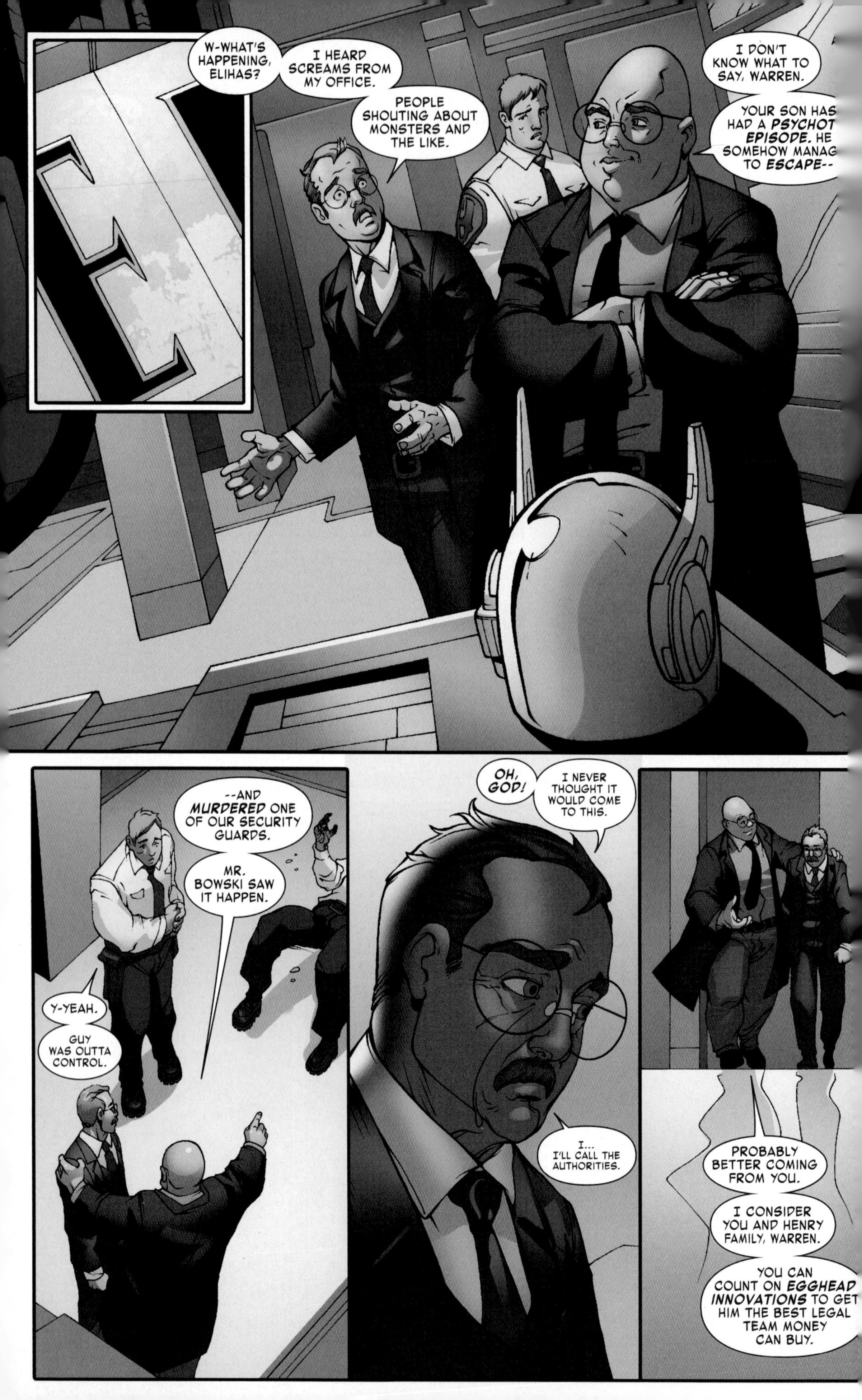
W-WHAT'S HAPPENING, ELIHAS?
I HEARD SCREAMS FROM MY OFFICE.
PEOPLE SHOUTING ABOUT MONSTERS AND THE LIKE.
I DON'T KNOW WHAT TO SAY, WARREN.
YOUR SON HAS HAD A PSYCHOT EPISODE. HE SOMEHOW MANAG TO ESCAPE--
--AND MURDERED ONE OF OUR SECURITY GUARDS.
MR. BOWSKI SAW IT HAPPEN.
Y-YEAH.
GUY WAS OUTTA CONTROL.
OH, GOD!
I NEVER THOUGHT IT WOULD COME TO THIS.
I... I'LL CALL THE AUTHORITIES.
PROBABLY BETTER COMING FROM YOU.
I CONSIDER YOU AND HENRY FAMILY, WARREN.
YOU CAN COUNT ON EGGHEAD INNOVATIONS TO GET HIM THE BEST LEGAL TEAM MONEY CAN BUY.

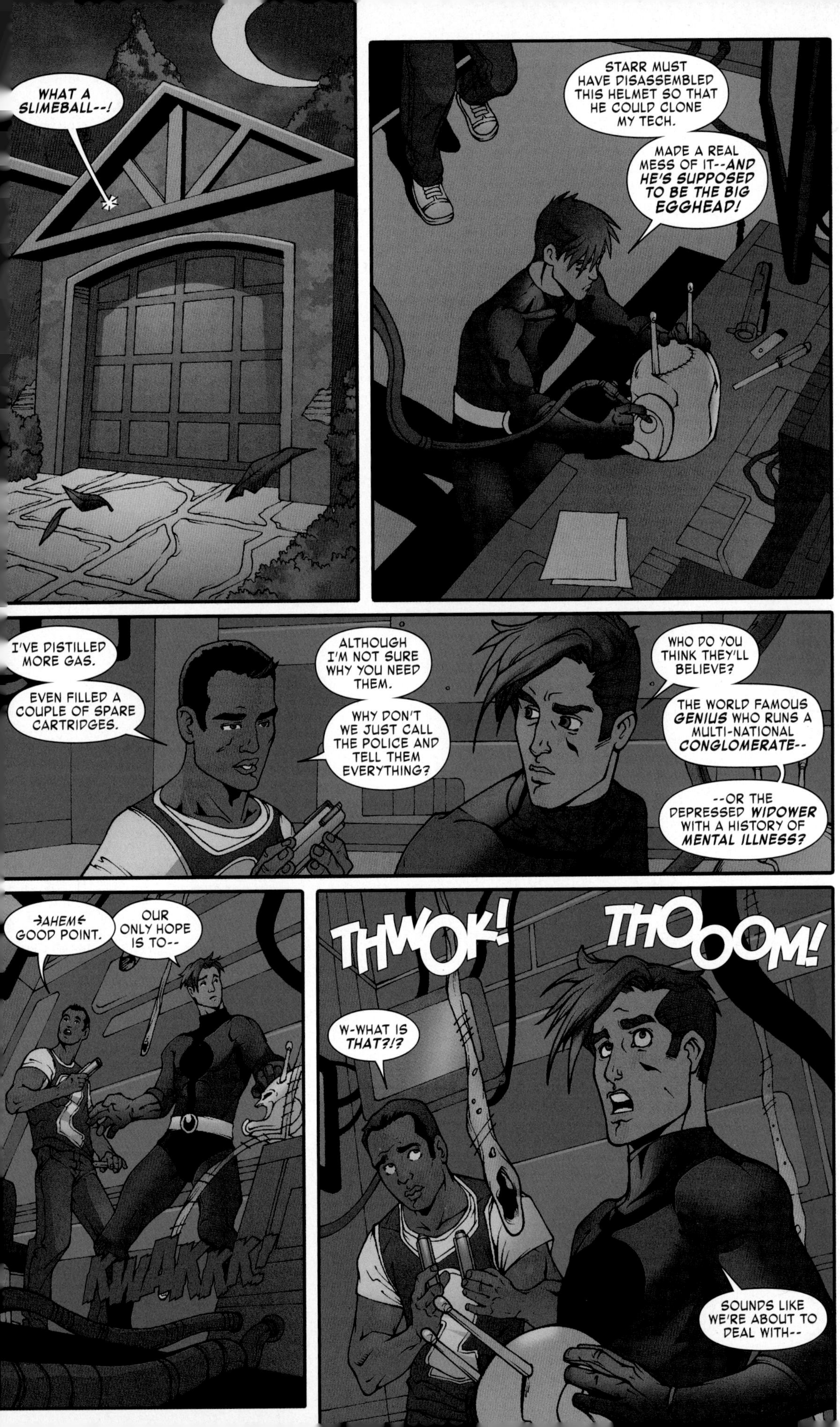
WHAT A SLIMEBALL--!
STARR MUST HAVE DISASSEMBLED THIS HELMET SO THAT HE COULD CLONE MY TECH.
MADE A REAL MESS OF IT--AND HE'S SUPPOSED TO BE THE BIG EGGHEAD!
I'VE DISTILLED MORE GAS.
EVEN FILLED A COUPLE OF SPARE CARTRIDGES.
ALTHOUGH I'M NOT SURE WHY YOU NEED THEM.
WHY DON'T WE JUST CALL THE POLICE AND TELL THEM EVERYTHING?
WHO DO YOU THINK THEY'LL BELIEVE?
THE WORLD FAMOUS GENIUS WHO RUNS A MULTI-NATIONAL CONGLOMERATE--
--OR THE DEPRESSED WIDOWER WITH A HISTORY OF MENTAL ILLNESS?
AHEM GOOD POINT.
OUR ONLY HOPE IS TO--
KWAKK!
THWOK!
THOOOM!
W-WHAT IS THAT?!?
SOUNDS LIKE WE'RE ABOUT TO DEAL WITH--

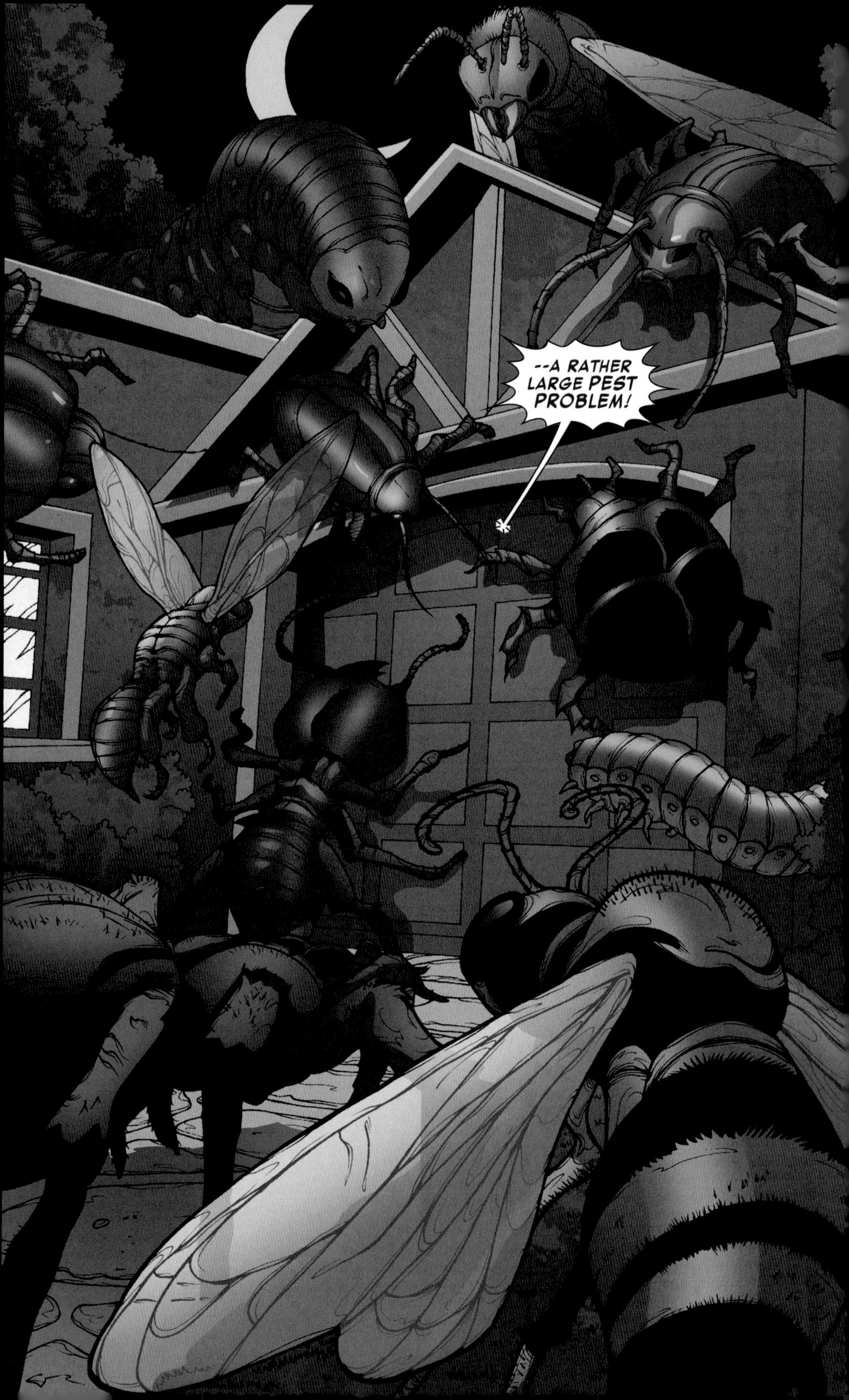
--A RATHER LARGE PEST PROBLEM!

THWAK! KWOOM! THWAM!

UHHH... HANK?

READY FOR THE BIG RESCUE ANY TIME NOW.

ABOUT THAT--

--I KNOW I SAID I COULD *PROBABLY* ADJUST MY HELMET TO COMMUNICATE WITH THE GIANT-SIZED INSECTS *ELIHAS STARR* SENT TO KILL US.

DON'T RECALL NO *"PROBABLY."*

WHATEVER!

I NEED MORE TIME.

WHY DON'T YOU ASK FOR AN *M-16* WHILE YOU'RE AT IT?

NOT TO WORRY! I HAVE A BACKUP PLAN.

I'M GOING TO FOLLOW YOUR SUGGESTION AND--

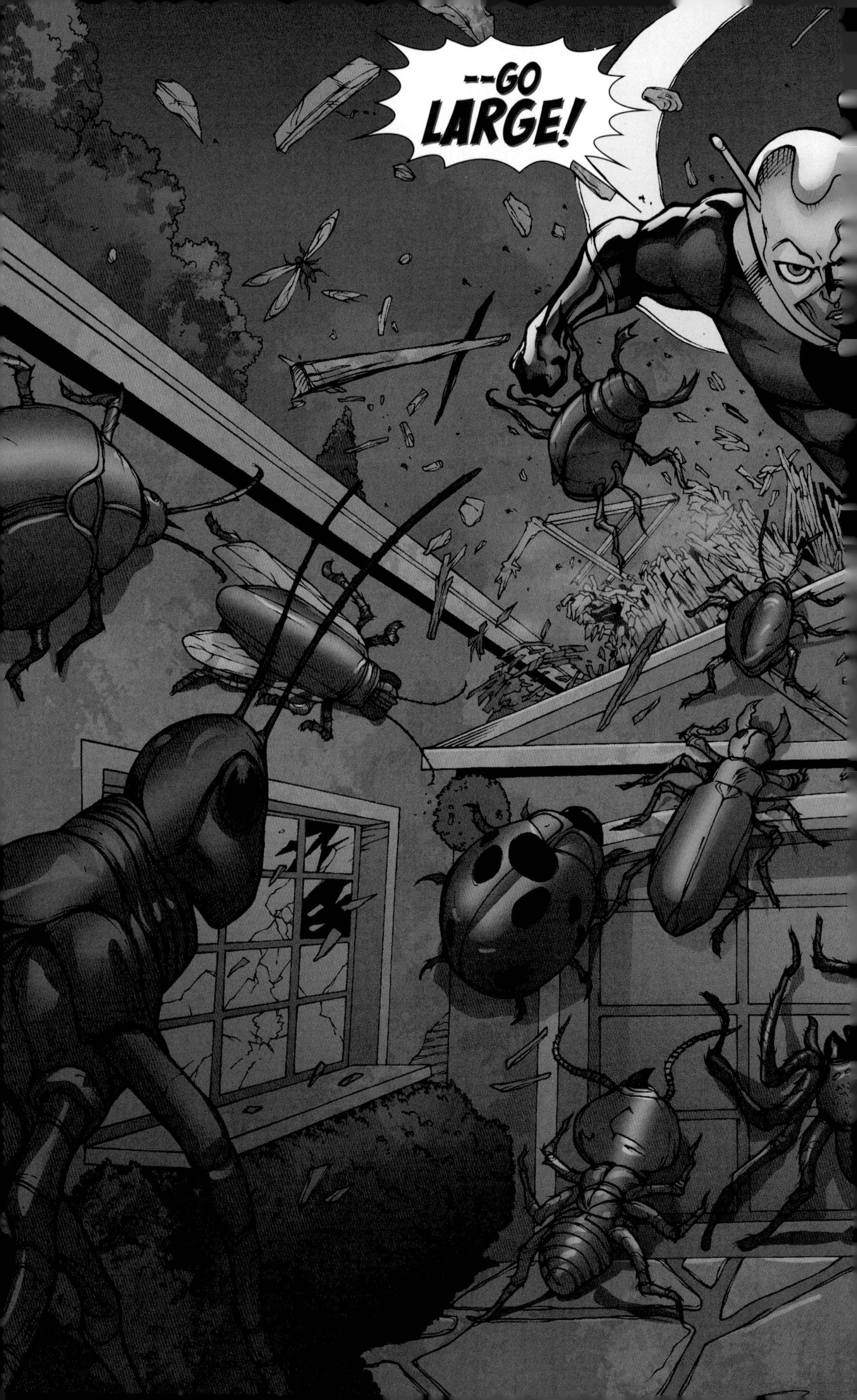
--GO LARGE!

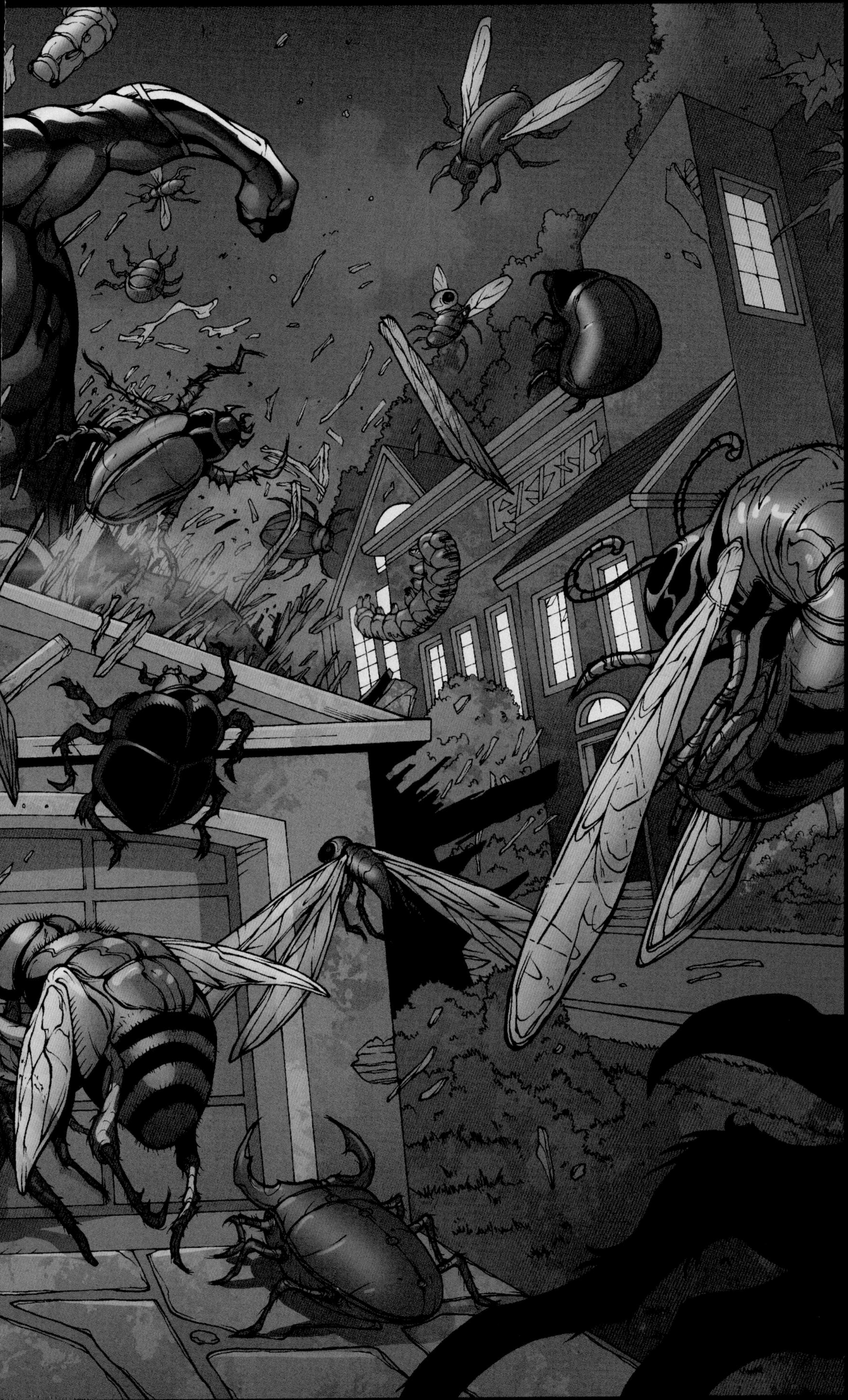

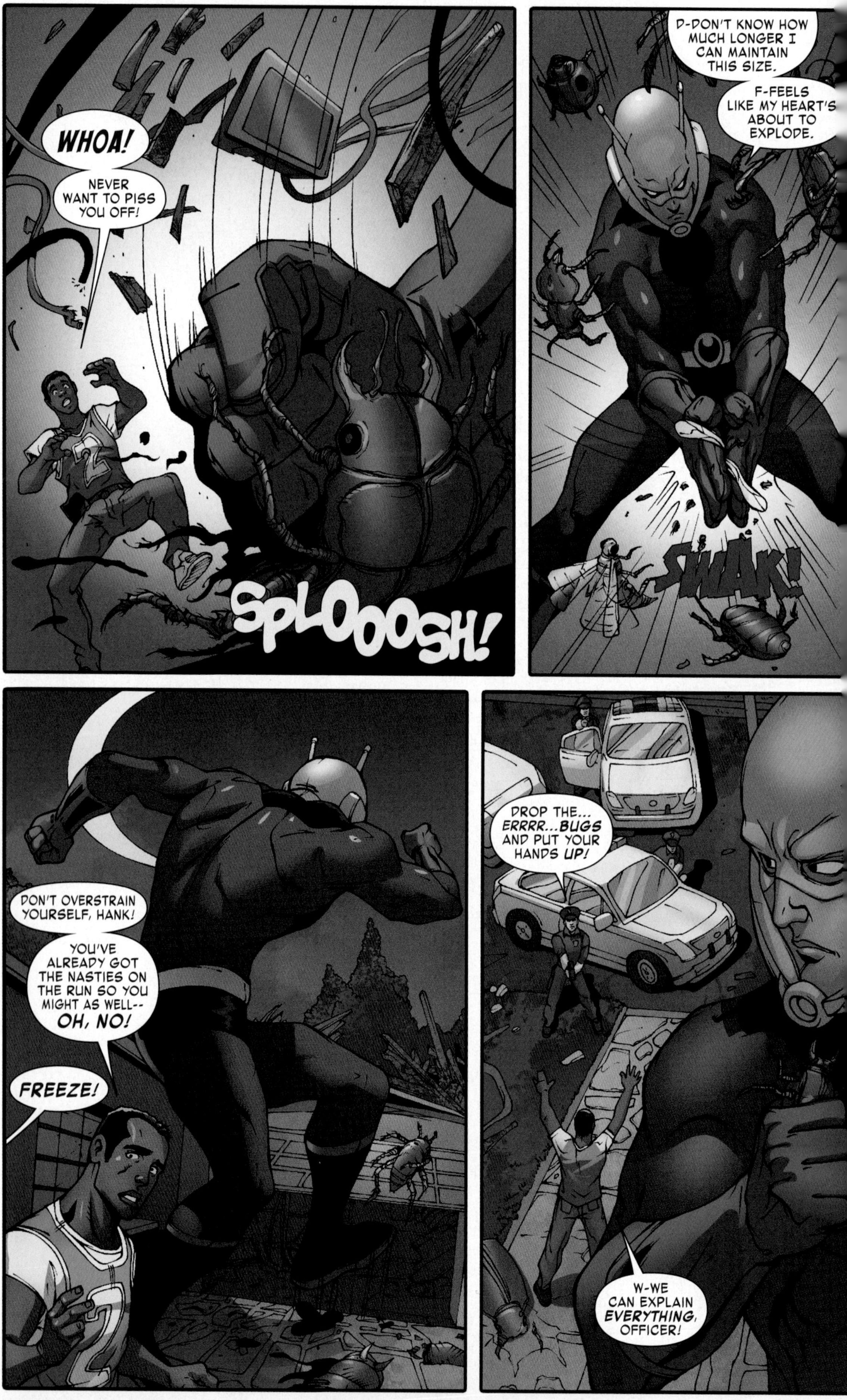
WHOA!
NEVER WANT TO PISS YOU OFF!
SPLOOOSH!
D-DON'T KNOW HOW MUCH LONGER I CAN MAINTAIN THIS SIZE.
F-FEELS LIKE MY HEART'S ABOUT TO EXPLODE.
SWAK!
DON'T OVERSTRAIN YOURSELF, HANK!
YOU'VE ALREADY GOT THE NASTIES ON THE RUN SO YOU MIGHT AS WELL-- OH, NO!
FREEZE!
DROP THE... ERRRR...BUGS AND PUT YOUR HANDS UP!
W-WE CAN EXPLAIN EVERYTHING, OFFICER!

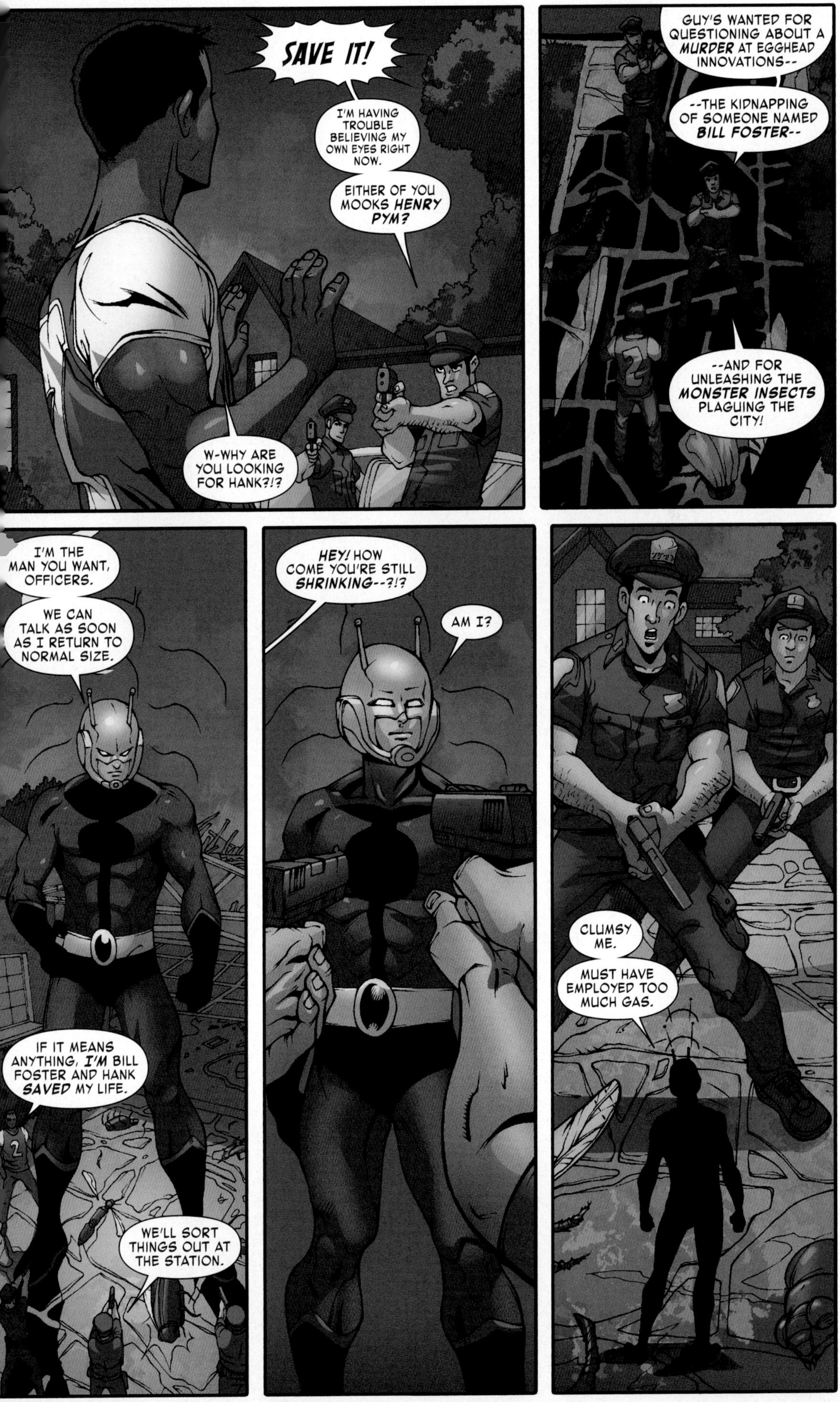
SAVE IT!
I'M HAVING TROUBLE BELIEVING MY OWN EYES RIGHT NOW.
EITHER OF YOU MOOKS HENRY PYM?
W-WHY ARE YOU LOOKING FOR HANK?!?
GUY'S WANTED FOR QUESTIONING ABOUT A MURDER AT EGGHEAD INNOVATIONS--
--THE KIDNAPPING OF SOMEONE NAMED BILL FOSTER--
--AND FOR UNLEASHING THE MONSTER INSECTS PLAGUING THE CITY!
I'M THE MAN YOU WANT, OFFICERS.
WE CAN TALK AS SOON AS I RETURN TO NORMAL SIZE.
IF IT MEANS ANYTHING, I'M BILL FOSTER AND HANK SAVED MY LIFE.
WE'LL SORT THINGS OUT AT THE STATION.
HEY! HOW COME YOU'RE STILL SHRINKING--?!?
AM I?
CLUMSY ME.
MUST HAVE EMPLOYED TOO MUCH GAS.

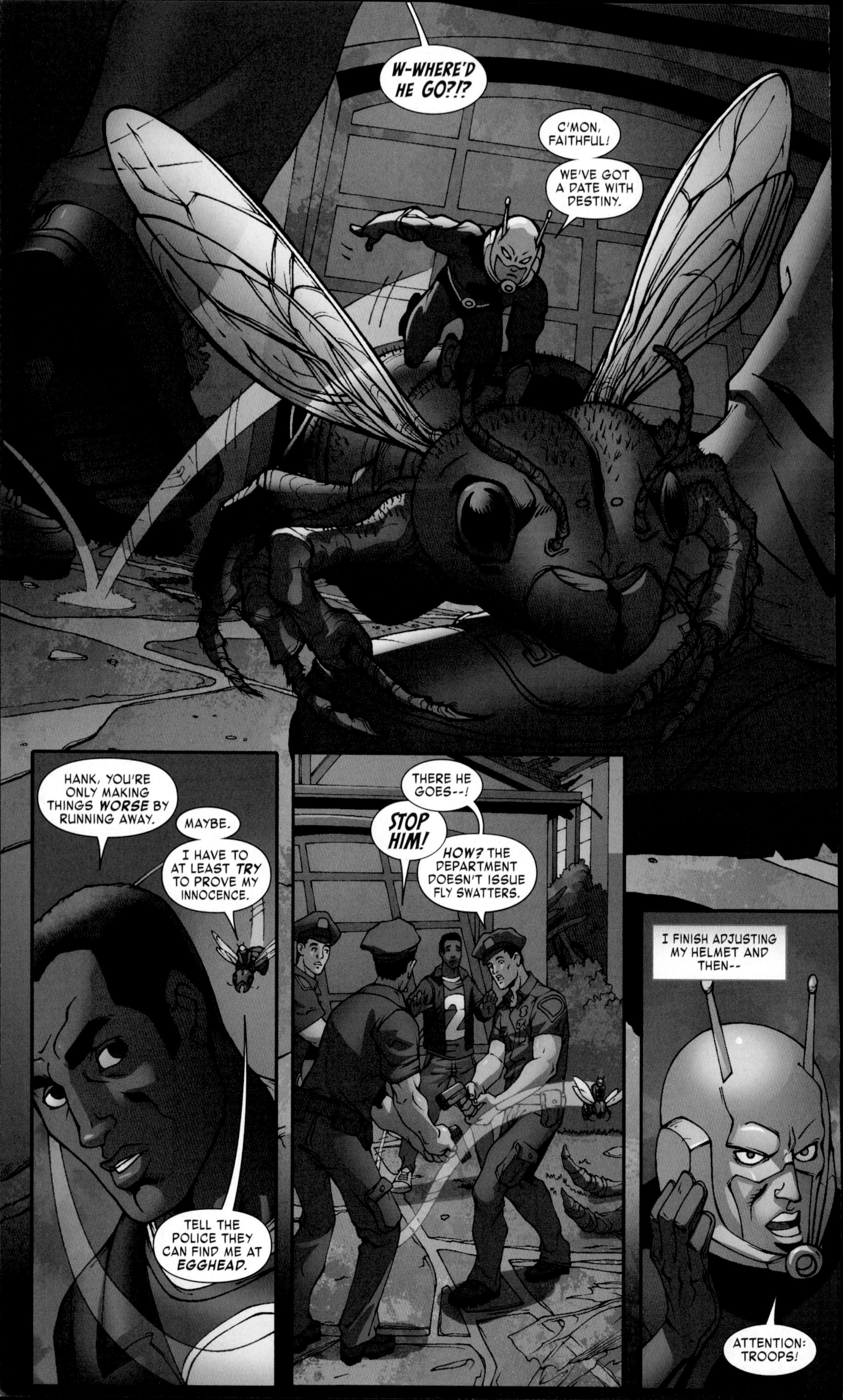

W-WHERE'D HE GO?!?
C'MON, FAITHFUL!
WE'VE GOT A DATE WITH DESTINY.
HANK, YOU'RE ONLY MAKING THINGS WORSE BY RUNNING AWAY.
MAYBE.
I HAVE TO AT LEAST TRY TO PROVE MY INNOCENCE.
TELL THE POLICE THEY CAN FIND ME AT EGGHEAD.
THERE HE GOES--!
STOP HIM!
HOW? THE DEPARTMENT DOESN'T ISSUE FLY SWATTERS.
I FINISH ADJUSTING MY HELMET AND THEN--
ATTENTION: TROOPS!

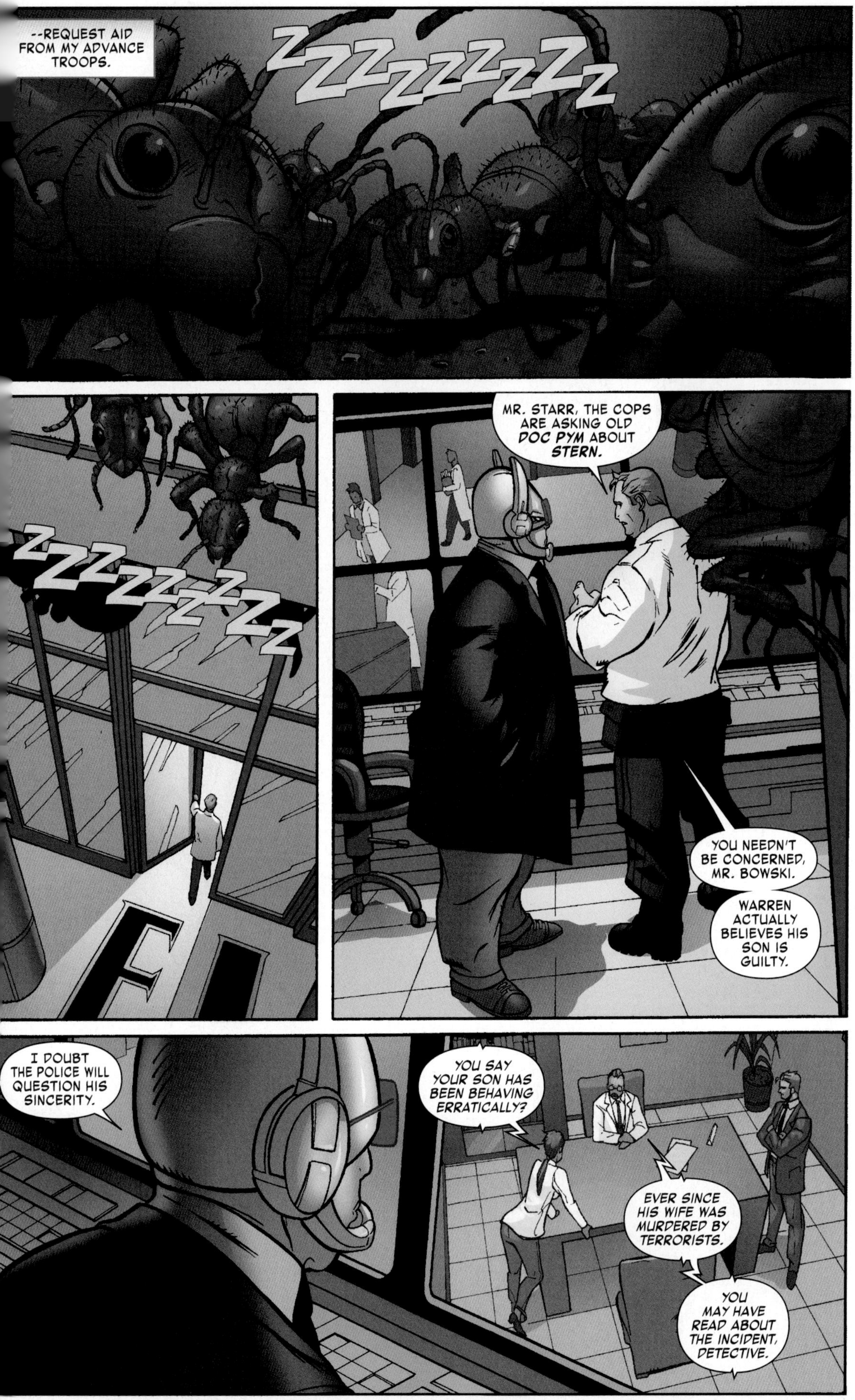
--REQUEST AID FROM MY ADVANCE TROOPS.
ZZZZZZZZZZZ
ZZZZZZZZZZZ
MR. STARR, THE COPS ARE ASKING OLD DOC PYM ABOUT STERN.
YOU NEEDN'T BE CONCERNED, MR. BOWSKI.
WARREN ACTUALLY BELIEVES HIS SON IS GUILTY.
I DOUBT THE POLICE WILL QUESTION HIS SINCERITY.
YOU SAY YOUR SON HAS BEEN BEHAVING ERRATICALLY?
EVER SINCE HIS WIFE WAS MURDERED BY TERRORISTS.
YOU MAY HAVE READ ABOUT THE INCIDENT, DETECTIVE.

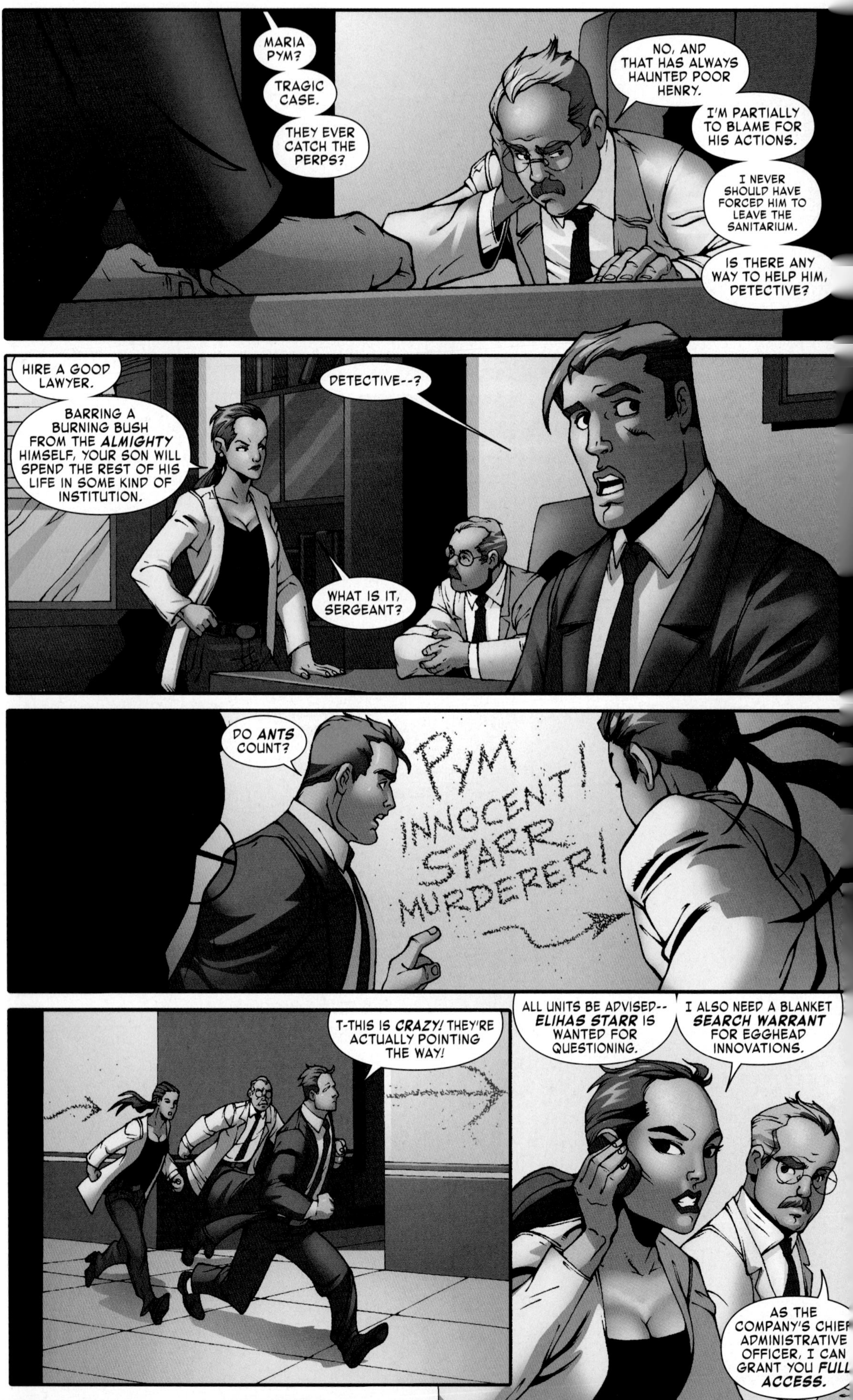
MARIA PYM?
TRAGIC CASE.
THEY EVER CATCH THE PERPS?
NO, AND THAT HAS ALWAYS HAUNTED POOR HENRY.
I'M PARTIALLY TO BLAME FOR HIS ACTIONS.
I NEVER SHOULD HAVE FORCED HIM TO LEAVE THE SANITARIUM.
IS THERE ANY WAY TO HELP HIM, DETECTIVE?
HIRE A GOOD LAWYER.
BARRING A BURNING BUSH FROM THE ALMIGHTY HIMSELF, YOUR SON WILL SPEND THE REST OF HIS LIFE IN SOME KIND OF INSTITUTION.
DETECTIVE--?
WHAT IS IT, SERGEANT?
DO ANTS COUNT?
PYM INNOCENT! STARR MURDERER!
T-THIS IS CRAZY! THEY'RE ACTUALLY POINTING THE WAY!
ALL UNITS BE ADVISED-- ELIHAS STARR IS WANTED FOR QUESTIONING.
I ALSO NEED A BLANKET SEARCH WARRANT FOR EGGHEAD INNOVATIONS.
AS THE COMPANY'S CHIEF ADMINISTRATIVE OFFICER, I CAN GRANT YOU FULL ACCESS.

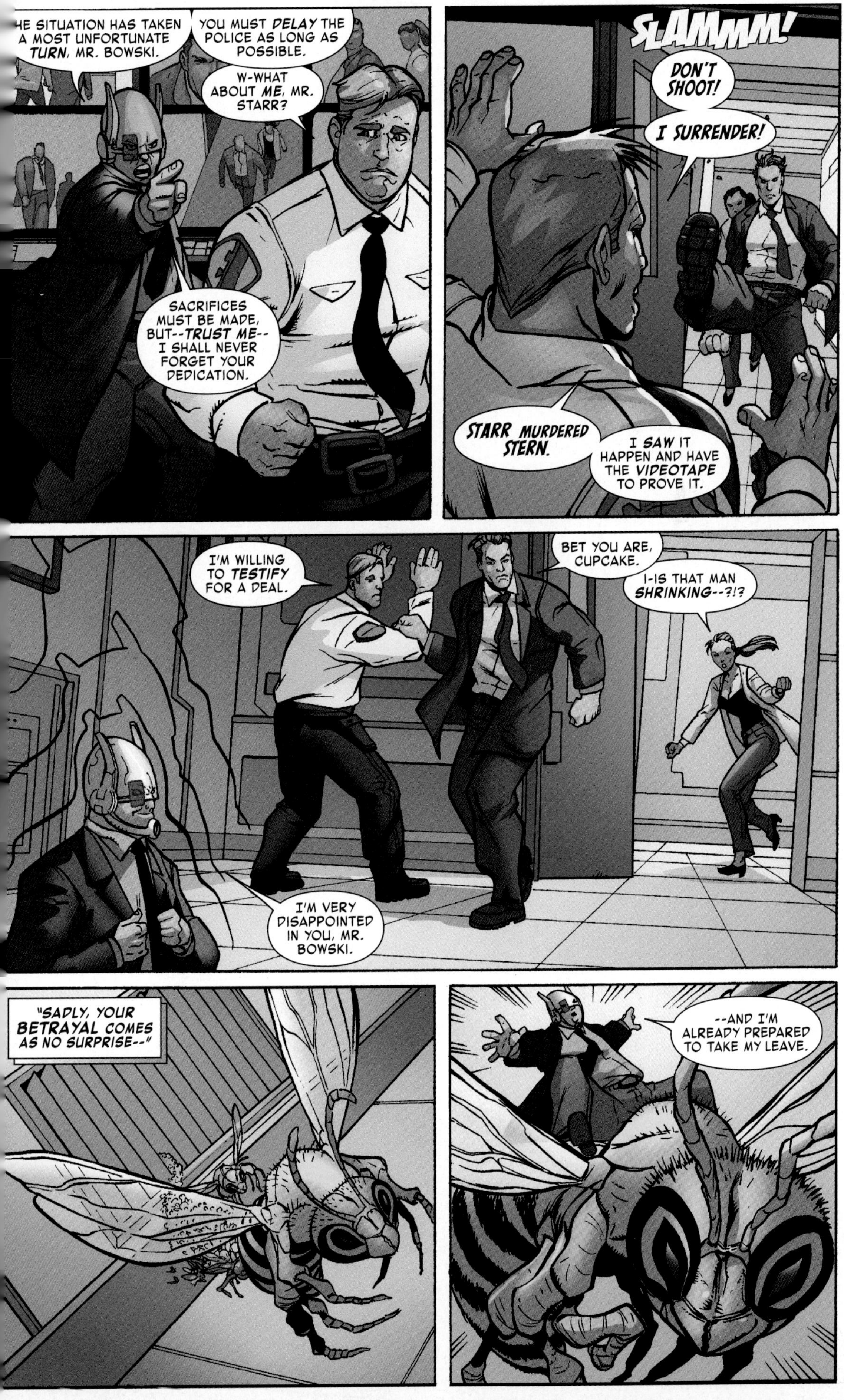
HE SITUATION HAS TAKEN A MOST UNFORTUNATE TURN, MR. BOWSKI.
YOU MUST DELAY THE POLICE AS LONG AS POSSIBLE.
W-WHAT ABOUT ME, MR. STARR?
SACRIFICES MUST BE MADE, BUT--TRUST ME--I SHALL NEVER FORGET YOUR DEDICATION.
SLAMMMM!
DON'T SHOOT!
I SURRENDER!
STARR MURDERED STERN.
I SAW IT HAPPEN AND HAVE THE VIDEOTAPE TO PROVE IT.
I'M WILLING TO TESTIFY FOR A DEAL.
BET YOU ARE, CUPCAKE.
I-IS THAT MAN SHRINKING--?!?
I'M VERY DISAPPOINTED IN YOU, MR. BOWSKI.
"SADLY, YOUR BETRAYAL COMES AS NO SURPRISE--"
--AND I'M ALREADY PREPARED TO TAKE MY LEAVE.

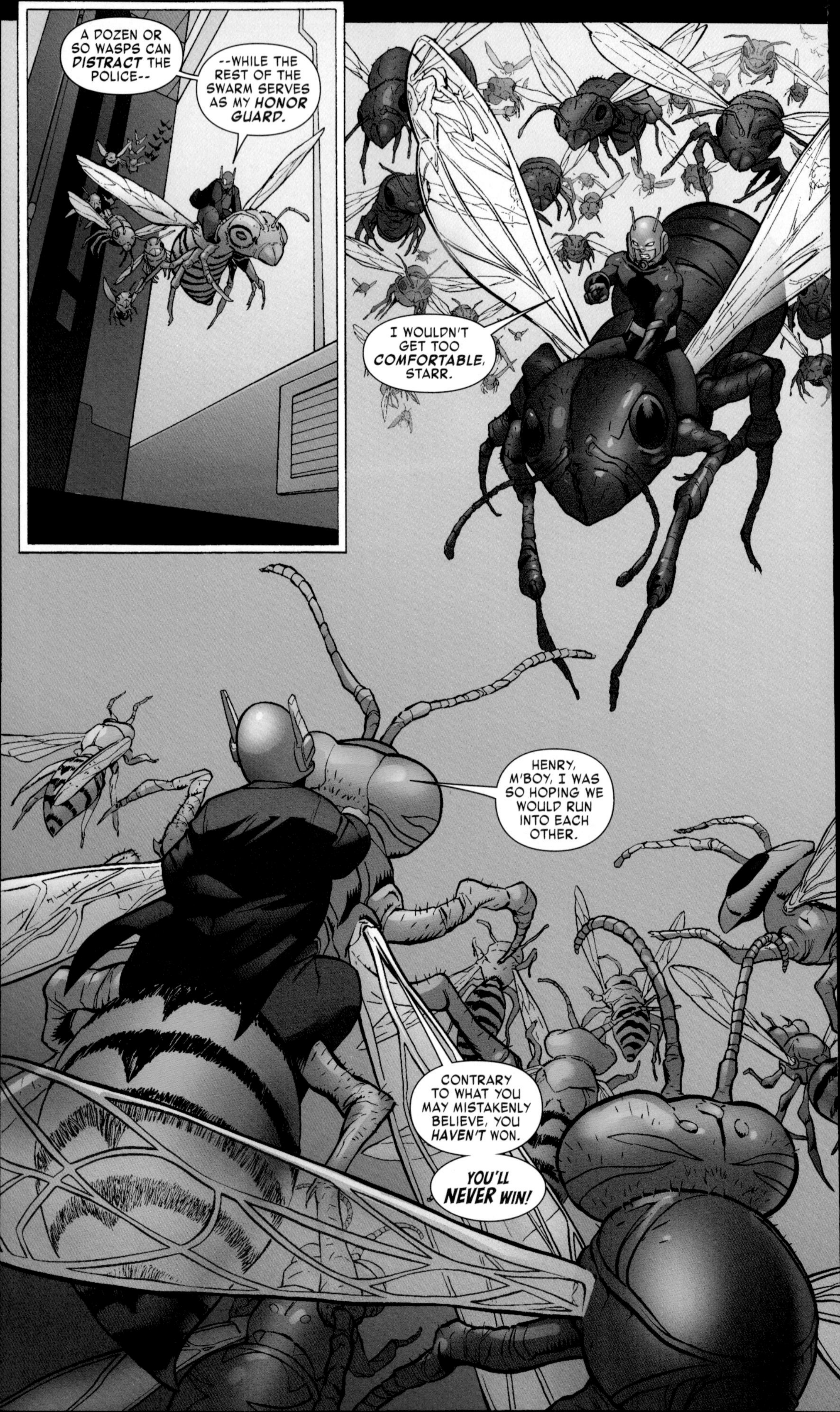
A DOZEN OR SO WASPS CAN *DISTRACT* THE POLICE--
--WHILE THE REST OF THE SWARM SERVES AS MY *HONOR GUARD.*
I WOULDN'T GET TOO *COMFORTABLE,* STARR.
HENRY, M'BOY, I WAS SO HOPING WE WOULD RUN INTO EACH OTHER.
CONTRARY TO WHAT YOU MAY MISTAKENLY BELIEVE, YOU *HAVEN'T* WON.
*YOU'LL NEVER WIN!*

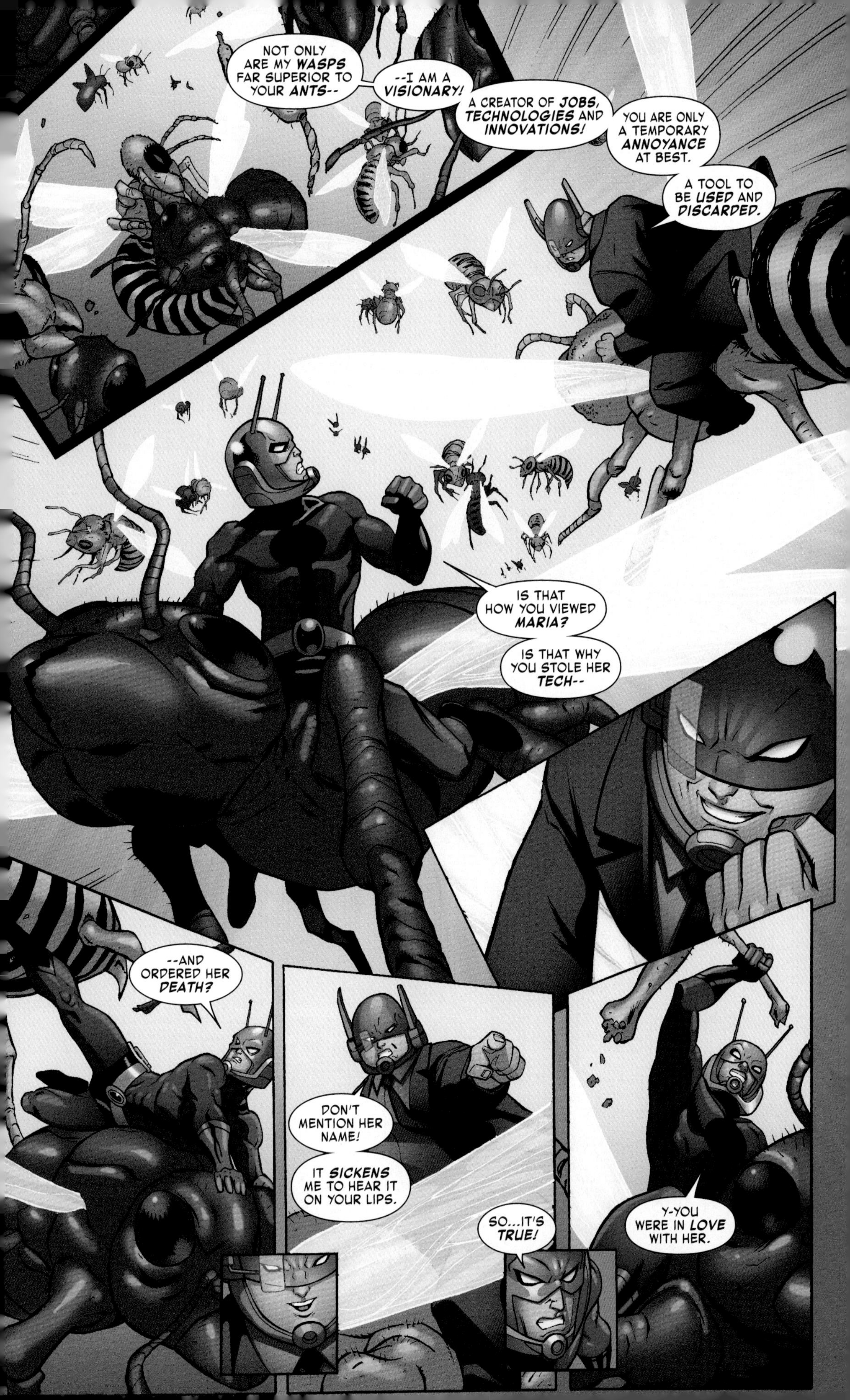
NOT ONLY ARE MY WASPS FAR SUPERIOR TO YOUR ANTS--
--I AM A VISIONARY!
A CREATOR OF JOBS, TECHNOLOGIES AND INNOVATIONS!
YOU ARE ONLY A TEMPORARY ANNOYANCE AT BEST.
A TOOL TO BE USED AND DISCARDED.
IS THAT HOW YOU VIEWED MARIA?
IS THAT WHY YOU STOLE HER TECH--
--AND ORDERED HER DEATH?
DON'T MENTION HER NAME!
IT SICKENS ME TO HEAR IT ON YOUR LIPS.
SO...IT'S TRUE!
Y-YOU WERE IN LOVE WITH HER.

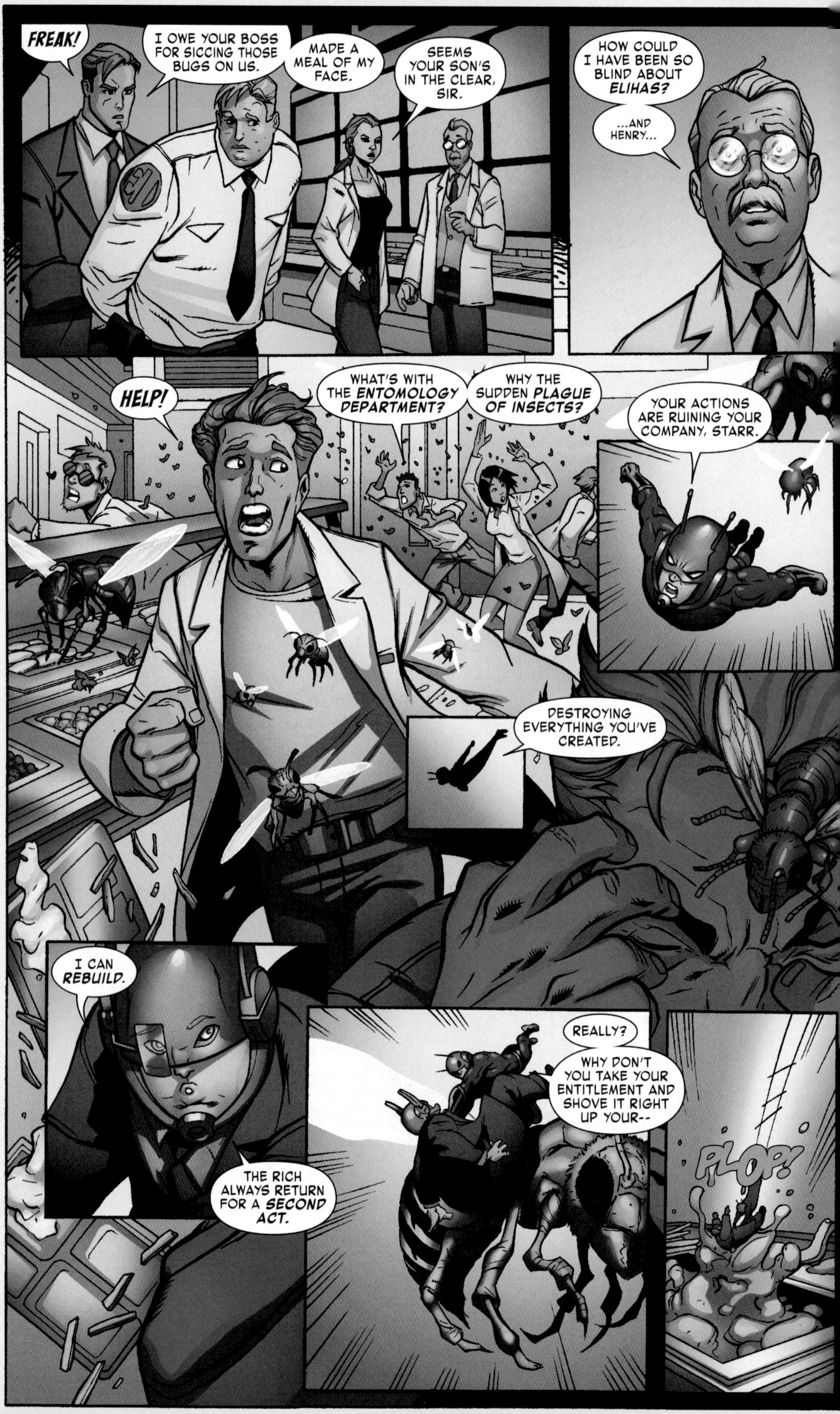
FREAK!
I OWE YOUR BOSS FOR SICCING THOSE BUGS ON US.
MADE A MEAL OF MY FACE.
SEEMS YOUR SON'S IN THE CLEAR, SIR.
HOW COULD I HAVE BEEN SO BLIND ABOUT ELIHAS?
...AND HENRY...
HELP!
WHAT'S WITH THE ENTOMOLOGY DEPARTMENT?
WHY THE SUDDEN PLAGUE OF INSECTS?
YOUR ACTIONS ARE RUINING YOUR COMPANY, STARR.
DESTROYING EVERYTHING YOU'VE CREATED.
I CAN REBUILD.
THE RICH ALWAYS RETURN FOR A SECOND ACT.
REALLY?
WHY DON'T YOU TAKE YOUR ENTITLEMENT AND SHOVE IT RIGHT UP YOUR--
PLOP!

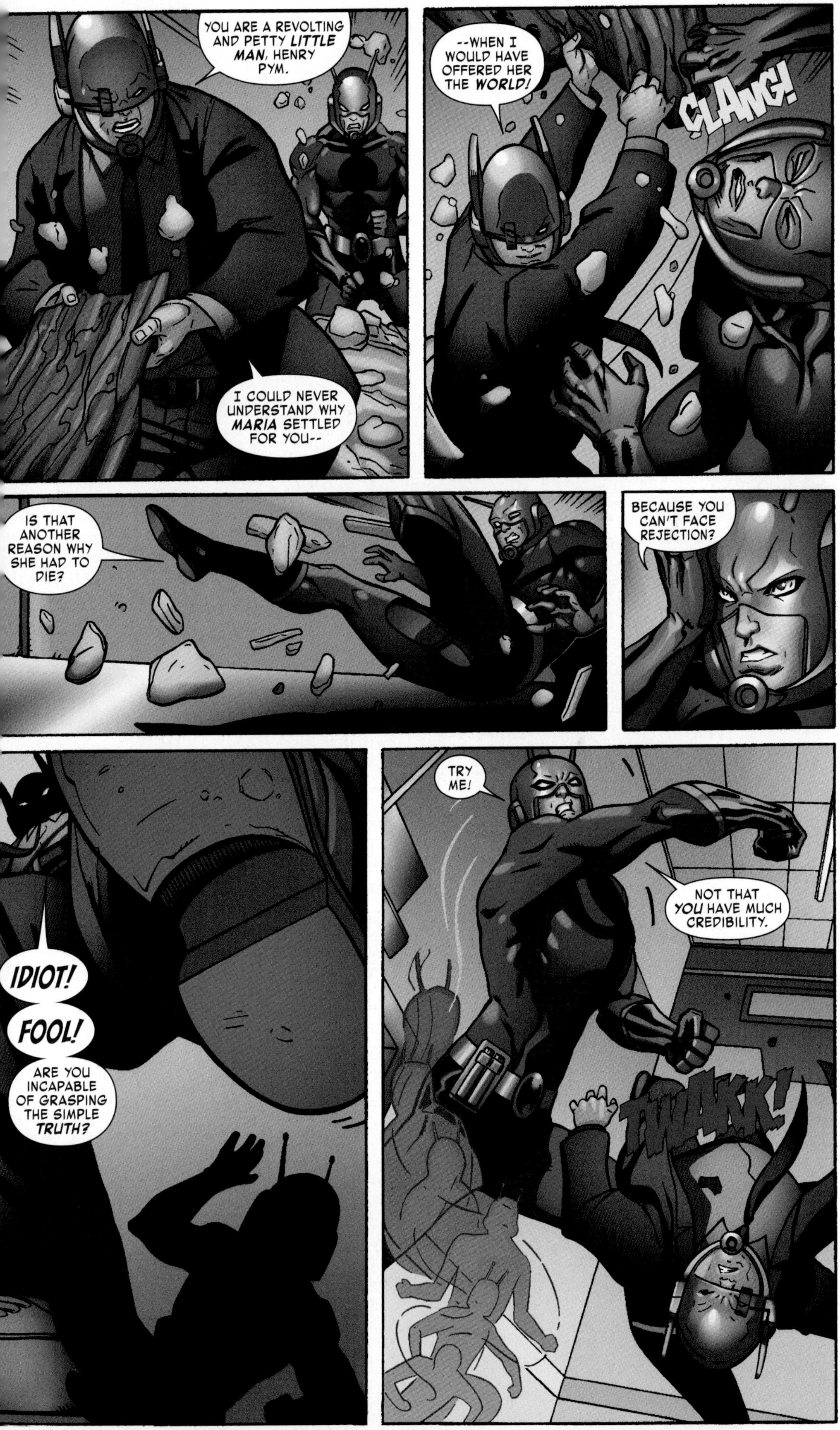
YOU ARE A REVOLTING AND PETTY LITTLE MAN, HENRY PYM.
I COULD NEVER UNDERSTAND WHY MARIA SETTLED FOR YOU--
--WHEN I WOULD HAVE OFFERED HER THE WORLD!
CLANG!
IS THAT ANOTHER REASON WHY SHE HAD TO DIE?
BECAUSE YOU CAN'T FACE REJECTION?
IDIOT!
FOOL!
ARE YOU INCAPABLE OF GRASPING THE SIMPLE TRUTH?
TRY ME!
NOT THAT YOU HAVE MUCH CREDIBILITY.
TWAKK!

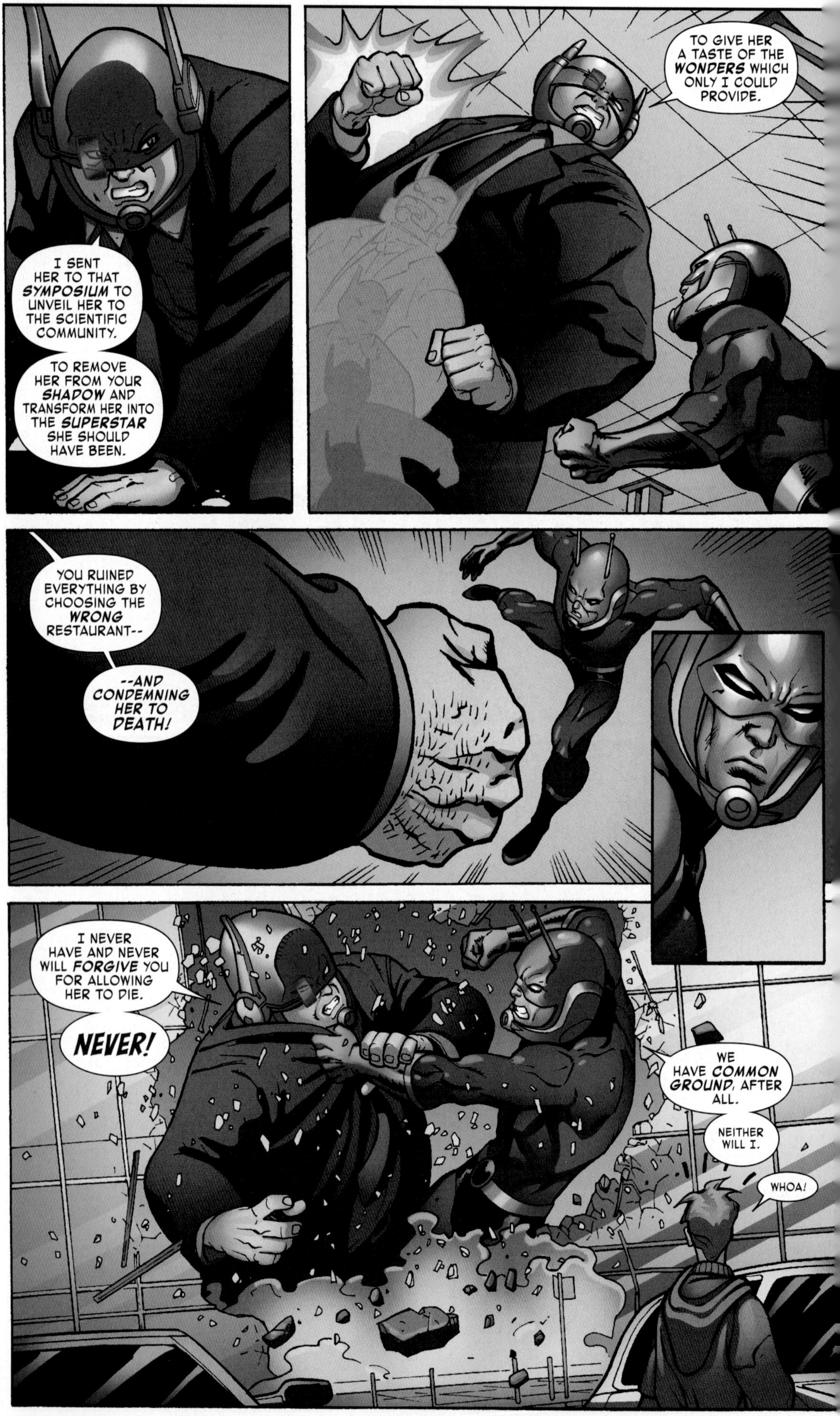

I SENT HER TO THAT SYMPOSIUM TO UNVEIL HER TO THE SCIENTIFIC COMMUNITY.
TO REMOVE HER FROM YOUR SHADOW AND TRANSFORM HER INTO THE SUPERSTAR SHE SHOULD HAVE BEEN.
TO GIVE HER A TASTE OF THE WONDERS WHICH ONLY I COULD PROVIDE.
YOU RUINED EVERYTHING BY CHOOSING THE WRONG RESTAURANT--
--AND CONDEMNING HER TO DEATH!
I NEVER HAVE AND NEVER WILL FORGIVE YOU FOR ALLOWING HER TO DIE.
NEVER!
WE HAVE COMMON GROUND, AFTER ALL.
NEITHER WILL I.
WHOA!

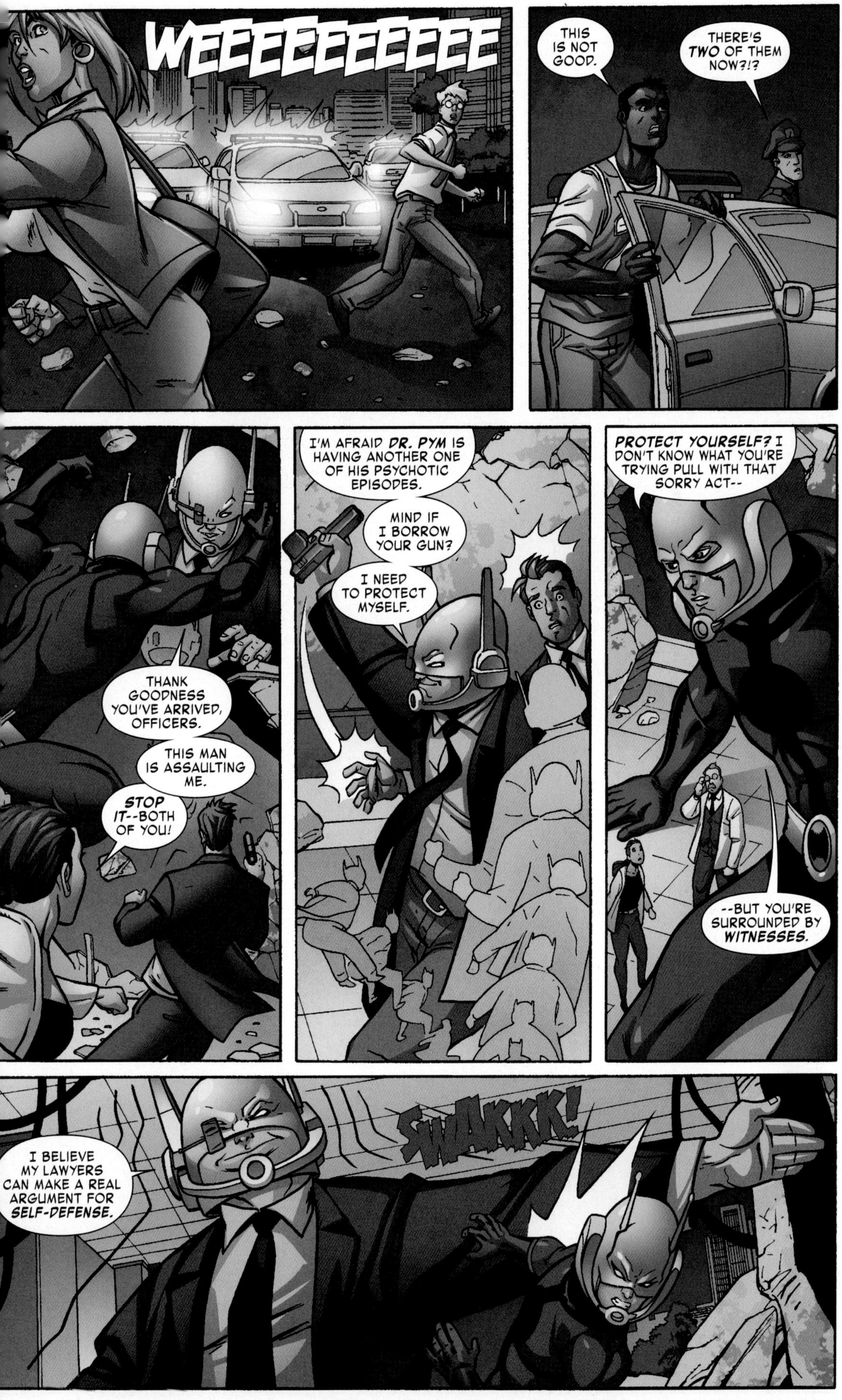
WEEEEEEEEEEE
THIS IS NOT GOOD.
THERE'S TWO OF THEM NOW?!?
THANK GOODNESS YOU'VE ARRIVED, OFFICERS.
THIS MAN IS ASSAULTING ME.
STOP IT--BOTH OF YOU!
I'M AFRAID DR. PYM IS HAVING ANOTHER ONE OF HIS PSYCHOTIC EPISODES.
MIND IF I BORROW YOUR GUN?
I NEED TO PROTECT MYSELF.
PROTECT YOURSELF? I DON'T KNOW WHAT YOU'RE TRYING PULL WITH THAT SORRY ACT--
--BUT YOU'RE SURROUNDED BY WITNESSES.
SWAKKK!
I BELIEVE MY LAWYERS CAN MAKE A REAL ARGUMENT FOR SELF-DEFENSE.

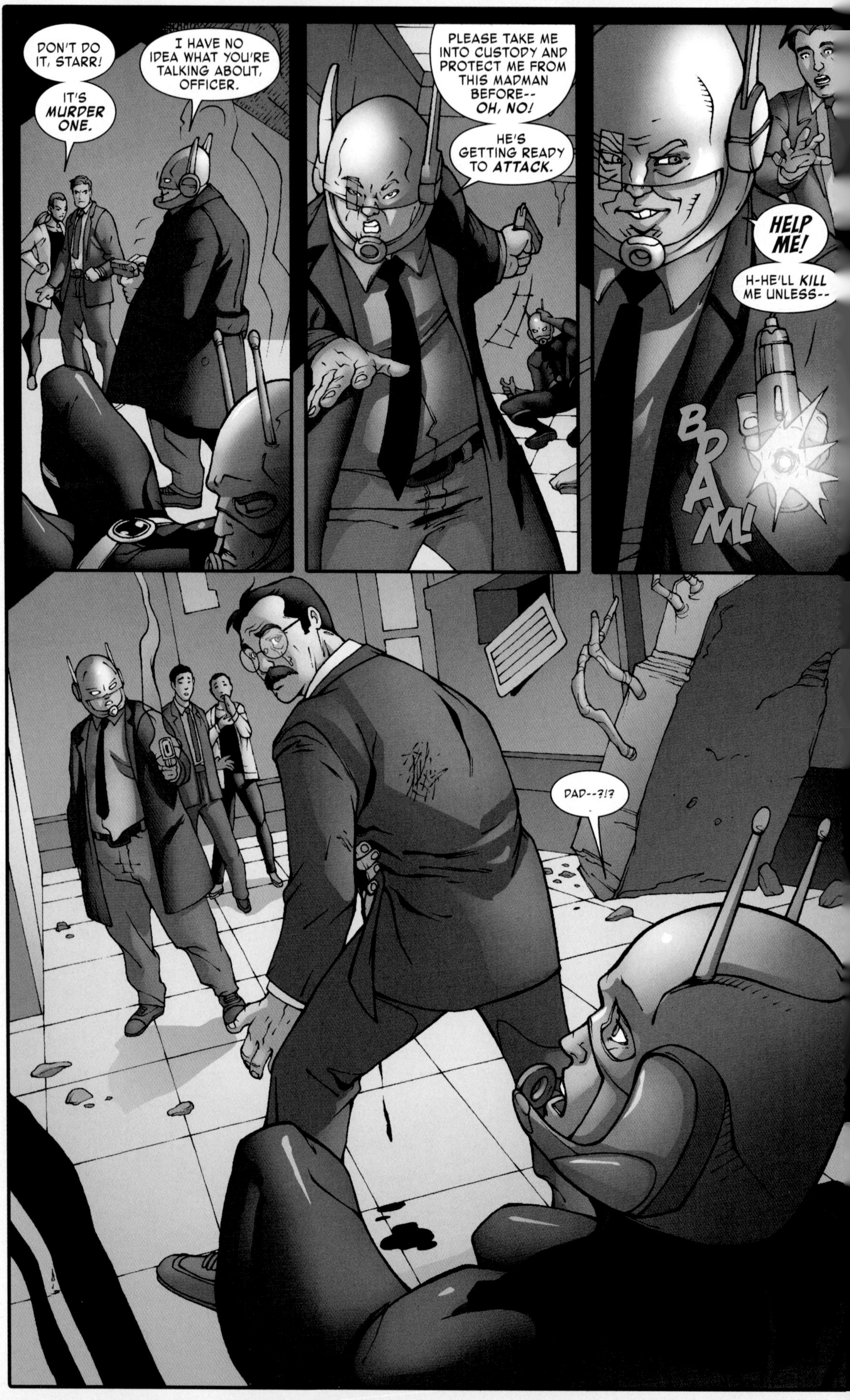
DON'T DO IT, STARR!
IT'S MURDER ONE.
I HAVE NO IDEA WHAT YOU'RE TALKING ABOUT, OFFICER.
PLEASE TAKE ME INTO CUSTODY AND PROTECT ME FROM THIS MADMAN BEFORE-- OH, NO!
HE'S GETTING READY TO ATTACK.
HELP ME!
H-HE'LL KILL ME UNLESS--
BDAM!
DAD--?!?

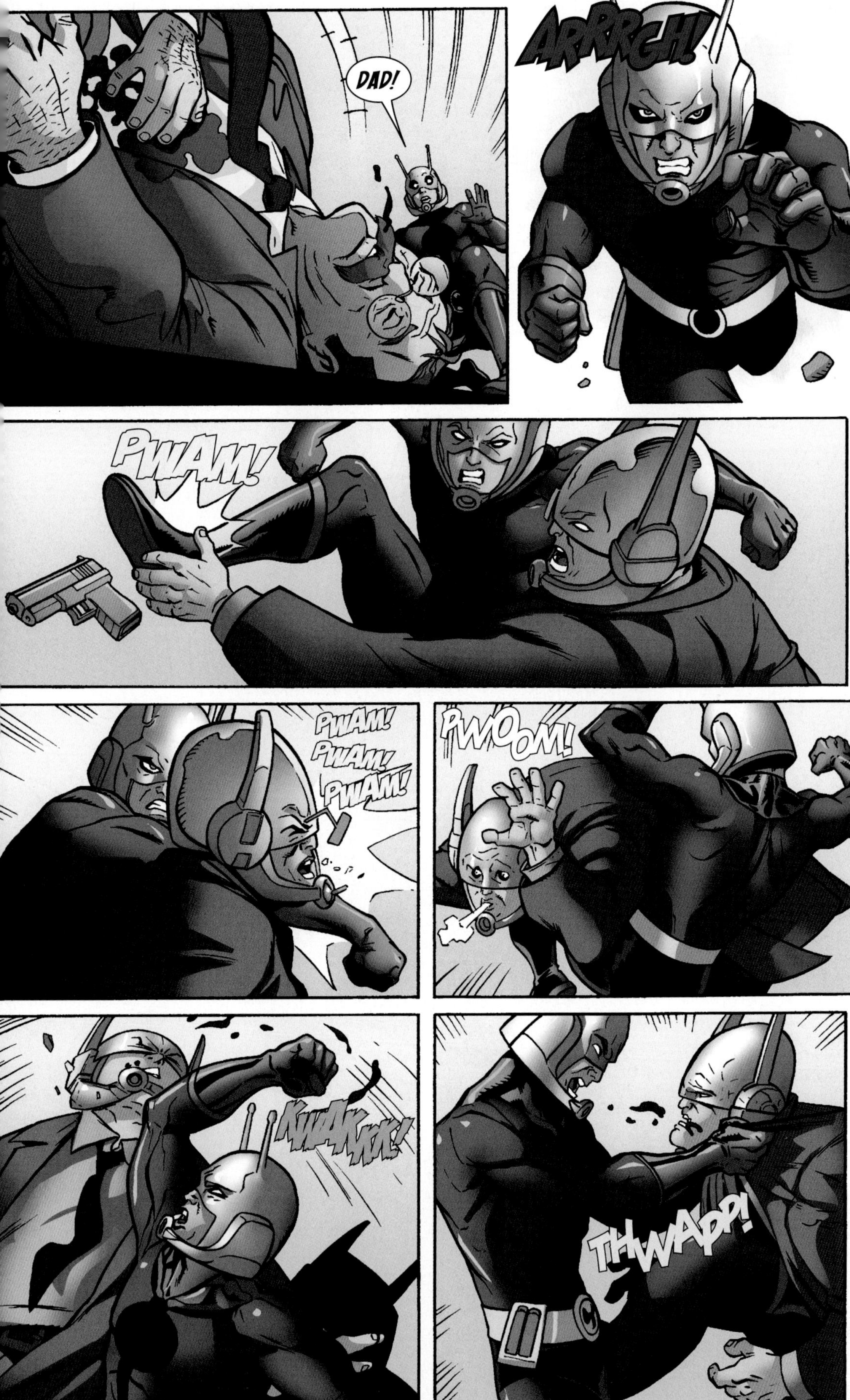

DAD!
ARRRGH!
PWAM!
PWAM!
PWAM!
PWAM!
PWOOM!
KWAKKK!
THWAPP!

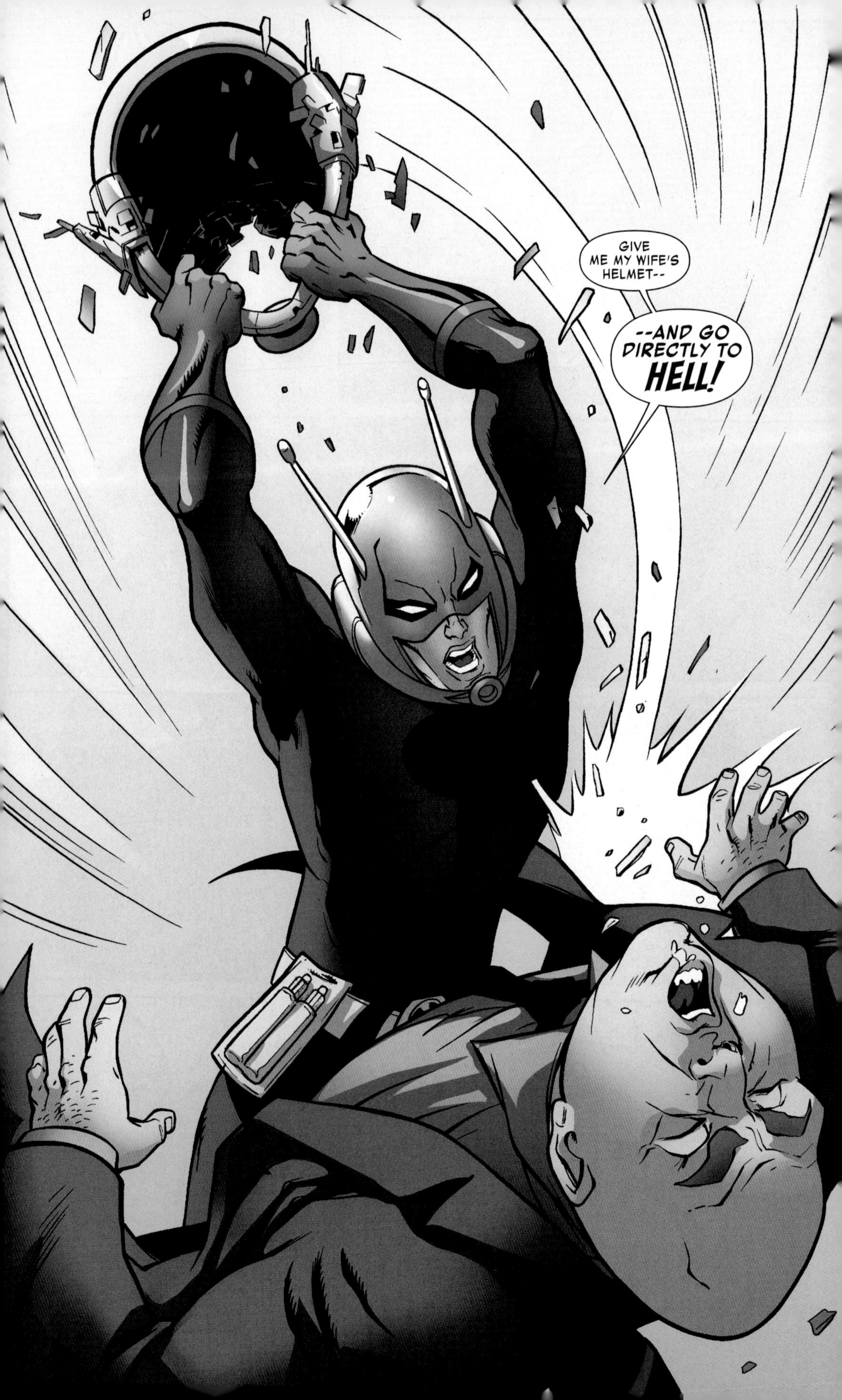
GIVE ME MY WIFE'S HELMET--
--AND GO DIRECTLY TO HELL!

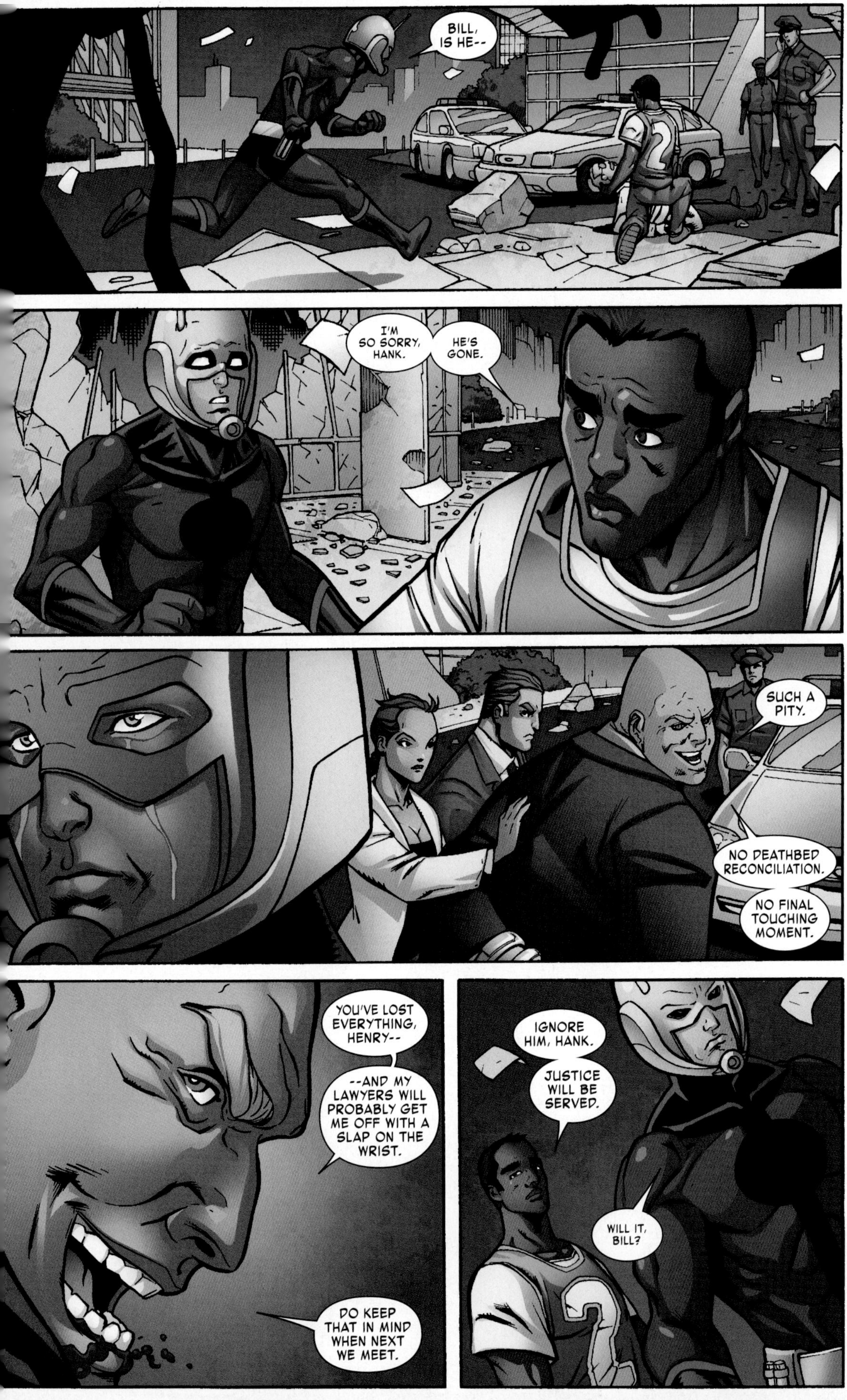
BILL, IS HE--
I'M SO SORRY, HANK.
HE'S GONE.
SUCH A PITY.
NO DEATHBED RECONCILIATION.
NO FINAL TOUCHING MOMENT.
YOU'VE LOST EVERYTHING, HENRY--
--AND MY LAWYERS WILL PROBABLY GET ME OFF WITH A SLAP ON THE WRIST.
DO KEEP THAT IN MIND WHEN NEXT WE MEET.
IGNORE HIM, HANK.
JUSTICE WILL BE SERVED.
WILL IT, BILL?

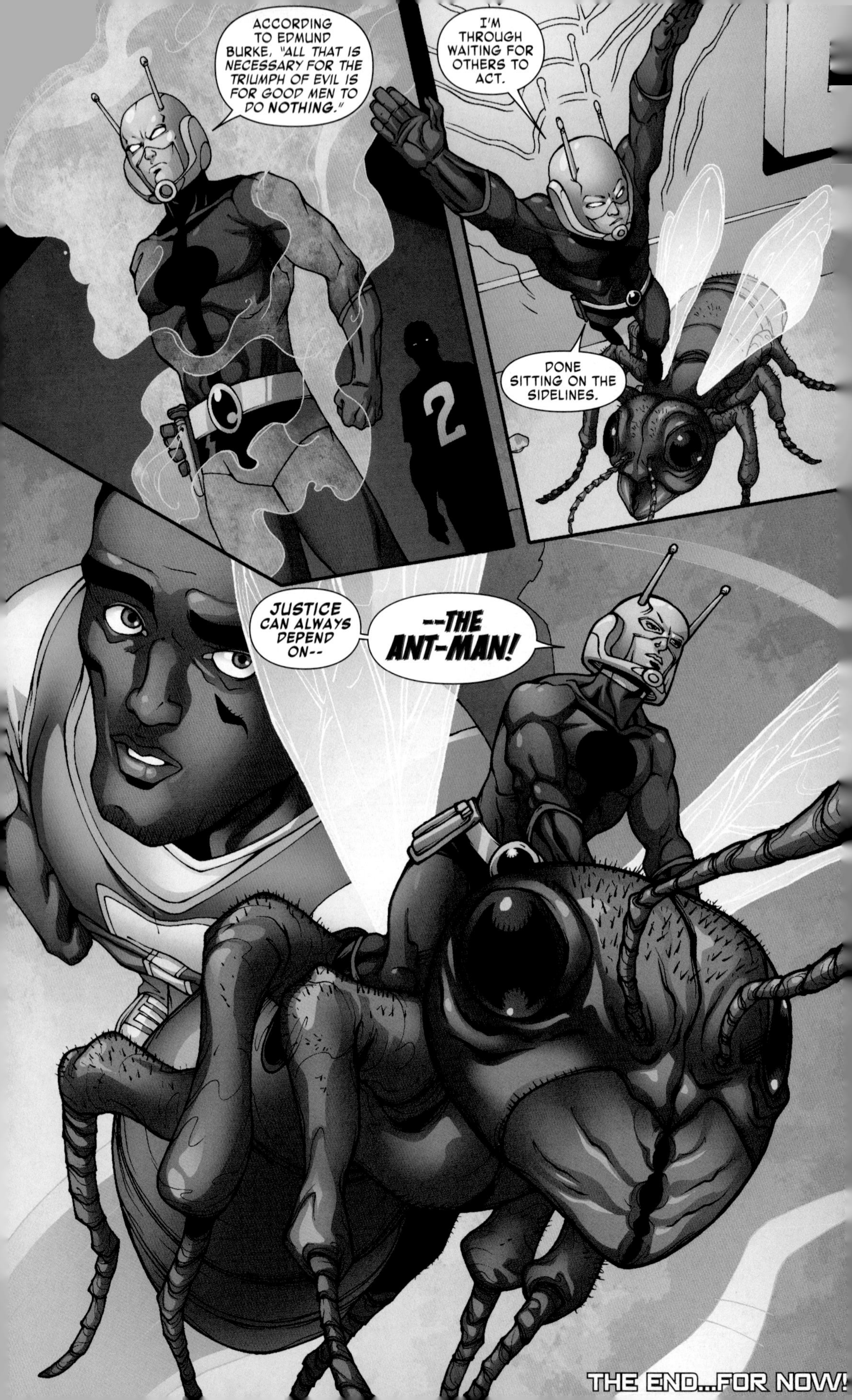
ACCORDING TO EDMUND BURKE, "ALL THAT IS NECESSARY FOR THE TRIUMPH OF EVIL IS FOR GOOD MEN TO DO NOTHING."
I'M THROUGH WAITING FOR OTHERS TO ACT.
DONE SITTING ON THE SIDELINES.
JUSTICE CAN ALWAYS DEPEND ON--
--THE ANT-MAN!
THE END...FOR NOW!

**WHERE ARE THEY NOW?** *ANT-MAN (2015) #1* SCOTT LANG WILL DO ANYTHING FOR HIS DAUGHTER, BUT CAN HE SURVIVE A HIGH-STAKES JOB ERVIEW SO HE CAN STAY A PART OF HER LIFE? SCOTT IS SURE TO SHRINK TO THE OCCASION IN WRITER NICK SPENCER'S FIRST ASTONISHING ISSUE!

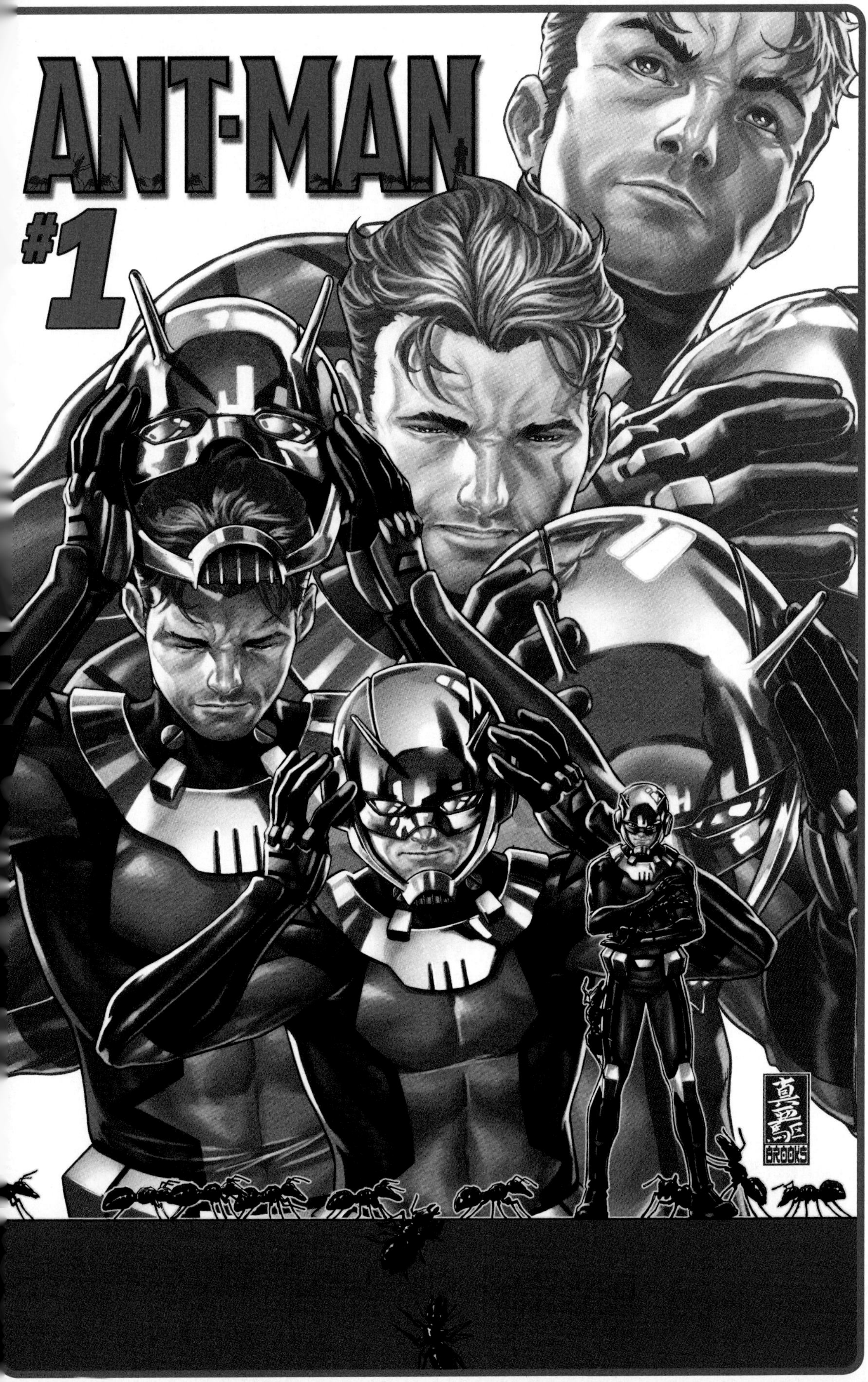
ANT-MAN
#1
BROOKS

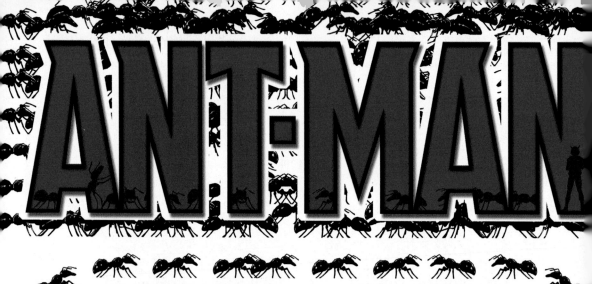

# ANT·MAN

WHEN HANK PYM, THE ORIGINAL ANT-MAN, RETIRED FROM THE JOB, ANOTHER MAN ROSE TO THE OCCASION (ERR, STOLE THE COSTUME) – NONE OTHER THAN SCOTT LANG! HIS SOMEWHAT SORDID PAST BEHIND HIM, SCOTT TOOK ON THE SIZE-CHANGING, ANT-COMMUNICATING ABILITIES OF ANT-MAN!

**NICK SPENCER**
WRITER

**RAMON ROSANAS**
ARTIST

**JORDAN BOYD**
COLORIST

**VC'S TRAVIS LANHAM**
LETTERER

**IDETTE WINECOOR**
DESIGNER

**MARK BROOKS**
COVER ARTIST

SKOTTIE YOUNG; ED MCGUINNESS & MARTE GRACIA; JASON PEARSON; CHRIS SAMNEE & MATTHEW WILSON SALVADOR LARROCA & ISRAEL SILVA; ANDY PARK
VARIANT COVER ARTISTS

**JON MOISAN**
ASSISTANT EDITOR

**WIL MOSS**
EDITOR

**AXEL ALONSO**
EDITOR IN CHIEF

**JOE QUESADA**
CHIEF CREATIVE OFFICER

**DAN BUCKLEY**
PUBLISHER

**ALAN FINE**
EXECUTIVE PRODUCER

SPECIAL THANKS TO **JIM BOYLE**

ANT-MAN CREATED BY **STAN LEE, LARRY LIEBER & JACK KIRBY**

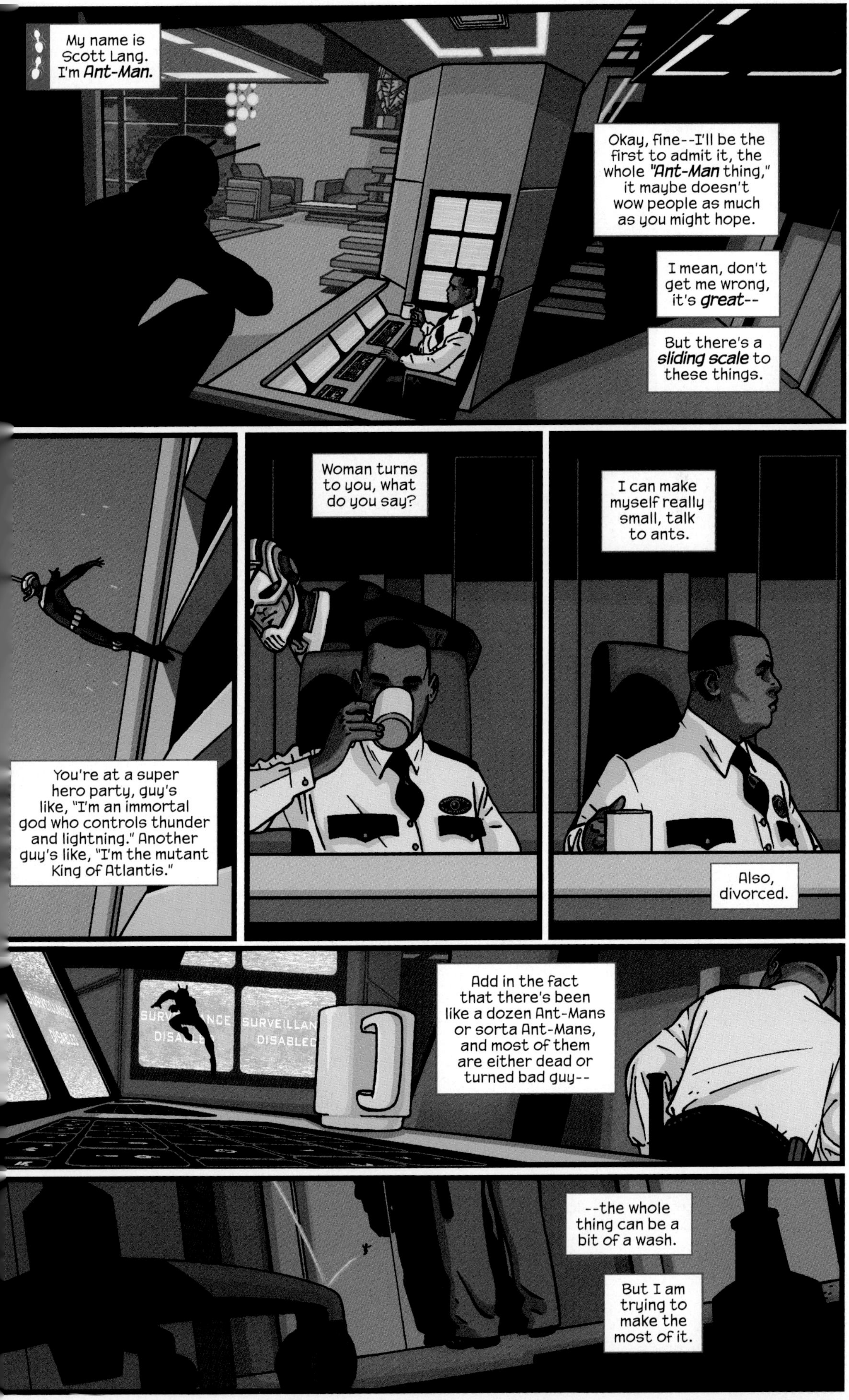
My name is Scott Lang. I'm *Ant-Man.*
Okay, fine--I'll be the first to admit it, the whole *"Ant-Man* thing," it maybe doesn't wow people as much as you might hope.
I mean, don't get me wrong, it's *great*--
But there's a *sliding scale* to these things.
You're at a super hero party, guy's like, "I'm an immortal god who controls thunder and lightning." Another guy's like, "I'm the mutant King of Atlantis."
Woman turns to you, what do you say?
I can make myself really small, talk to ants.
Also, divorced.
SURVEILLANCE DISABLED
Add in the fact that there's been like a dozen Ant-Mans or sorta Ant-Mans, and most of them are either dead or turned bad guy--
--the whole thing can be a bit of a wash.
But I am trying to make the most of it.

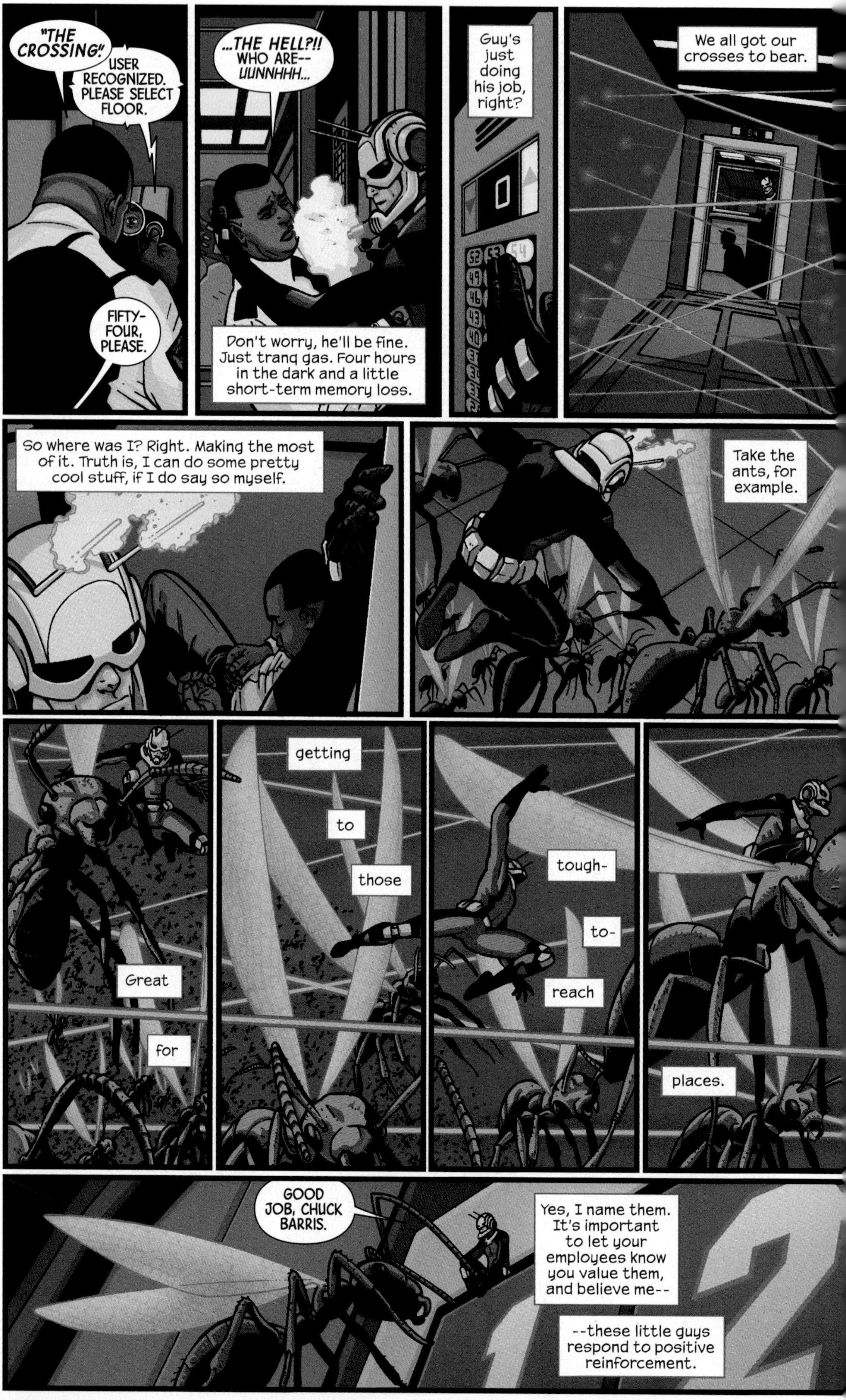
"THE CROSSING."
USER RECOGNIZED. PLEASE SELECT FLOOR.
FIFTY-FOUR, PLEASE.
...THE HELL?!! WHO ARE-- UUNNHHH...
Don't worry, he'll be fine. Just tranq gas. Four hours in the dark and a little short-term memory loss.
Guy's just doing his job, right?
We all got our crosses to bear.
So where was I? Right. Making the most of it. Truth is, I can do some pretty cool stuff, if I do say so myself.
Take the ants, for example.
Great
for
getting
to
those
tough-
to-
reach
places.
GOOD JOB, CHUCK BARRIS.
Yes, I name them. It's important to let your employees know you value them, and believe me--
--these little guys respond to positive reinforcement.

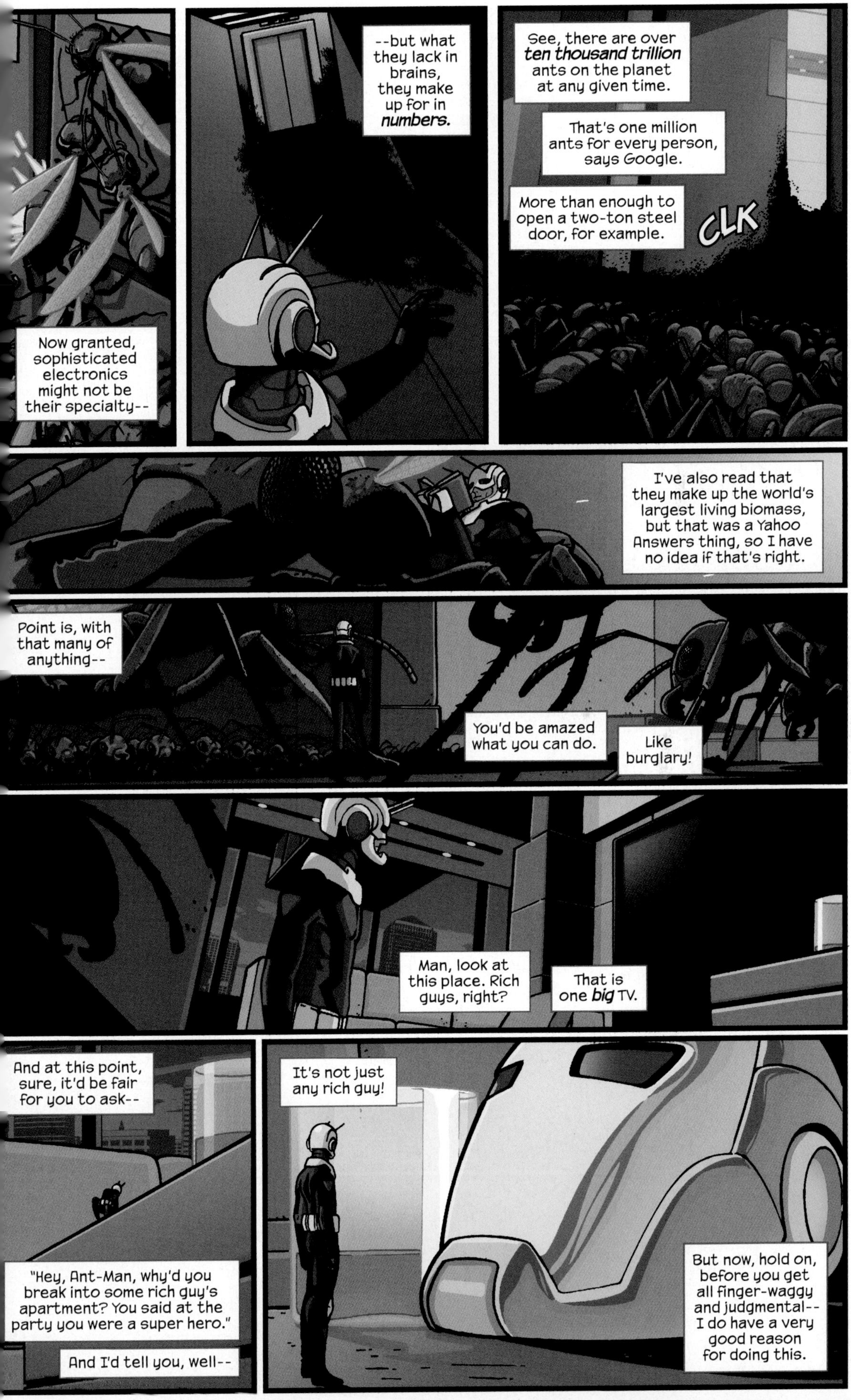
Now granted, sophisticated electronics might not be their specialty--
--but what they lack in brains, they make up for in *numbers.*
See, there are over ***ten thousand trillion*** ants on the planet at any given time.
That's one million ants for every person, says Google.
More than enough to open a two-ton steel door, for example.
CLK
I've also read that they make up the world's largest living biomass, but that was a Yahoo Answers thing, so I have no idea if that's right.
Point is, with that many of anything--
You'd be amazed what you can do.
Like burglary!
Man, look at this place. Rich guys, right?
That is one *big* TV.
And at this point, sure, it'd be fair for you to ask--
"Hey, Ant-Man, why'd you break into some rich guy's apartment? You said at the party you were a super hero."
And I'd tell you, well--
It's not just any rich guy!
But now, hold on, before you get all finger-waggy and judgmental--I do have a very good reason for doing this.

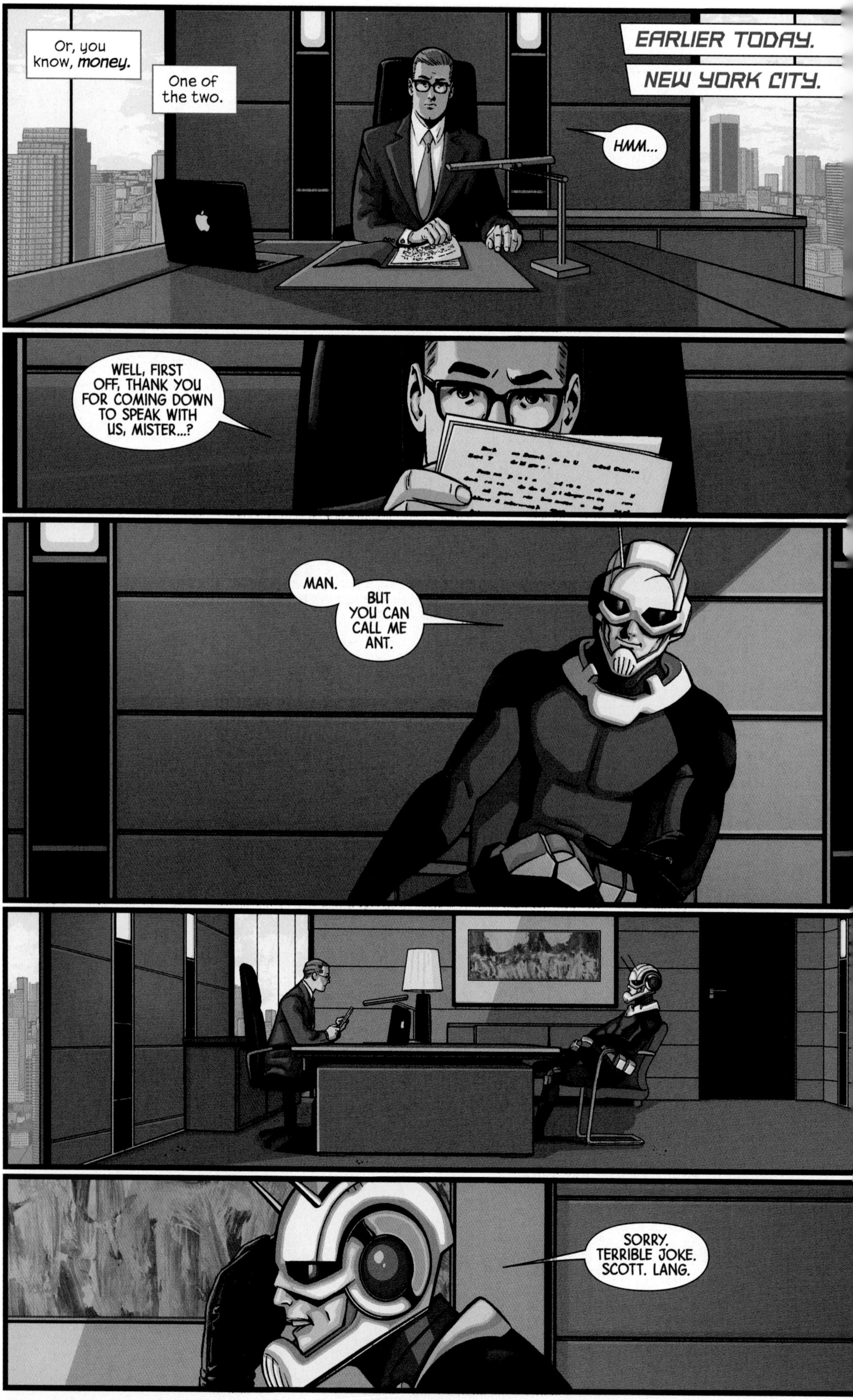
Or, you know, *money.*
One of the two.
EARLIER TODAY.
NEW YORK CITY.
HMM...
WELL, FIRST OFF, THANK YOU FOR COMING DOWN TO SPEAK WITH US, MISTER...?
MAN.
BUT YOU CAN CALL ME ANT.
SORRY. TERRIBLE JOKE. SCOTT. LANG.

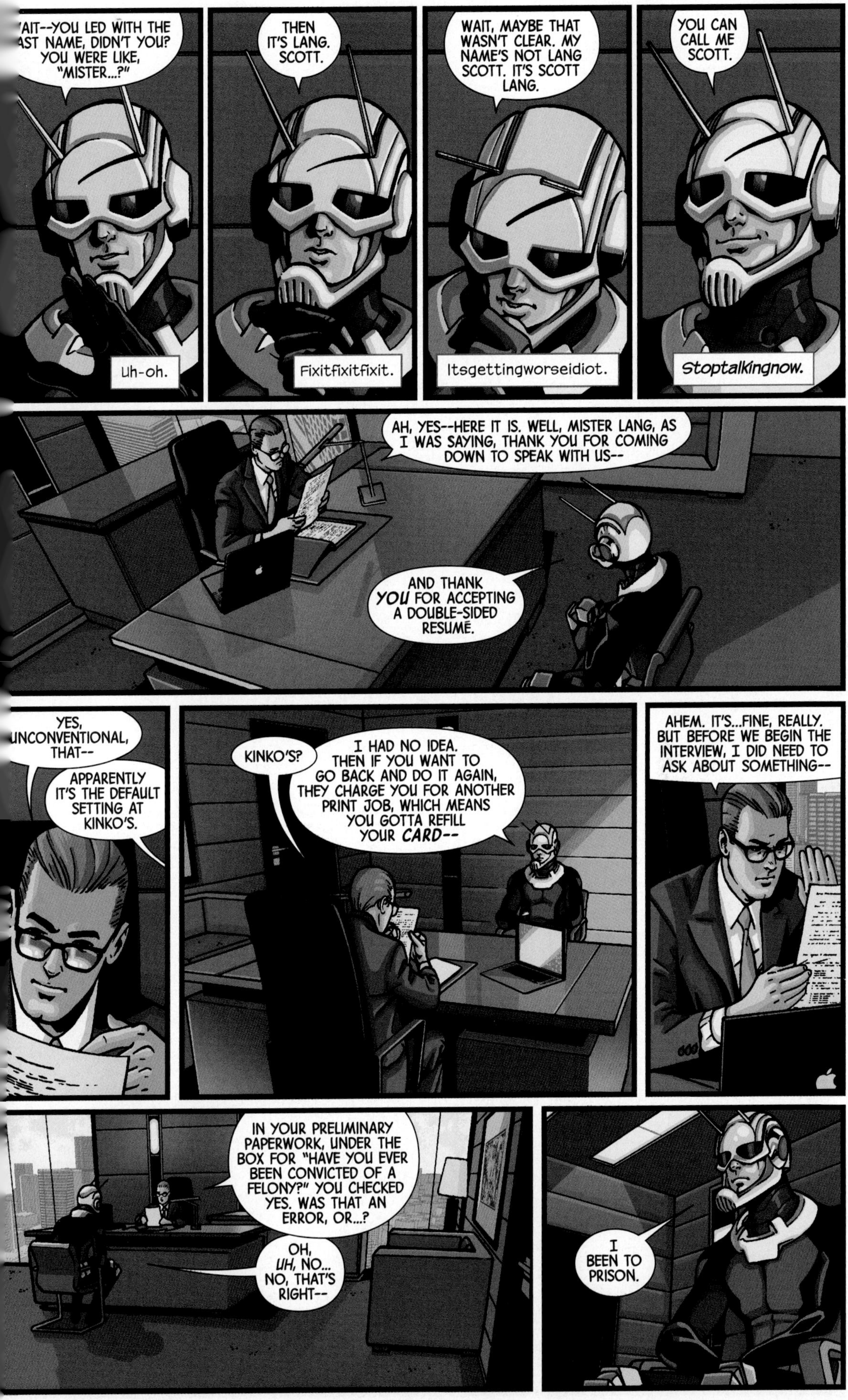

WAIT--YOU LED WITH THE LAST NAME, DIDN'T YOU? YOU WERE LIKE, "MISTER...?"
Uh-oh.
THEN IT'S LANG. SCOTT.
Fixitfixitfixit.
WAIT, MAYBE THAT WASN'T CLEAR. MY NAME'S NOT LANG SCOTT. IT'S SCOTT LANG.
Itsgettingworseidiot.
YOU CAN CALL ME SCOTT.
Stoptalkingnow.
AH, YES--HERE IT IS. WELL, MISTER LANG, AS I WAS SAYING, THANK YOU FOR COMING DOWN TO SPEAK WITH US--
AND THANK YOU FOR ACCEPTING A DOUBLE-SIDED RESUMÉ.
YES, UNCONVENTIONAL, THAT--
APPARENTLY IT'S THE DEFAULT SETTING AT KINKO'S.
KINKO'S?
I HAD NO IDEA. THEN IF YOU WANT TO GO BACK AND DO IT AGAIN, THEY CHARGE YOU FOR ANOTHER PRINT JOB, WHICH MEANS YOU GOTTA REFILL YOUR CARD--
AHEM. IT'S...FINE, REALLY. BUT BEFORE WE BEGIN THE INTERVIEW, I DID NEED TO ASK ABOUT SOMETHING--
IN YOUR PRELIMINARY PAPERWORK, UNDER THE BOX FOR "HAVE YOU EVER BEEN CONVICTED OF A FELONY?" YOU CHECKED YES. WAS THAT AN ERROR, OR...?
OH, UH, NO... NO, THAT'S RIGHT--
I BEEN TO PRISON.

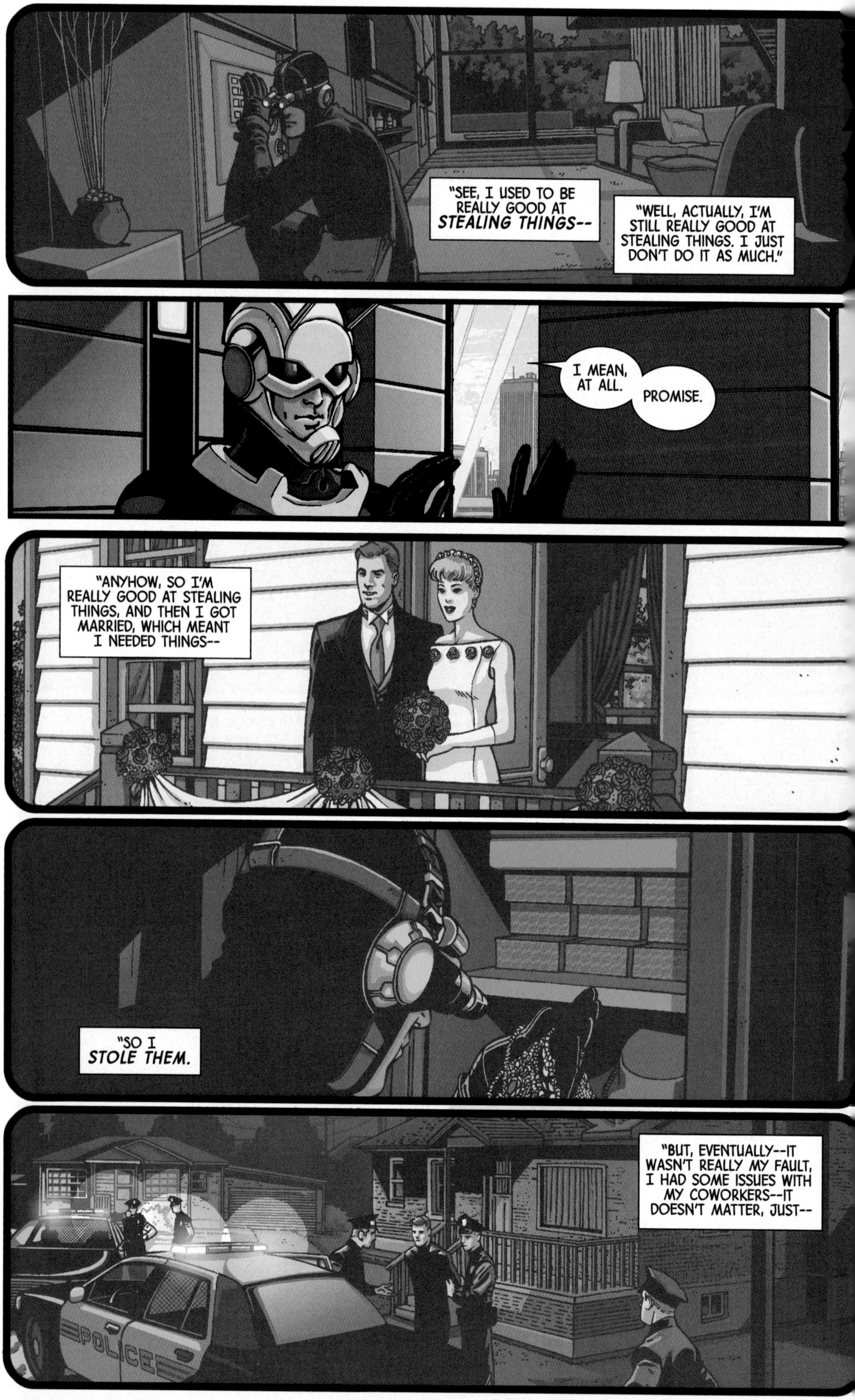
"SEE, I USED TO BE REALLY GOOD AT STEALING THINGS--
"WELL, ACTUALLY, I'M STILL REALLY GOOD AT STEALING THINGS. I JUST DON'T DO IT AS MUCH."
I MEAN, AT ALL.
PROMISE.
"ANYHOW, SO I'M REALLY GOOD AT STEALING THINGS, AND THEN I GOT MARRIED, WHICH MEANT I NEEDED THINGS--
"SO I STOLE THEM.
"BUT, EVENTUALLY--IT WASN'T REALLY MY FAULT, I HAD SOME ISSUES WITH MY COWORKERS--IT DOESN'T MATTER, JUST--
POLICE

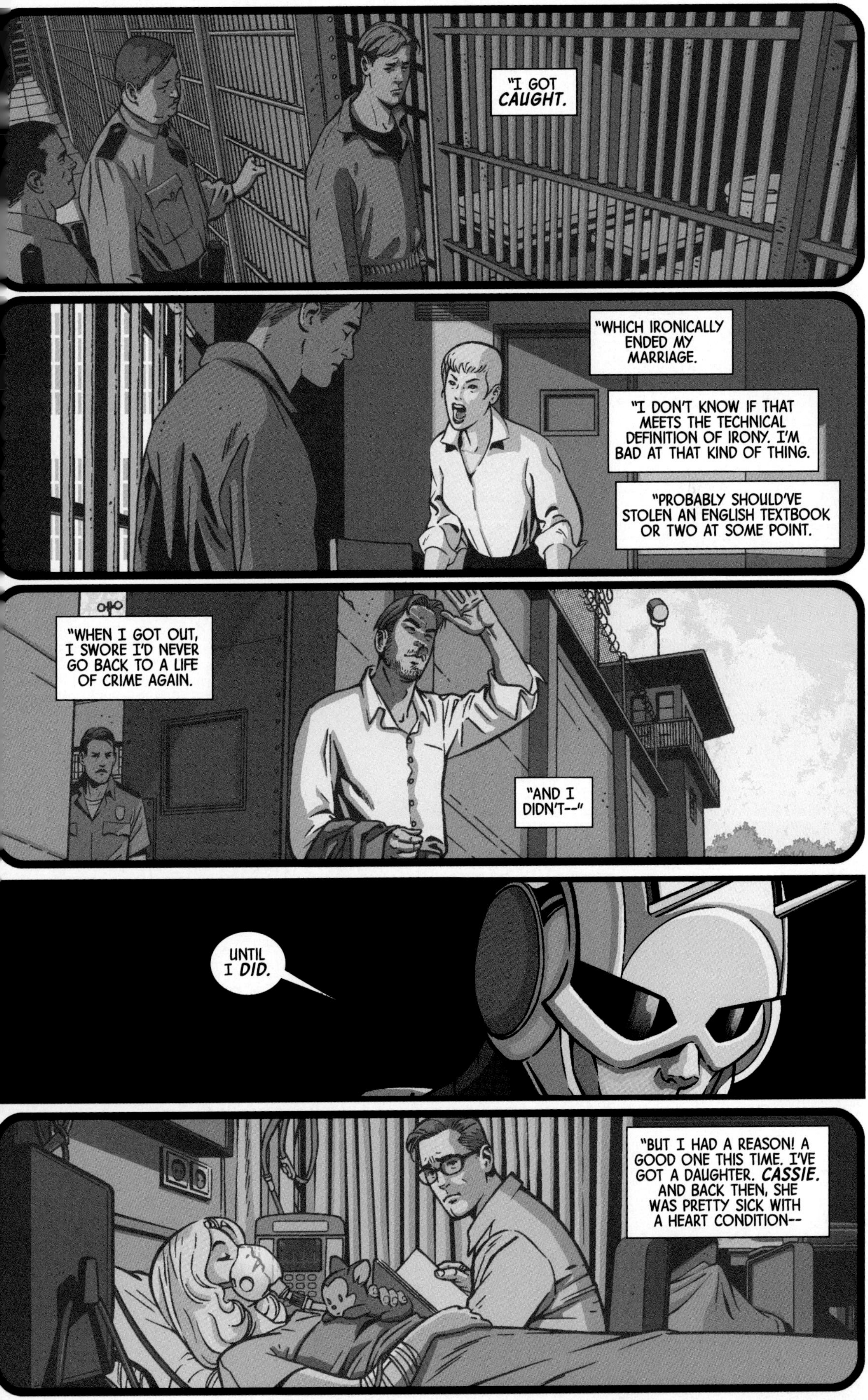
"I GOT CAUGHT.
"WHICH IRONICALLY ENDED MY MARRIAGE.
"I DON'T KNOW IF THAT MEETS THE TECHNICAL DEFINITION OF IRONY. I'M BAD AT THAT KIND OF THING.
"PROBABLY SHOULD'VE STOLEN AN ENGLISH TEXTBOOK OR TWO AT SOME POINT.
"WHEN I GOT OUT, I SWORE I'D NEVER GO BACK TO A LIFE OF CRIME AGAIN.
"AND I DIDN'T--"
UNTIL I DID.
"BUT I HAD A REASON! A GOOD ONE THIS TIME. I'VE GOT A DAUGHTER. CASSIE. AND BACK THEN, SHE WAS PRETTY SICK WITH A HEART CONDITION--

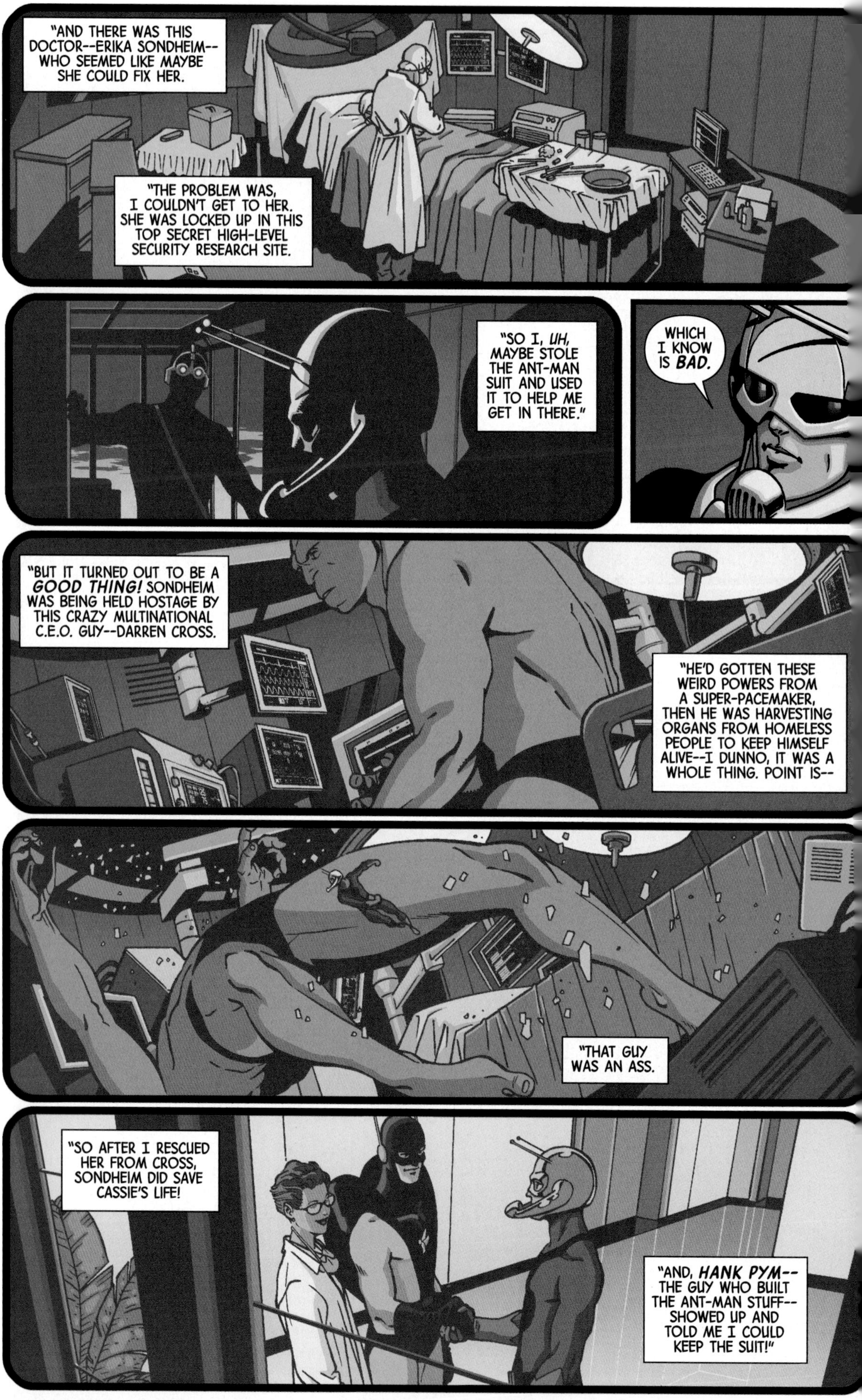
"AND THERE WAS THIS DOCTOR--ERIKA SONDHEIM--WHO SEEMED LIKE MAYBE SHE COULD FIX HER.
"THE PROBLEM WAS, I COULDN'T GET TO HER. SHE WAS LOCKED UP IN THIS TOP SECRET HIGH-LEVEL SECURITY RESEARCH SITE.
"SO I, *UH*, MAYBE STOLE THE ANT-MAN SUIT AND USED IT TO HELP ME GET IN THERE."
WHICH I KNOW IS ***BAD.***
"BUT IT TURNED OUT TO BE A ***GOOD THING!*** SONDHEIM WAS BEING HELD HOSTAGE BY THIS CRAZY MULTINATIONAL C.E.O. GUY--DARREN CROSS.
"HE'D GOTTEN THESE WEIRD POWERS FROM A SUPER-PACEMAKER, THEN HE WAS HARVESTING ORGANS FROM HOMELESS PEOPLE TO KEEP HIMSELF ALIVE--I DUNNO, IT WAS A WHOLE THING. POINT IS--
"THAT GUY WAS AN ASS.
"SO AFTER I RESCUED HER FROM CROSS, SONDHEIM DID SAVE CASSIE'S LIFE!
"AND, ***HANK PYM***--THE GUY WHO BUILT THE ANT-MAN STUFF--SHOWED UP AND TOLD ME I COULD KEEP THE SUIT!"

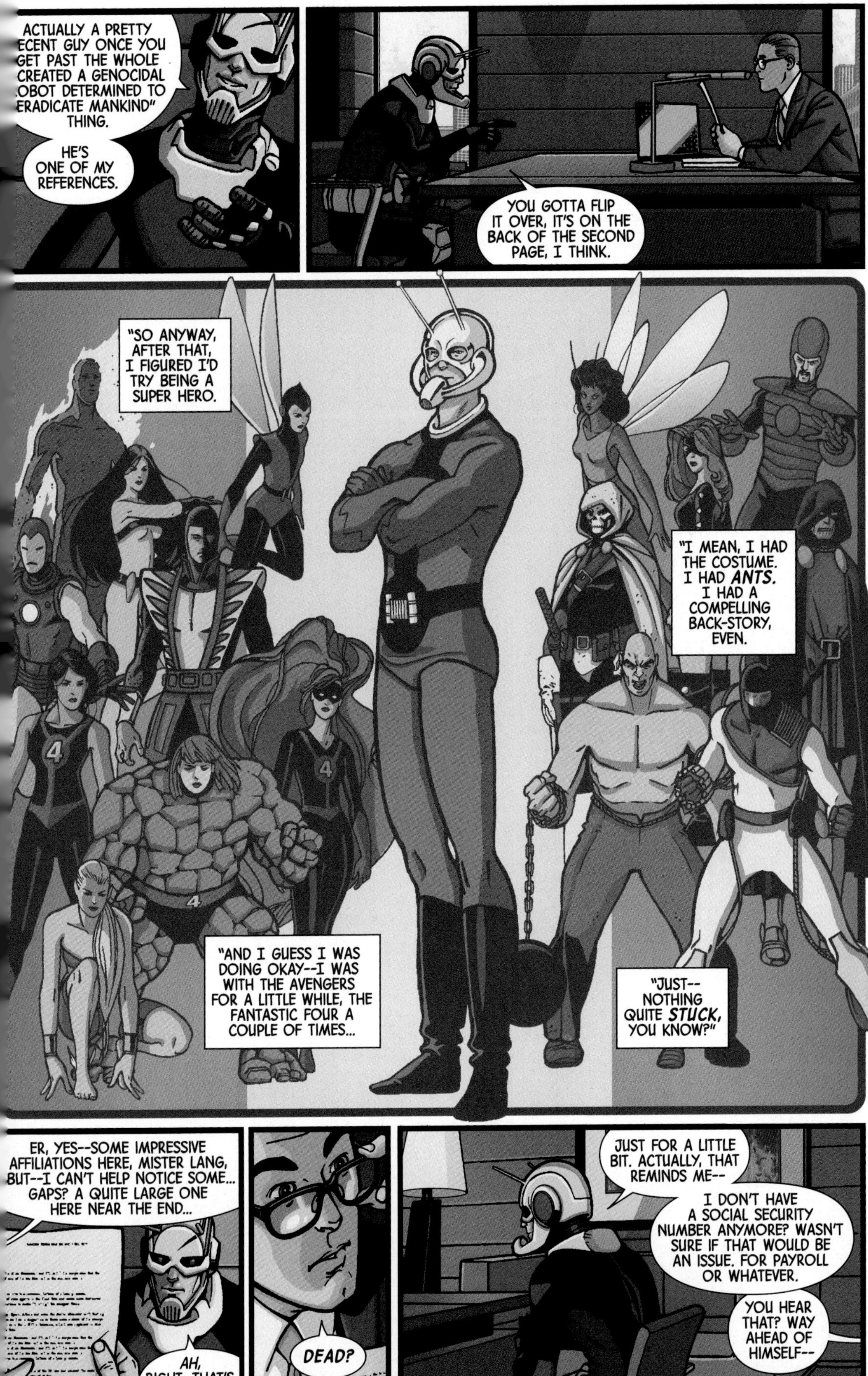
ACTUALLY A PRETTY DECENT GUY ONCE YOU GET PAST THE WHOLE "CREATED A GENOCIDAL ROBOT DETERMINED TO ERADICATE MANKIND" THING.
HE'S ONE OF MY REFERENCES.
YOU GOTTA FLIP IT OVER, IT'S ON THE BACK OF THE SECOND PAGE, I THINK.
"SO ANYWAY, AFTER THAT, I FIGURED I'D TRY BEING A SUPER HERO.
"I MEAN, I HAD THE COSTUME. I HAD ANTS. I HAD A COMPELLING BACK-STORY, EVEN.
"AND I GUESS I WAS DOING OKAY--I WAS WITH THE AVENGERS FOR A LITTLE WHILE, THE FANTASTIC FOUR A COUPLE OF TIMES...
"JUST--NOTHING QUITE STUCK, YOU KNOW?"
ER, YES--SOME IMPRESSIVE AFFILIATIONS HERE, MISTER LANG, BUT--I CAN'T HELP NOTICE SOME... GAPS? A QUITE LARGE ONE HERE NEAR THE END...
AH, RIGHT. THAT'S WHEN I WAS DEAD.
DEAD?
JUST FOR A LITTLE BIT. ACTUALLY, THAT REMINDS ME--
I DON'T HAVE A SOCIAL SECURITY NUMBER ANYMORE? WASN'T SURE IF THAT WOULD BE AN ISSUE. FOR PAYROLL OR WHATEVER.
YOU HEAR THAT? WAY AHEAD OF HIMSELF--

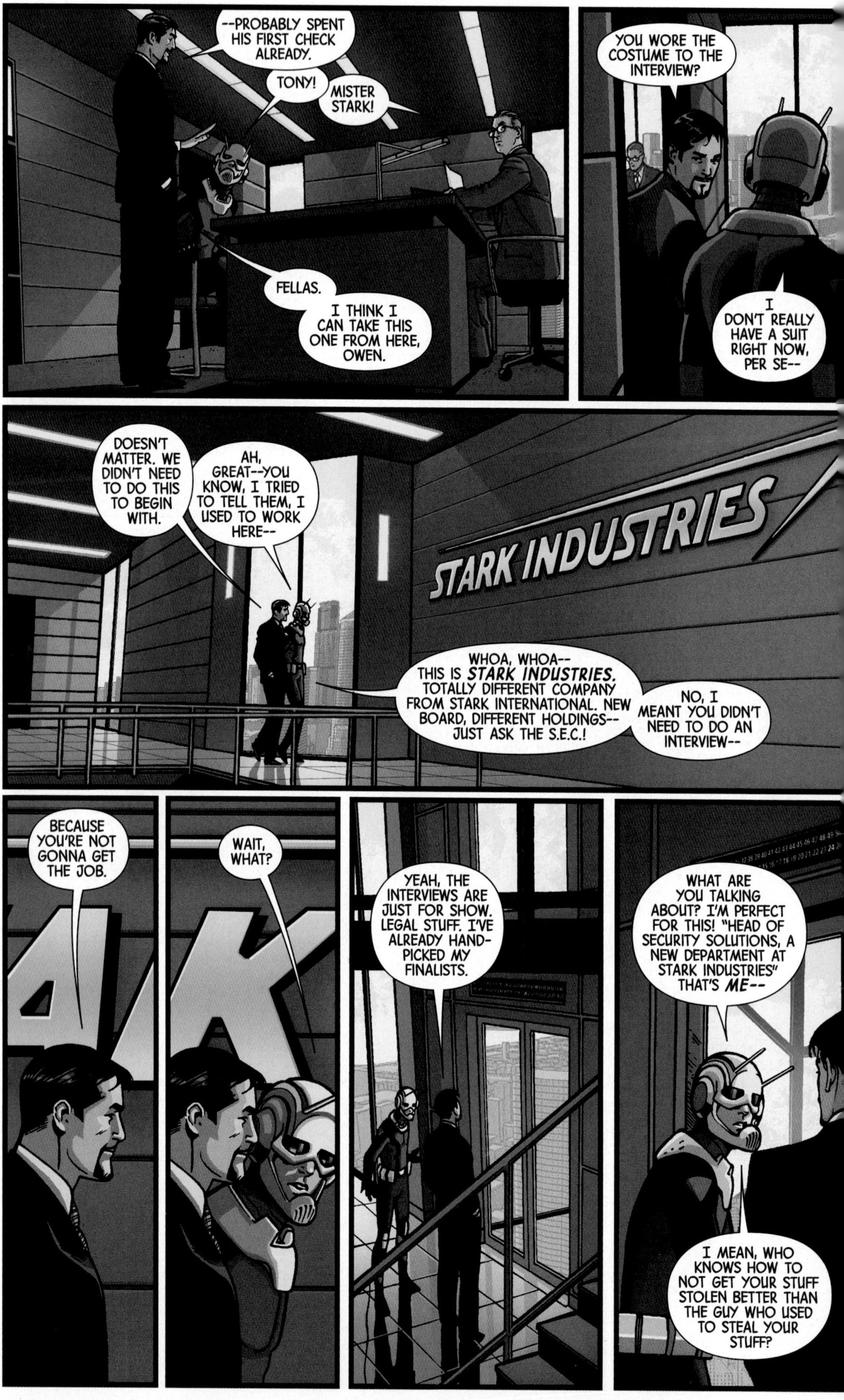
--PROBABLY SPENT HIS FIRST CHECK ALREADY.
TONY!
MISTER STARK!
FELLAS.
I THINK I CAN TAKE THIS ONE FROM HERE, OWEN.
YOU WORE THE COSTUME TO THE INTERVIEW?
I DON'T REALLY HAVE A SUIT RIGHT NOW, PER SE--
DOESN'T MATTER. WE DIDN'T NEED TO DO THIS TO BEGIN WITH.
AH, GREAT--YOU KNOW, I TRIED TO TELL THEM, I USED TO WORK HERE--
STARK INDUSTRIES
WHOA, WHOA-- THIS IS STARK INDUSTRIES. TOTALLY DIFFERENT COMPANY FROM STARK INTERNATIONAL. NEW BOARD, DIFFERENT HOLDINGS-- JUST ASK THE S.E.C.!
NO, I MEANT YOU DIDN'T NEED TO DO AN INTERVIEW--
BECAUSE YOU'RE NOT GONNA GET THE JOB.
WAIT, WHAT?
YEAH, THE INTERVIEWS ARE JUST FOR SHOW. LEGAL STUFF. I'VE ALREADY HAND-PICKED MY FINALISTS.
WHAT ARE YOU TALKING ABOUT? I'M PERFECT FOR THIS! "HEAD OF SECURITY SOLUTIONS, A NEW DEPARTMENT AT STARK INDUSTRIES" THAT'S ME--
I MEAN, WHO KNOWS HOW TO NOT GET YOUR STUFF STOLEN BETTER THAN THE GUY WHO USED TO STEAL YOUR STUFF?

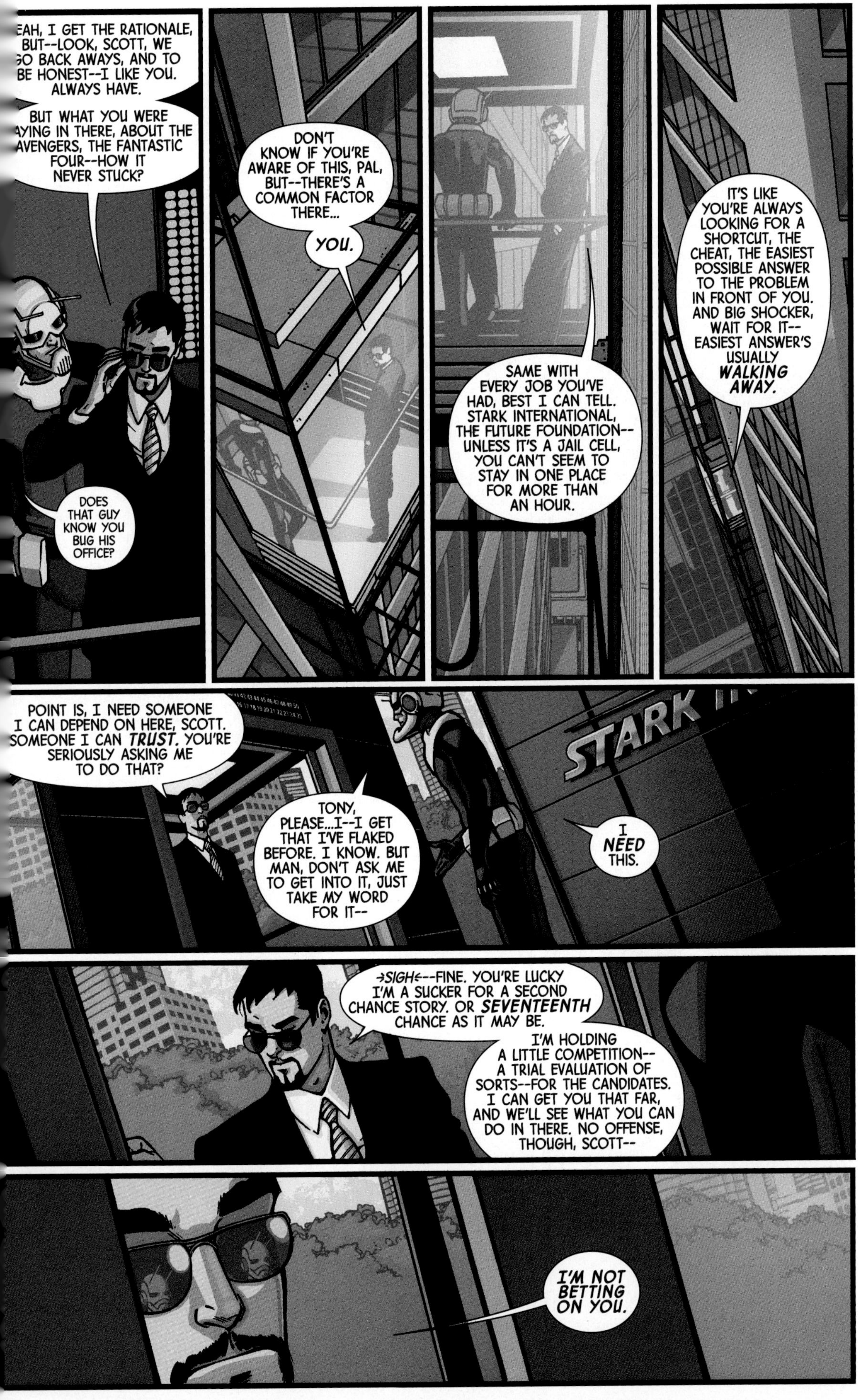

EAH, I GET THE RATIONALE, BUT--LOOK, SCOTT, WE GO BACK AWAYS, AND TO BE HONEST--I LIKE YOU. ALWAYS HAVE.
BUT WHAT YOU WERE AYING IN THERE, ABOUT THE AVENGERS, THE FANTASTIC FOUR--HOW IT NEVER STUCK?
DOES THAT GUY KNOW YOU BUG HIS OFFICE?
DON'T KNOW IF YOU'RE AWARE OF THIS, PAL, BUT--THERE'S A COMMON FACTOR THERE...
YOU.
SAME WITH EVERY JOB YOU'VE HAD, BEST I CAN TELL. STARK INTERNATIONAL, THE FUTURE FOUNDATION-- UNLESS IT'S A JAIL CELL, YOU CAN'T SEEM TO STAY IN ONE PLACE FOR MORE THAN AN HOUR.
IT'S LIKE YOU'RE ALWAYS LOOKING FOR A SHORTCUT, THE CHEAT, THE EASIEST POSSIBLE ANSWER TO THE PROBLEM IN FRONT OF YOU. AND BIG SHOCKER, WAIT FOR IT-- EASIEST ANSWER'S USUALLY WALKING AWAY.
POINT IS, I NEED SOMEONE I CAN DEPEND ON HERE, SCOTT. SOMEONE I CAN TRUST. YOU'RE SERIOUSLY ASKING ME TO DO THAT?
STARK
TONY, PLEASE...I--I GET THAT I'VE FLAKED BEFORE. I KNOW. BUT MAN, DON'T ASK ME TO GET INTO IT, JUST TAKE MY WORD FOR IT--
I NEED THIS.
→SIGH←--FINE. YOU'RE LUCKY I'M A SUCKER FOR A SECOND CHANCE STORY. OR SEVENTEENTH CHANCE AS IT MAY BE.
I'M HOLDING A LITTLE COMPETITION-- A TRIAL EVALUATION OF SORTS--FOR THE CANDIDATES. I CAN GET YOU THAT FAR, AND WE'LL SEE WHAT YOU CAN DO IN THERE. NO OFFENSE, THOUGH, SCOTT--
I'M NOT BETTING ON YOU.

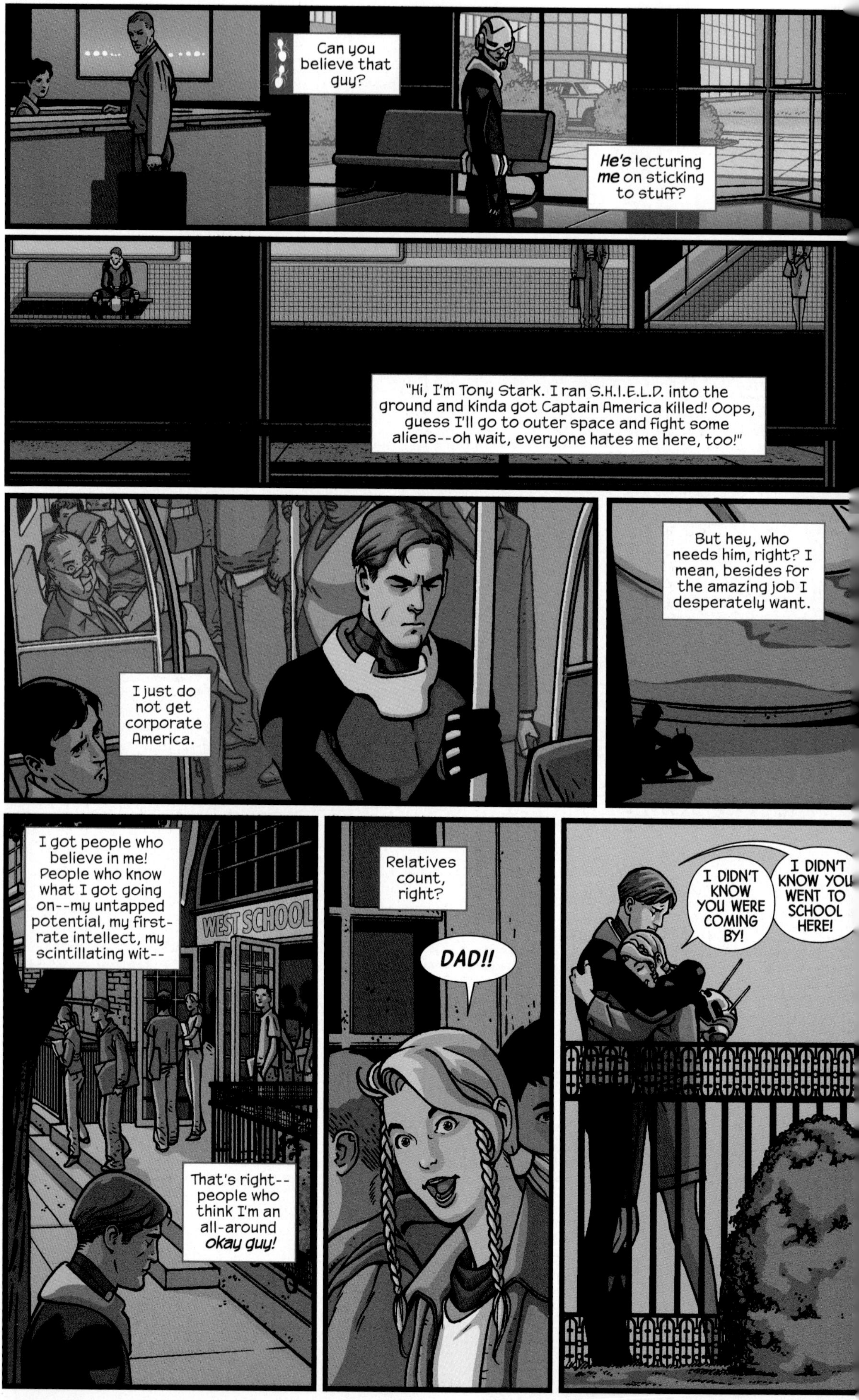

Can you believe that guy?
He's lecturing me on sticking to stuff?
"Hi, I'm Tony Stark. I ran S.H.I.E.L.D. into the ground and kinda got Captain America killed! Oops, guess I'll go to outer space and fight some aliens--oh wait, everyone hates me here, too!"
I just do not get corporate America.
But hey, who needs him, right? I mean, besides for the amazing job I desperately want.
I got people who believe in me! People who know what I got going on--my untapped potential, my first-rate intellect, my scintillating wit--
WEST SCHOOL
That's right--people who think I'm an all-around okay guy!
Relatives count, right?
DAD!!
I DIDN'T KNOW YOU WERE COMING BY!
I DIDN'T KNOW YOU WENT TO SCHOOL HERE!

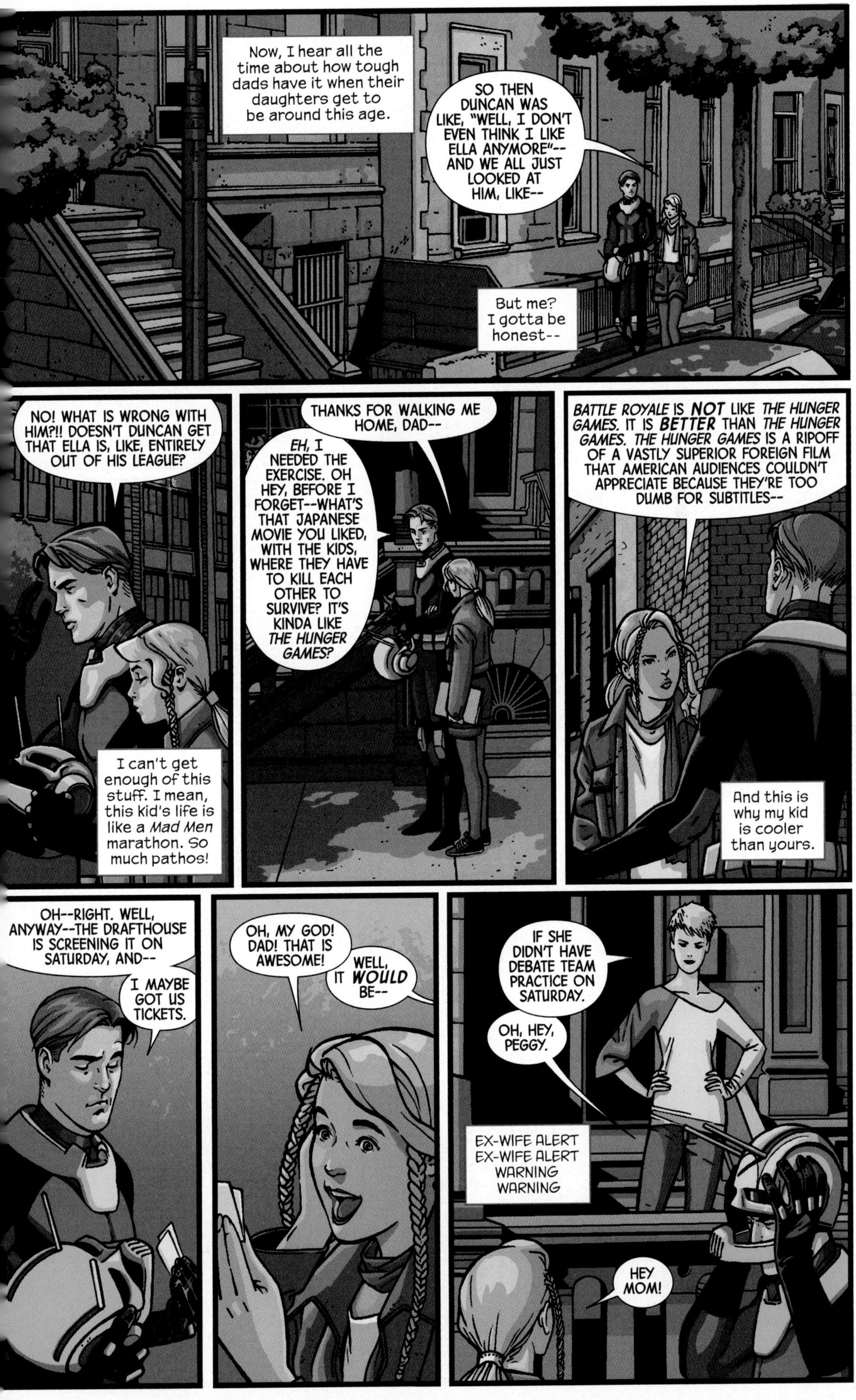
Now, I hear all the time about how tough dads have it when their daughters get to be around this age.
SO THEN DUNCAN WAS LIKE, "WELL, I DON'T EVEN THINK I LIKE ELLA ANYMORE"-- AND WE ALL JUST LOOKED AT HIM, LIKE--
But me? I gotta be honest--
NO! WHAT IS WRONG WITH HIM?!! DOESN'T DUNCAN GET THAT ELLA IS, LIKE, ENTIRELY OUT OF HIS LEAGUE?
I can't get enough of this stuff. I mean, this kid's life is like a *Mad Men* marathon. So much pathos!
THANKS FOR WALKING ME HOME, DAD--
*EH,* I NEEDED THE EXERCISE. OH HEY, BEFORE I FORGET--WHAT'S THAT JAPANESE MOVIE YOU LIKED, WITH THE KIDS, WHERE THEY HAVE TO KILL EACH OTHER TO SURVIVE? IT'S KINDA LIKE *THE HUNGER GAMES?*
*BATTLE ROYALE* IS **NOT** LIKE *THE HUNGER GAMES.* IT IS **BETTER** THAN *THE HUNGER GAMES. THE HUNGER GAMES* IS A RIPOFF OF A VASTLY SUPERIOR FOREIGN FILM THAT AMERICAN AUDIENCES COULDN'T APPRECIATE BECAUSE THEY'RE TOO DUMB FOR SUBTITLES--
And this is why my kid is cooler than yours.
OH--RIGHT. WELL, ANYWAY--THE DRAFTHOUSE IS SCREENING IT ON SATURDAY, AND--
I MAYBE GOT US TICKETS.
OH, MY GOD! DAD! THAT IS AWESOME!
WELL, IT ***WOULD*** BE--
IF SHE DIDN'T HAVE DEBATE TEAM PRACTICE ON SATURDAY.
OH, HEY, PEGGY.
EX-WIFE ALERT
EX-WIFE ALERT
WARNING
WARNING
HEY MOM!

IT'S IN THE GOOGLE CALENDAR.

I KINDA GOT SOME *INTERNET CONNECTIVITY* ISSUES RIGHT NOW.

CASSIE. HOMEWORK TIME.

BYE, DADDY.

PRAY TO WHATEVER GODS WILL HEAR YOU.

INTERNET CONNECTIVITY ISSUES? PAY A *BILL*, SCOTT.

MAYBE I'M PROTESTING ALL THESE *MERGERS*-- THEY'RE BAD FOR CONSUMERS, YOU KNOW!

WHAT IS THIS?

WHAT DO YOU MEAN?

YOU'RE PICKING HER UP FROM *SCHOOL* NOW?

LOOK, I KNOW WHAT YOU'RE GONNA SAY, BUT--I JUST HAPPENED TO BE THERE--

YOU JUST *HAPPENED* TO BE AT A MIDDLE SCHOOL?

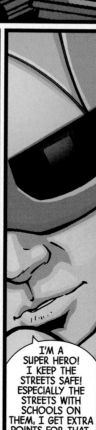

I'M A SUPER HERO! I KEEP THE STREETS SAFE! ESPECIALLY THE STREETS WITH SCHOOLS ON THEM, I GET EXTRA POINTS FOR THAT. BESIDES, THE JUDGE SAYS I HAVE--

*VISITATION.* NOT CUSTODY. YOU'RE SUPPOSED TO CLEAR IT WITH ME *FIRST.*

YEAH, WELL, MAYBE IF I GOT A *WEEKEND* ONCE IN A WHILE--

*UH-UH.* SHE'S GOT WAY TOO MUCH SCHOOL TO CATCH UP ON. AND YOU LIVE IN A STUDIO, SCOTT. YOU DON'T HAVE ROOM--

I DON'T *NEED* ROOM. I TOLD YOU, I CAN SHRINK HER DOWN WITH ME--

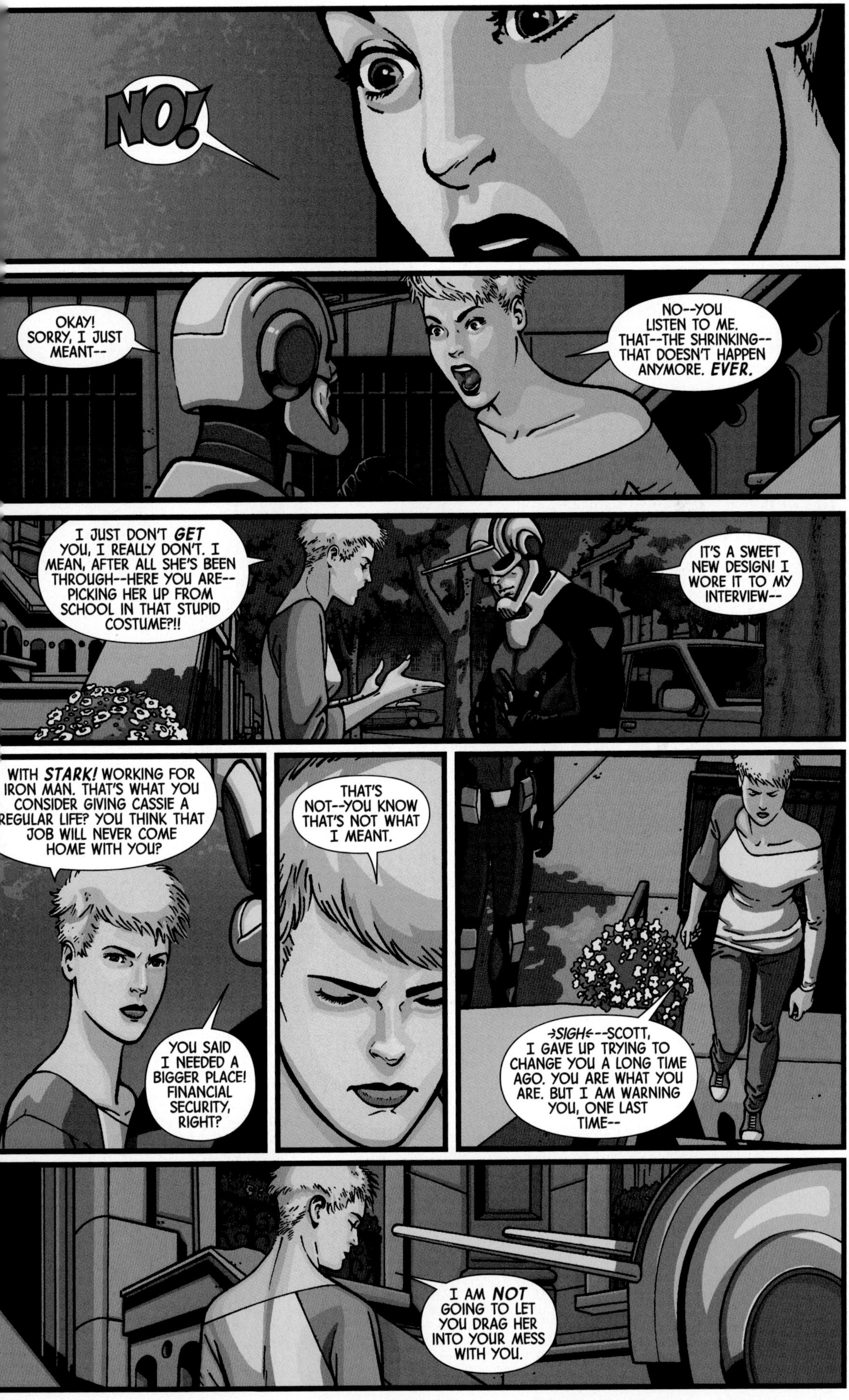
NO!
OKAY! SORRY, I JUST MEANT--
NO--YOU LISTEN TO ME. THAT--THE SHRINKING--THAT DOESN'T HAPPEN ANYMORE. EVER.
I JUST DON'T GET YOU, I REALLY DON'T. I MEAN, AFTER ALL SHE'S BEEN THROUGH--HERE YOU ARE--PICKING HER UP FROM SCHOOL IN THAT STUPID COSTUME?!!
IT'S A SWEET NEW DESIGN! I WORE IT TO MY INTERVIEW--
WITH STARK! WORKING FOR IRON MAN. THAT'S WHAT YOU CONSIDER GIVING CASSIE A REGULAR LIFE? YOU THINK THAT JOB WILL NEVER COME HOME WITH YOU?
YOU SAID I NEEDED A BIGGER PLACE! FINANCIAL SECURITY, RIGHT?
THAT'S NOT--YOU KNOW THAT'S NOT WHAT I MEANT.
→SIGH←--SCOTT, I GAVE UP TRYING TO CHANGE YOU A LONG TIME AGO. YOU ARE WHAT YOU ARE. BUT I AM WARNING YOU, ONE LAST TIME--
I AM NOT GOING TO LET YOU DRAG HER INTO YOUR MESS WITH YOU.

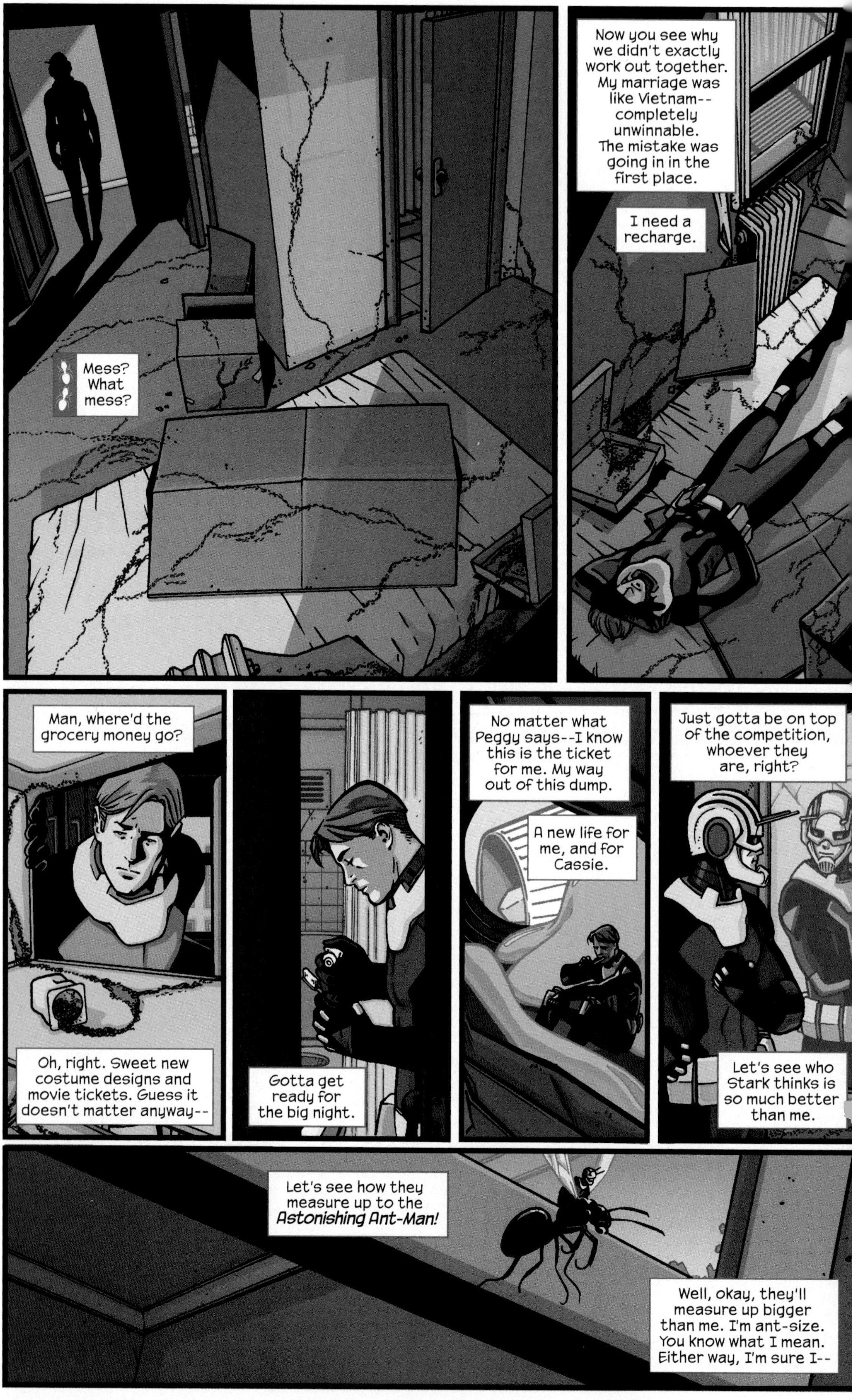
Mess? What mess?
Now you see why we didn't exactly work out together. My marriage was like Vietnam--completely unwinnable. The mistake was going in in the first place.
I need a recharge.
Man, where'd the grocery money go?
Oh, right. Sweet new costume designs and movie tickets. Guess it doesn't matter anyway--
Gotta get ready for the big night.
No matter what Peggy says--I know this is the ticket for me. My way out of this dump.
A new life for me, and for Cassie.
Just gotta be on top of the competition, whoever they are, right?
Let's see who Stark thinks is so much better than me.
Let's see how they measure up to the *Astonishing Ant-Man!*
Well, okay, they'll measure up bigger than me. I'm ant-size. You know what I mean. Either way, I'm sure I--

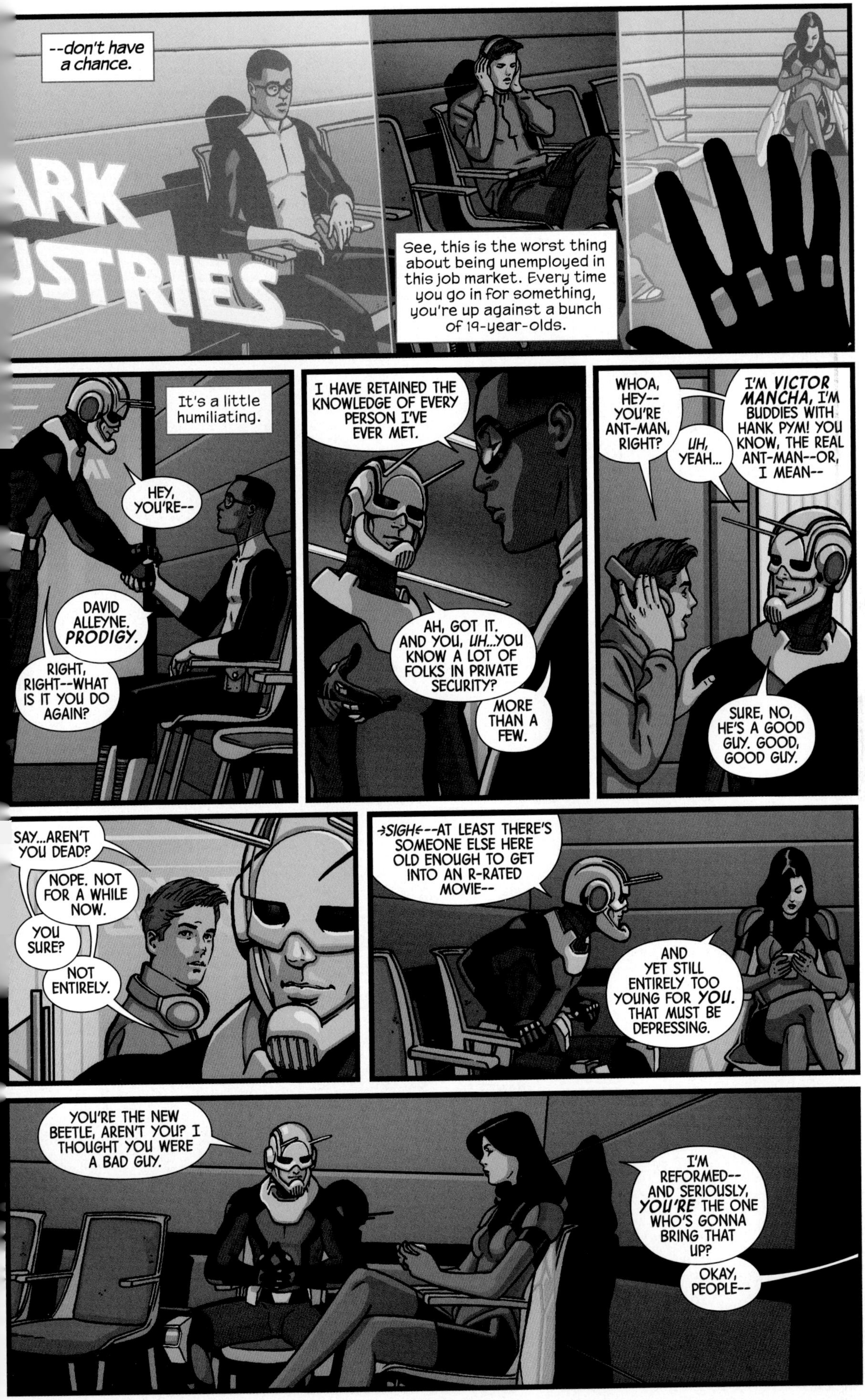
--don't have a chance.
ARK
USTRIES
See, this is the worst thing about being unemployed in this job market. Every time you go in for something, you're up against a bunch of 19-year-olds.
It's a little humiliating.
HEY, YOU'RE--
DAVID ALLEYNE. PRODIGY.
RIGHT, RIGHT--WHAT IS IT YOU DO AGAIN?
I HAVE RETAINED THE KNOWLEDGE OF EVERY PERSON I'VE EVER MET.
AH, GOT IT. AND YOU, UH...YOU KNOW A LOT OF FOLKS IN PRIVATE SECURITY?
MORE THAN A FEW.
WHOA, HEY-- YOU'RE ANT-MAN, RIGHT?
UH, YEAH...
I'M VICTOR MANCHA, I'M BUDDIES WITH HANK PYM! YOU KNOW, THE REAL ANT-MAN--OR, I MEAN--
SURE, NO, HE'S A GOOD GUY. GOOD, GOOD GUY.
SAY...AREN'T YOU DEAD?
NOPE. NOT FOR A WHILE NOW.
YOU SURE?
NOT ENTIRELY.
→SIGH←--AT LEAST THERE'S SOMEONE ELSE HERE OLD ENOUGH TO GET INTO AN R-RATED MOVIE--
AND YET STILL ENTIRELY TOO YOUNG FOR YOU. THAT MUST BE DEPRESSING.
YOU'RE THE NEW BEETLE, AREN'T YOU? I THOUGHT YOU WERE A BAD GUY.
I'M REFORMED-- AND SERIOUSLY, YOU'RE THE ONE WHO'S GONNA BRING THAT UP?
OKAY, PEOPLE--

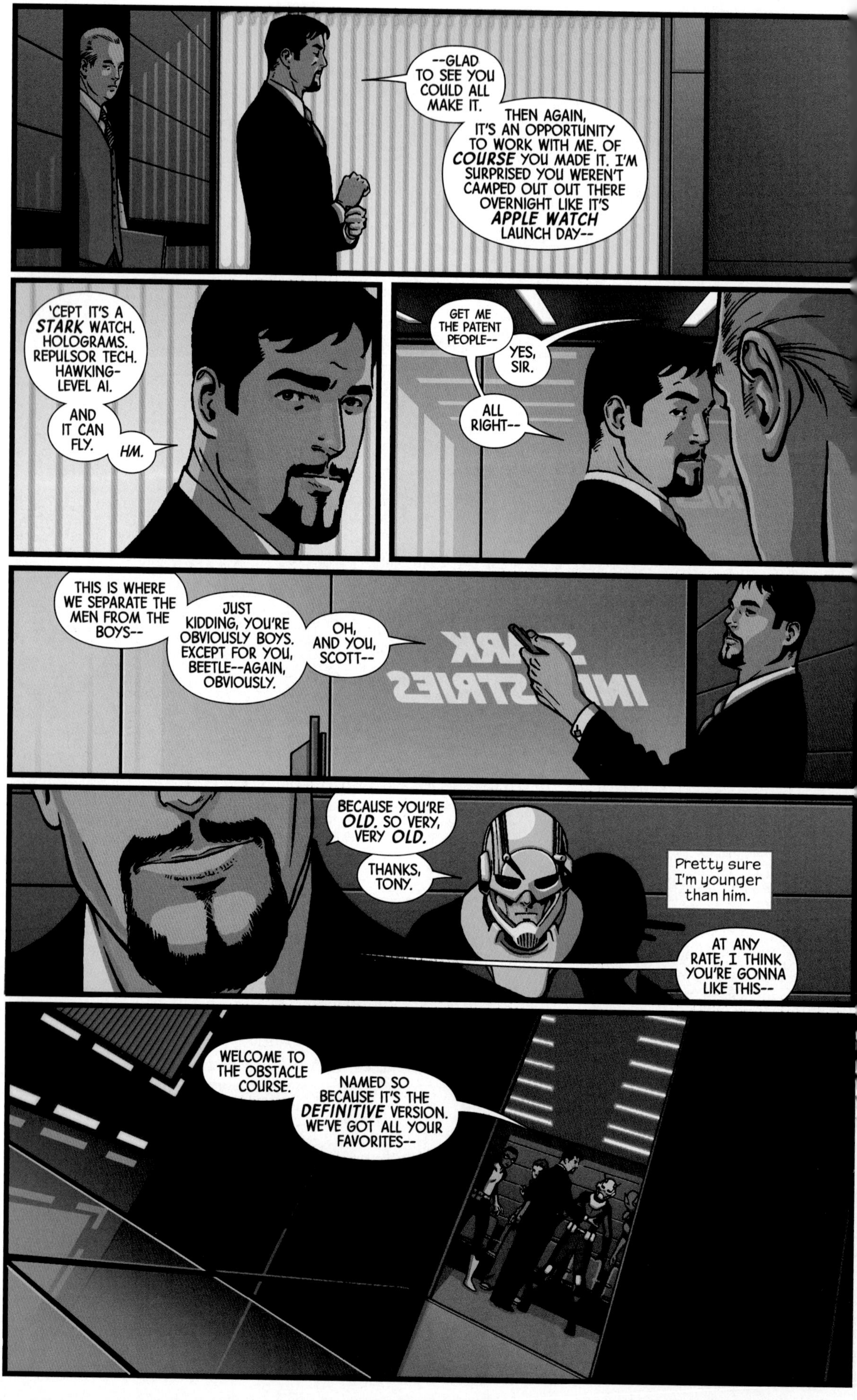
--GLAD TO SEE YOU COULD ALL MAKE IT.
THEN AGAIN, IT'S AN OPPORTUNITY TO WORK WITH ME. OF COURSE YOU MADE IT. I'M SURPRISED YOU WEREN'T CAMPED OUT OUT THERE OVERNIGHT LIKE IT'S APPLE WATCH LAUNCH DAY--
'CEPT IT'S A STARK WATCH. HOLOGRAMS. REPULSOR TECH. HAWKING-LEVEL AI.
AND IT CAN FLY.
HM.
GET ME THE PATENT PEOPLE--
YES, SIR.
ALL RIGHT--
THIS IS WHERE WE SEPARATE THE MEN FROM THE BOYS--
JUST KIDDING, YOU'RE OBVIOUSLY BOYS. EXCEPT FOR YOU, BEETLE--AGAIN, OBVIOUSLY.
OH, AND YOU, SCOTT--
BECAUSE YOU'RE OLD. SO VERY, VERY OLD.
THANKS, TONY.
Pretty sure I'm younger than him.
AT ANY RATE, I THINK YOU'RE GONNA LIKE THIS--
WELCOME TO THE OBSTACLE COURSE.
NAMED SO BECAUSE IT'S THE DEFINITIVE VERSION. WE'VE GOT ALL YOUR FAVORITES--

"SOME OVER-EAGER HUNTER KILLER DRONES--"

ACK! SHUT UP!

"A SOPHISTICATED RANGE-MOTION SENSOR BEAM NETWORK--"

MIKHAIL SOLOVSKY, MOSCOW BALLET. WONDERING WHEN THAT WOULD COME IN HANDY.

"EVEN ONE OR TWO VIBRANIUM-REINFORCED STOPWALLS--"

THERE BETTER BE A GIANT PILE OF MONEY IN THE SHAPE OF A V BEHIND THIS THING!

"AND FINALLY, THE *PIECE DE RESISTANCE*-- THE MOTHER CODE. THE ACCESS PASSWORD THAT TRUMPS ALL STARK SYSTEMS."

Enter code

CRACK THIS, AND I'LL KNOW YOU'VE GOT WHAT IT TAKES TO BREAK DOWN ANY SECURITY SYSTEM, WHICH MEANS YOU'VE GOT WHAT IT TAKES TO BUILD A *BETTER* ONE. SO--

*IMPRESS ME.*

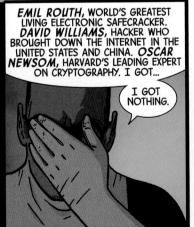

*EMIL ROUTH,* WORLD'S GREATEST LIVING ELECTRONIC SAFECRACKER. *DAVID WILLIAMS,* HACKER WHO BROUGHT DOWN THE INTERNET IN THE UNITED STATES AND CHINA. *OSCAR NEWSOM,* HARVARD'S LEADING EXPERT ON CRYPTOGRAPHY. I GOT...

I GOT NOTHING.

TONY, YOUR COMPUTER HATES YOU. IT'S GIVING UP YOUR FINANCIALS, YOUR BROWSING HISTORY--*GROSS,* MAN-- NOT TO MENTION THE PHOTOS FOLDER--

STILL NOT GIVING UP THE CODE, THOUGH.

EH. I GIVE UP.

WELL, SCOTT-- YOU GONNA SHOW THESE KIDS HOW IT'S DONE?

WITH *PLEASURE,* TONY.

Or deep, unrelenting agony.

I mean, if Knows Everything Kid and Living Computer Lad can't do this, how the hell am I supposed to?

Luckily I do have one secret super-power none of the others have--

Enter code

The power to fake *sick.*

See, with the Pym Particles, I can actually shrink individual parts of my body. Now this is not something most guys are usually in a rush to do, but in the case of the *digestive* system--

Can come in handy.

BLERGH!!

EWW!

OH MAN--

INSIDE THE HELMET!

OKAY, THAT'S ENOUGH--

TONY, I'M SORRY, I--I SHOULD'VE SAID SOMETHING. BEEN DEALING WITH A STOMACH FLU-- THOUGHT I COULD TOUGH IT OUT--

→SIGH←-- IT'S FINE--

LOOK, ALL OF YOU, HERE'S WHAT WE'RE GONNA DO. WE'LL RECONVENE TOMORROW MORNING AND GO THROUGH ALL OF THIS AGAIN, SEE IF WE GET SOME DIFFERENT RESULTS.

AND GOD KNOWS WE BETTER. I HAVE TO HIRE ONE OF YOU PEOPLE. RHODEY WON'T EVEN RETURN MY CALLS.

At least it buys me a second chance. I was way out of my depth in there. The only way I'm going to crack that code is if I put my head down and come up with something *great,* something outside the box.

Or, wait-- that's not actually the *only* way...

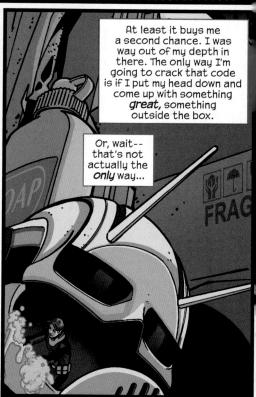

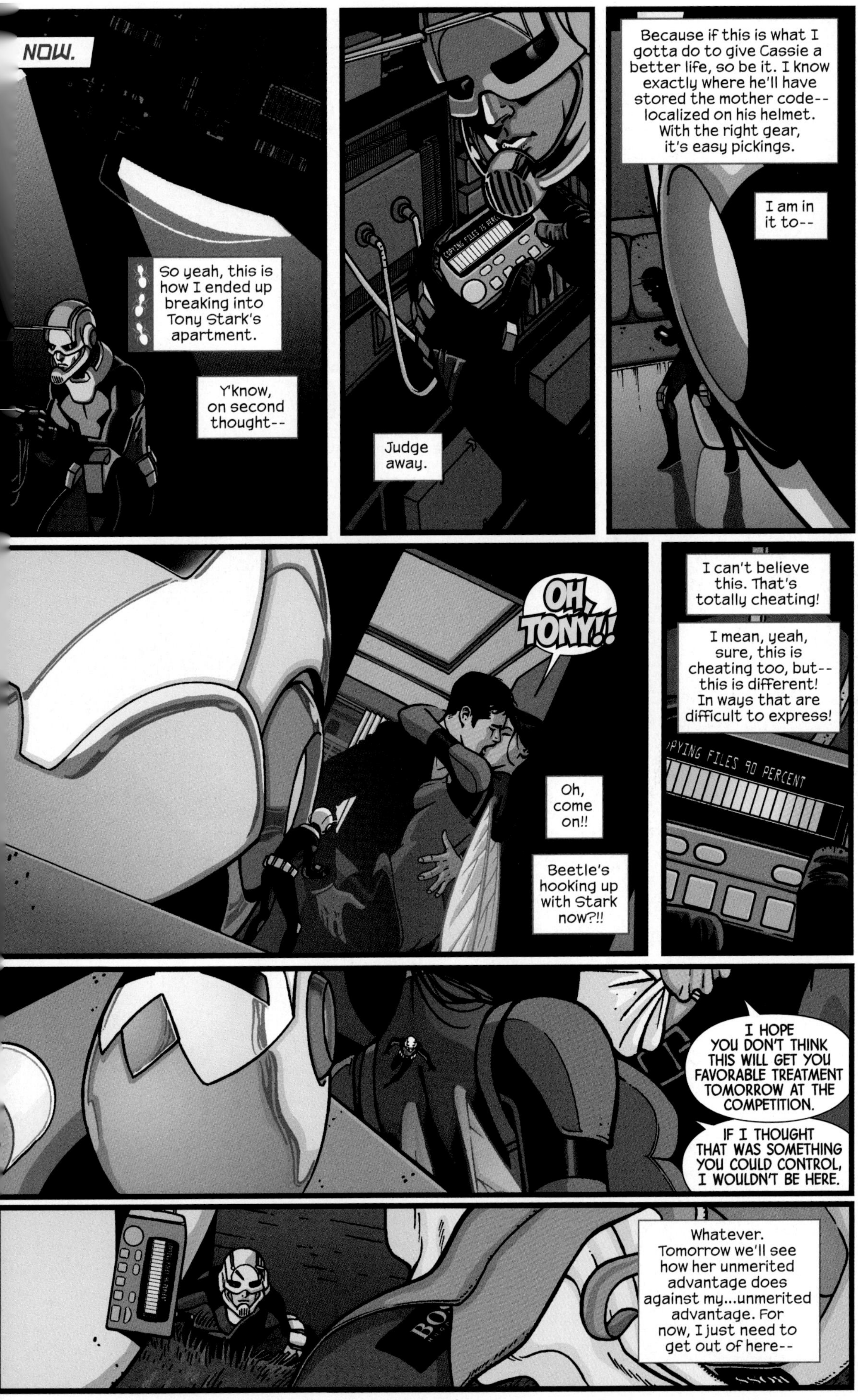
NOW.
So yeah, this is how I ended up breaking into Tony Stark's apartment.
Y'know, on second thought--
Judge away.
Because if this is what I gotta do to give Cassie a better life, so be it. I know exactly where he'll have stored the mother code--localized on his helmet. With the right gear, it's easy pickings.
I am in it to--
OH, TONY!!
Oh, come on!!
Beetle's hooking up with Stark now?!!
I can't believe this. That's totally cheating!
I mean, yeah, sure, this is cheating too, but--this is different! In ways that are difficult to express!
PYING FILES 90 PERCENT
I HOPE YOU DON'T THINK THIS WILL GET YOU FAVORABLE TREATMENT TOMORROW AT THE COMPETITION.
IF I THOUGHT THAT WAS SOMETHING YOU COULD CONTROL, I WOULDN'T BE HERE.
Whatever. Tomorrow we'll see how her unmerited advantage does against my...unmerited advantage. For now, I just need to get out of here--

--before things get awkward.

Please god let this thing get done before I have to see--

Too late.

Always too late.

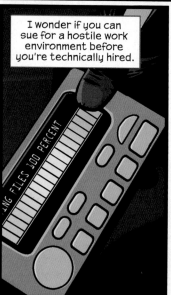

I wonder if you can sue for a hostile work environment before you're technically hired.

Either way, this better have been worth it. Let's see what the mother code is--man, this thing is loading slow--

Huh?

CONGRATULATIONS!

CLAP CLAP

CLAP

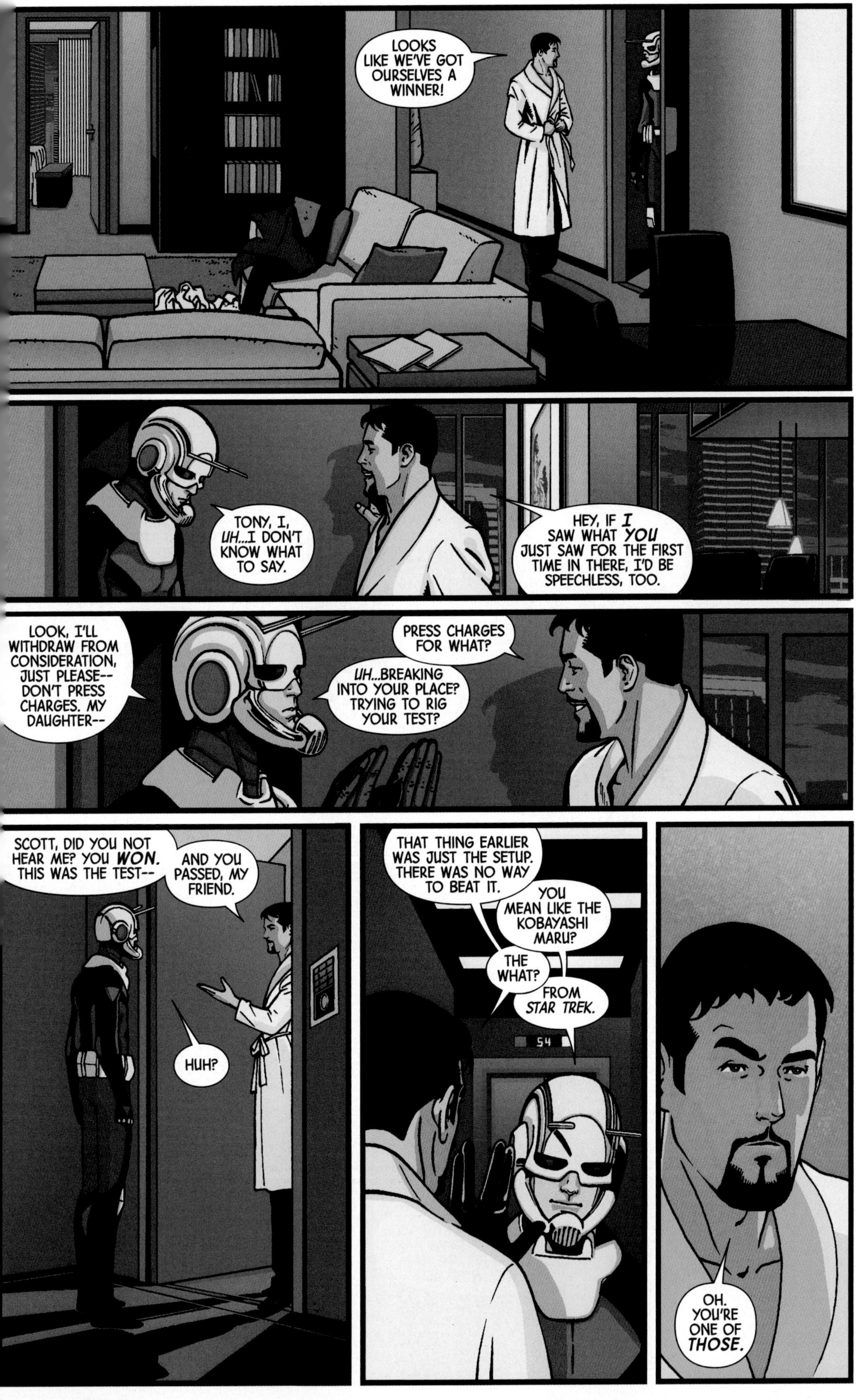

LOOKS LIKE WE'VE GOT OURSELVES A WINNER!
TONY, I, UH...I DON'T KNOW WHAT TO SAY.
HEY, IF I SAW WHAT YOU JUST SAW FOR THE FIRST TIME IN THERE, I'D BE SPEECHLESS, TOO.
LOOK, I'LL WITHDRAW FROM CONSIDERATION, JUST PLEASE--DON'T PRESS CHARGES. MY DAUGHTER--
PRESS CHARGES FOR WHAT?
UH...BREAKING INTO YOUR PLACE? TRYING TO RIG YOUR TEST?
SCOTT, DID YOU NOT HEAR ME? YOU WON. THIS WAS THE TEST--
AND YOU PASSED, MY FRIEND.
HUH?
THAT THING EARLIER WAS JUST THE SETUP. THERE WAS NO WAY TO BEAT IT.
YOU MEAN LIKE THE KOBAYASHI MARU?
THE WHAT?
FROM STAR TREK.
54
OH. YOU'RE ONE OF THOSE.

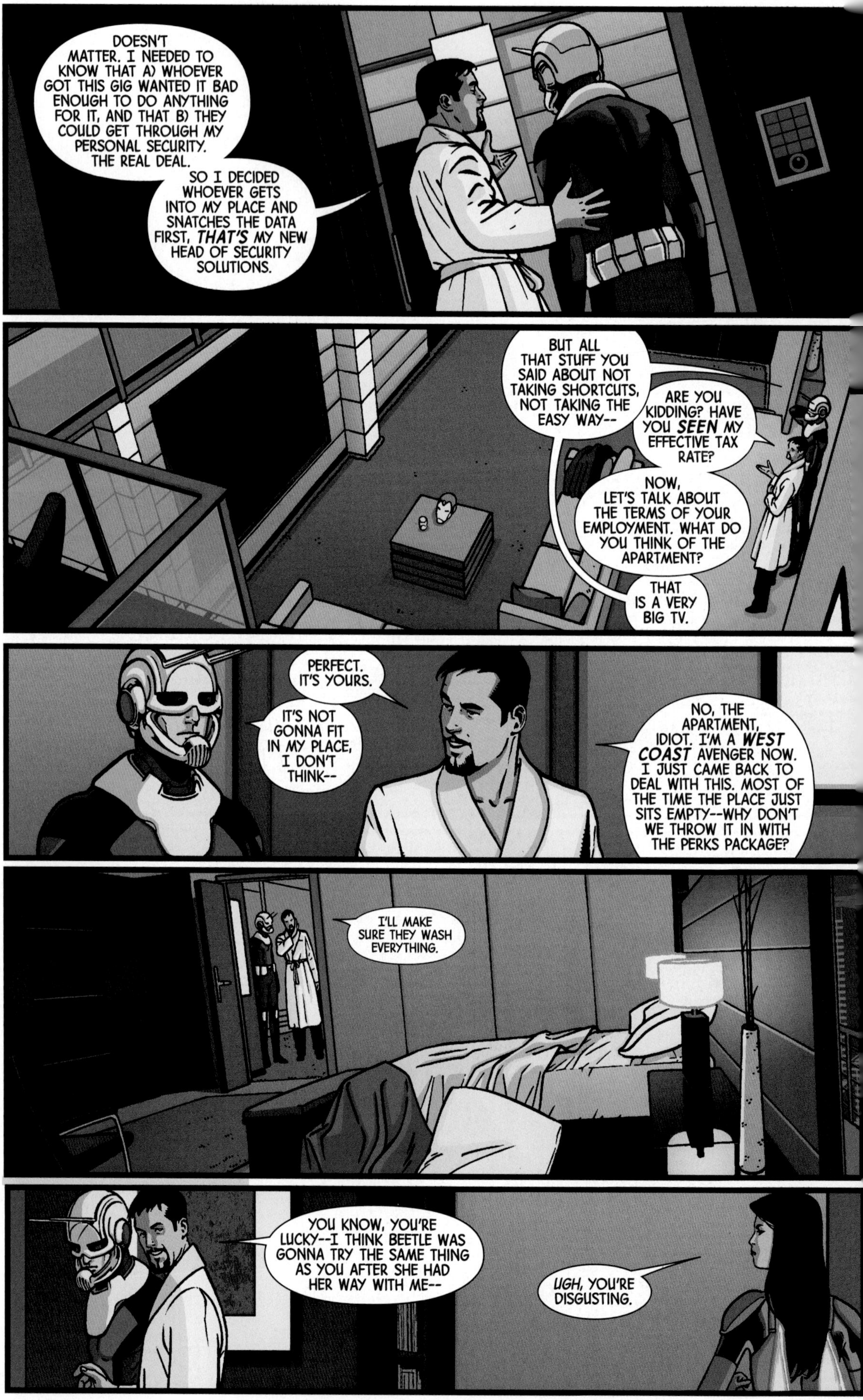
DOESN'T MATTER. I NEEDED TO KNOW THAT A) WHOEVER GOT THIS GIG WANTED IT BAD ENOUGH TO DO ANYTHING FOR IT, AND THAT B) THEY COULD GET THROUGH MY PERSONAL SECURITY. THE REAL DEAL.
SO I DECIDED WHOEVER GETS INTO MY PLACE AND SNATCHES THE DATA FIRST, THAT'S MY NEW HEAD OF SECURITY SOLUTIONS.
BUT ALL THAT STUFF YOU SAID ABOUT NOT TAKING SHORTCUTS, NOT TAKING THE EASY WAY--
ARE YOU KIDDING? HAVE YOU SEEN MY EFFECTIVE TAX RATE?
NOW, LET'S TALK ABOUT THE TERMS OF YOUR EMPLOYMENT. WHAT DO YOU THINK OF THE APARTMENT?
THAT IS A VERY BIG TV.
PERFECT. IT'S YOURS.
IT'S NOT GONNA FIT IN MY PLACE, I DON'T THINK--
NO, THE APARTMENT, IDIOT. I'M A WEST COAST AVENGER NOW. I JUST CAME BACK TO DEAL WITH THIS. MOST OF THE TIME THE PLACE JUST SITS EMPTY--WHY DON'T WE THROW IT IN WITH THE PERKS PACKAGE?
I'LL MAKE SURE THEY WASH EVERYTHING.
YOU KNOW, YOU'RE LUCKY--I THINK BEETLE WAS GONNA TRY THE SAME THING AS YOU AFTER SHE HAD HER WAY WITH ME--
UGH, YOU'RE DISGUSTING.

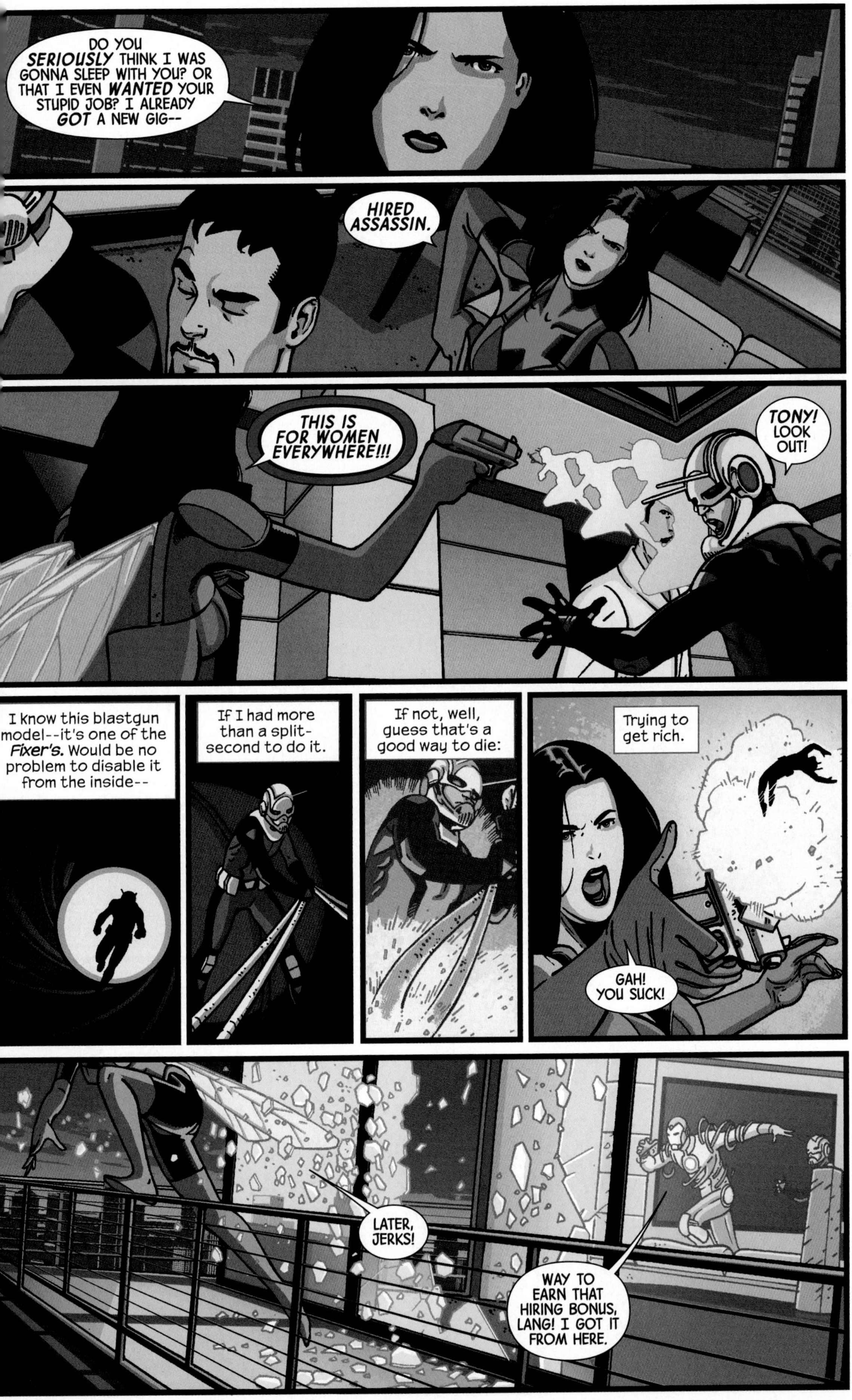

DO YOU SERIOUSLY THINK I WAS GONNA SLEEP WITH YOU? OR THAT I EVEN WANTED YOUR STUPID JOB? I ALREADY GOT A NEW GIG--
HIRED ASSASSIN.
THIS IS FOR WOMEN EVERYWHERE!!!
TONY! LOOK OUT!
I know this blastgun model--it's one of the Fixer's. Would be no problem to disable it from the inside--
If I had more than a split-second to do it.
If not, well, guess that's a good way to die:
Trying to get rich.
GAH! YOU SUCK!
LATER, JERKS!
WAY TO EARN THAT HIRING BONUS, LANG! I GOT IT FROM HERE.

Can you believe that guy?

I mean, how great is he?!!

Tony Stark, Man of the People!

Giving me the opportunity to show what I can do, putting me in a position to win--

Yes, sir, this is my ticket off the C-list!

No more "I thought you were Hank Pym!"

No more "So what else do you do besides talk to ants?"

Now to share the big news with--

CASS?

SHE'S NOT HERE, SCOTT.

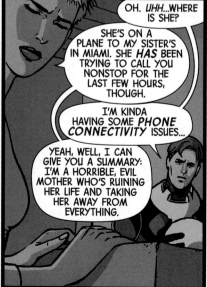

OH. UHH...WHERE IS SHE?

SHE'S ON A PLANE TO MY SISTER'S IN MIAMI. SHE **HAS** BEEN TRYING TO CALL YOU NONSTOP FOR THE LAST FEW HOURS, THOUGH.

I'M KINDA HAVING SOME **PHONE CONNECTIVITY** ISSUES...

YEAH, WELL, I CAN GIVE YOU A SUMMARY: I'M A HORRIBLE, EVIL MOTHER WHO'S RUINING HER LIFE AND TAKING HER AWAY FROM EVERYTHING.

I DON'T--WHAT'S GOING ON?

WHAT DOES IT LOOK LIKE?

AN AWESOME BOX FORT WAITING TO HAPPEN?

WE'RE *MOVING*, SCOTT. ACK HOME. WE'RE STAYING WITH TRINA FOR A BIT WHILE I FIND A PLACE.

YOU CAN'T JUST--I HAVE VISITATION!

AND YOU CAN VISIT WHENEVER YOU'D LIKE.

WHEN DID YOU DECIDE TO DO THIS?!!

BEEN THINKING ABOUT IT FOR A WHILE NOW. THEN, AFTER YOU SHOWED UP YESTERDAY-- WELL, FELT LIKE TIME FOR SOME DRASTIC ACTION.

I CAN'T--I CAN'T EVEN BELIEVE THIS. SHE'S MY *DAUGHTER*, PEGGY. YOU CAN'T JUST TAKE HER AWAY--

SCOTT, COME ON. SOMEONE HAS TO BE A GROWN-UP HERE. IT'S NOT EVEN JUST ABOUT YOU--THIS CITY, IT'S LOUSY WITH THIS COSTUME STUFF.

SHE ISN'T SAFE HERE.

I TOLD YOU, I CAN KEEP HER SAFE--

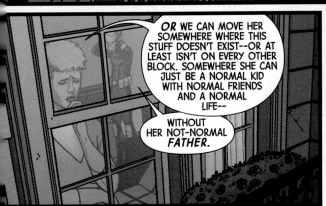

*OR* WE CAN MOVE HER SOMEWHERE WHERE THIS STUFF DOESN'T EXIST--OR AT LEAST ISN'T ON EVERY OTHER BLOCK. SOMEWHERE SHE CAN JUST BE A NORMAL KID WITH NORMAL FRIENDS AND A NORMAL LIFE--

WITHOUT HER NOT-NORMAL *FATHER*.

→SIGH←--I DON'T LIKE DOING THIS, SCOTT. I REALLY DON'T. YOU WERE NEVER A GOOD HUSBAND, BUT, AS A DAD--I DO KNOW HOW HARD YOU TRY.

AND I ALSO KNOW YOU WANT WHAT'S BEST FOR CASSIE--WHICH IS WHY I'M ASKING YOU TO REALLY THINK ABOUT THIS, ABOUT WHAT SHE-- *OUR DAUGHTER*-- WHAT KIND OF LIFE SHE DESERVES...IF YOU'RE HONEST WITH YOURSELF--

I THINK YOU ALREADY KNOW THE ANSWER.

Here's the thing, though--

I *don't*.

I mean, am I just being selfish? Is Cassie better off someplace else?

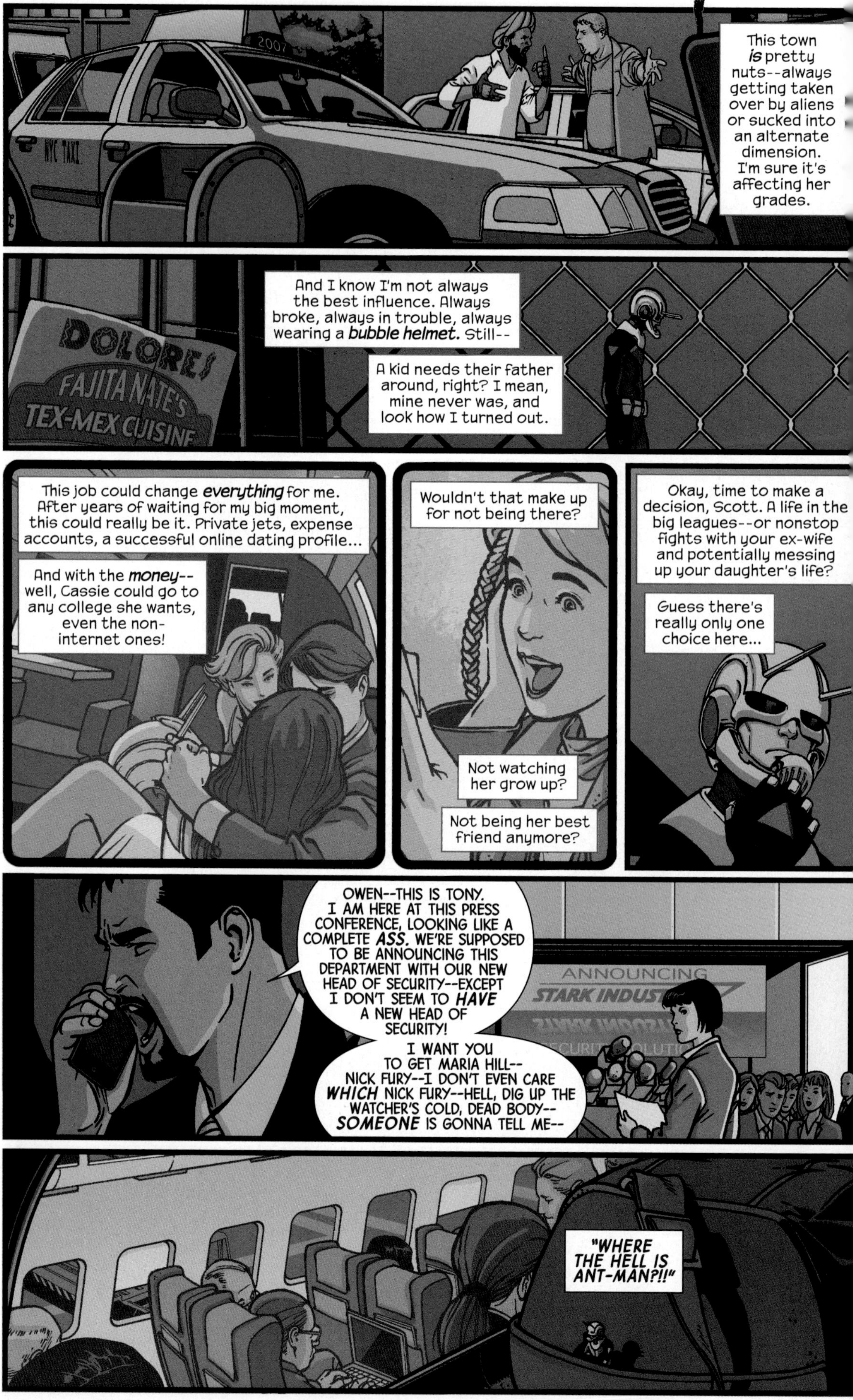

This town *is* pretty nuts--always getting taken over by aliens or sucked into an alternate dimension. I'm sure it's affecting her grades.
2007
NYC TAXI
And I know I'm not always the best influence. Always broke, always in trouble, always wearing a *bubble helmet.* Still--
A kid needs their father around, right? I mean, mine never was, and look how I turned out.
DOLORES
FAJITA NATE'S TEX-MEX CUISINE
This job could change *everything* for me. After years of waiting for my big moment, this could really be it. Private jets, expense accounts, a successful online dating profile...
And with the *money*--well, Cassie could go to any college she wants, even the non-internet ones!
Wouldn't that make up for not being there?
Not watching her grow up?
Not being her best friend anymore?
Okay, time to make a decision, Scott. A life in the big leagues--or nonstop fights with your ex-wife and potentially messing up your daughter's life?
Guess there's really only one choice here...
OWEN--THIS IS TONY. I AM HERE AT THIS PRESS CONFERENCE, LOOKING LIKE A COMPLETE *ASS.* WE'RE SUPPOSED TO BE ANNOUNCING THIS DEPARTMENT WITH OUR NEW HEAD OF SECURITY--EXCEPT I DON'T SEEM TO *HAVE* A NEW HEAD OF SECURITY!
I WANT YOU TO GET MARIA HILL--NICK FURY--I DON'T EVEN CARE *WHICH* NICK FURY--HELL, DIG UP THE WATCHER'S COLD, DEAD BODY--*SOMEONE* IS GONNA TELL ME--
ANNOUNCING
STARK INDUS
"WHERE THE HELL IS ANT-MAN?!!"

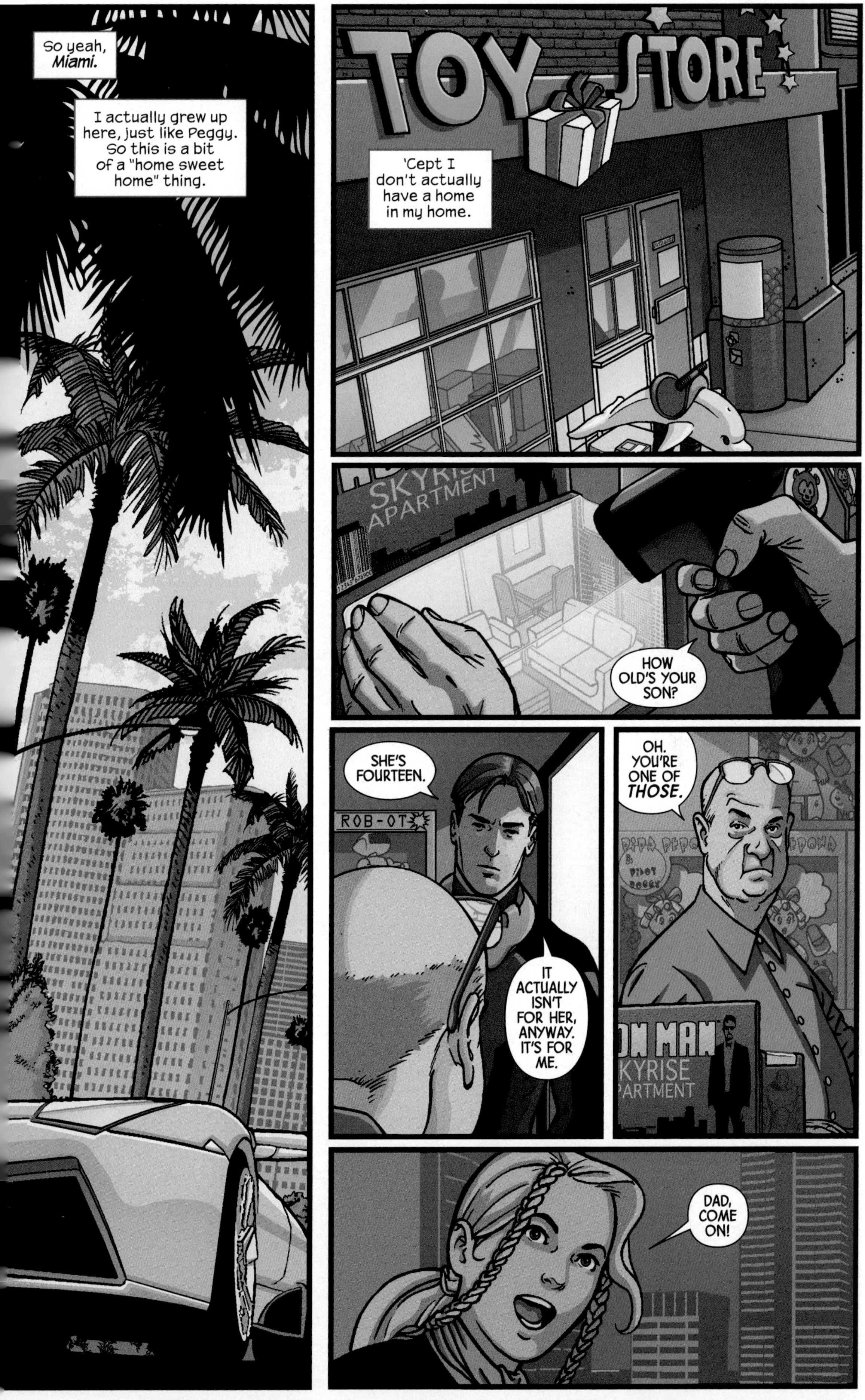
So yeah, *Miami.*
I actually grew up here, just like Peggy. So this is a bit of a "home sweet home" thing.
TOY STORE
'Cept I don't actually have a home in my home.
SKYRISE APARTMENT
HOW OLD'S YOUR SON?
SHE'S FOURTEEN.
ROB-OT
IT ACTUALLY ISN'T FOR HER, ANYWAY. IT'S FOR ME.
OH. YOU'RE ONE OF *THOSE.*
ON MAN
KYRISE
ARTMENT
DAD, COME ON!

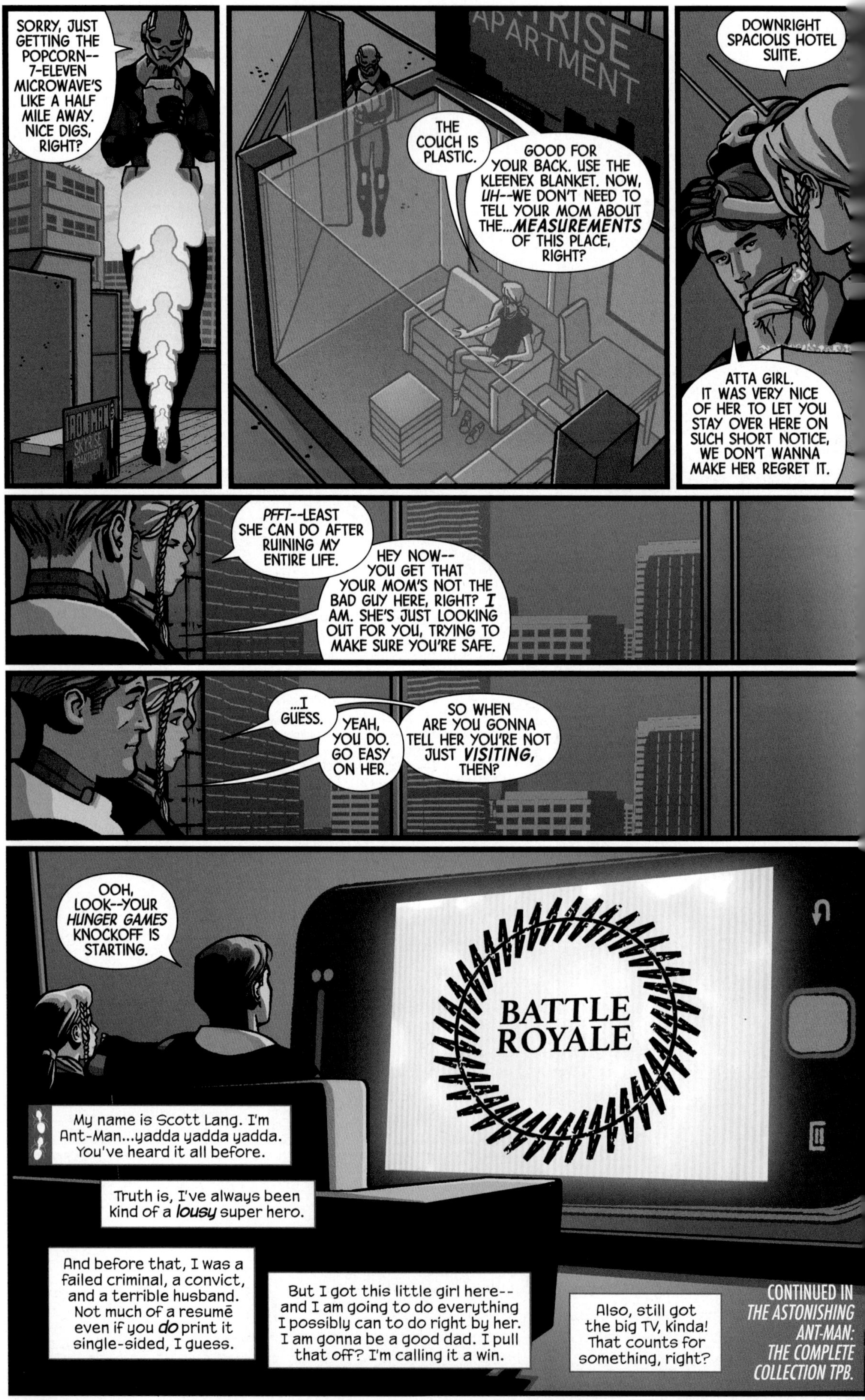
SORRY, JUST GETTING THE POPCORN-- 7-ELEVEN MICROWAVE'S LIKE A HALF MILE AWAY. NICE DIGS, RIGHT?
IRON MAN SKYRISE APARTMENT
THE COUCH IS PLASTIC.
GOOD FOR YOUR BACK. USE THE KLEENEX BLANKET. NOW, UH--WE DON'T NEED TO TELL YOUR MOM ABOUT THE...MEASUREMENTS OF THIS PLACE, RIGHT?
DOWNRIGHT SPACIOUS HOTEL SUITE.
ATTA GIRL. IT WAS VERY NICE OF HER TO LET YOU STAY OVER HERE ON SUCH SHORT NOTICE, WE DON'T WANNA MAKE HER REGRET IT.
PFFT--LEAST SHE CAN DO AFTER RUINING MY ENTIRE LIFE.
HEY NOW-- YOU GET THAT YOUR MOM'S NOT THE BAD GUY HERE, RIGHT? I AM. SHE'S JUST LOOKING OUT FOR YOU, TRYING TO MAKE SURE YOU'RE SAFE.
...I GUESS.
YEAH, YOU DO. GO EASY ON HER.
SO WHEN ARE YOU GONNA TELL HER YOU'RE NOT JUST VISITING, THEN?
OOH, LOOK--YOUR HUNGER GAMES KNOCKOFF IS STARTING.
BATTLE ROYALE
My name is Scott Lang. I'm Ant-Man...yadda yadda yadda. You've heard it all before.
Truth is, I've always been kind of a lousy super hero.
And before that, I was a failed criminal, a convict, and a terrible husband. Not much of a resumé even if you do print it single-sided, I guess.
But I got this little girl here-- and I am going to do everything I possibly can to do right by her. I am gonna be a good dad. I pull that off? I'm calling it a win.
Also, still got the big TV, kinda! That counts for something, right?
CONTINUED IN THE ASTONISHING ANT-MAN: THE COMPLETE COLLECTION TPB.

**Tom DeFalco**
**Ant-Man #1**
**Plot for 20 pages**

## PAGE 1

Our story opens somewhere in **Hungary** as an obviously expensive restaurant explodes in flame and fury, its concussion bursting outward to slam assorted passersby from their feet. One of these people is Hank Pym who was heading toward the restaurant.

## PAGE 2

Lying on the ground, his face covered with bruises and blood, Hank reacts is horror. (We will learn that his new wife—the former **Maria Trovaya**—was in that restaurant. She was attending a dinner connected to a scientific conference sponsored by her employer, Egghead Innovations. Hank was on his way to the dinner.)

Wel move closer to a horrified Hank—

—And then we will cut to a close up of a depressed Hank whose face is healed. (He has been relating the preceding panels in **flashback**. The bombing took place six months ago.)

Pulling back the camera, we discover that Hank is relating this incident to his psychiatrist. (Hank is currently a patient in a sanatorium. He suffered a nervous breakdown after the loss of his wife.)

## PAGE 3

An image of **Maria Pym** (she's a pretty brunette who looks somewhat, but not exactly like Janet Van Dyne) floats above his head as Hank explains that the authorities blamed the bombing on terrorists. He is now filled with paranoia, fearing that no one and no place is safe. No one can be trusted! (The terrorists can sneak into any place and kill any target at any time.)

As his psychiatrist assures Hank that he is safe in the sanatorium and that no one can sneak in to harm him here, we will have a three panel sequence that shows Hank noting an ant climbing up the leg of a desk or end table and walking across it.

Hank and the psychiatrist suddenly react as they hear shouting in the hallway.

## PAGE 4

**Warren Pym** suddenly bursts into the room, demanding that Hank stop coddling himself, grow up and get back to work. The malingering has gone on too long! (Hank's father Warren appeared in **"The Man In The Ant Hill,"** Page 2, Panel 7.)

The psychiatrist, of course, is outraged by Warren's appearance, but a haughty Warren reminds the good doctor that he (Warren) is paying for Hank's stay.
An angry Warren whips/turns toward a startled Hank, telling him to get ready to leave, actively pointing toward the door—

—And we have a **flashback** that shows a much younger Warren whipping/turning toward Hank's never-before-seen **mother**, telling her to get out of his house, actively pointing toward the door.

## PAGE 5

Over the psychiatrist's protests, Warren hustles Hank out the door—

—And they are soon driving away from the sanatorium. (As they drive, a stern Warren and the sulking Hank will talk and we'll learn about their relationship. Warren is disappointed in his son and wants him to grow up and be man. There's a correct order to things and it's time Hank stopped being the perpetual student and committed to a career.)

Warren is particularly interested in Hank's recent theories of "Pym Particles"—

—A term that confuses Hank until Warren explains that he took the liberty of naming Hank's recent discovery.

Sulking back in his seat, Hank explains that he intended to name his discovery after Maria as the car pulls up in front of **a distinctive and modern building** that is identified as **Egghead Innovations**.

## PAGE 6

Having entered the building, Warren escorts Hank past two distinctive security guards and their metal detector to introduce Hank to a serious Elihas "Egghead" Starr.

Elihas immediately expresses his sympathy for the loss of Maria, telling Hank that her death was a shock to everyone at the company.

As they walk down the hallway Elihas informs Hank that out of respect for Maria and Warren he has agreed to give Hank the use of a laboratory at Egghead Innovations.
Stating that he has heard about Hank's preliminary work on the so-called "Pym Particle", Elihas expects great things from him, but Hank tells Elihas not to expect too much because Hank only works on projects that appeal to his imagination.

In an redo of "The Man In The Ant Hill," Page 2, Panel 7, Warren will ask something like, "Ohhh...like what?" and Hank will give a serious and paranoid response.

## PAGE 7

The three enter an advanced **laboratory** to discover a smiling **Bill Foster** who is turning away from an experiment to greet the newcomers. (Elihas will mention that he took the liberty of hiring Hank an assistant.)

Foster is very excited to be working with Hank and extends his hand. (Foster has read a number of Hank's published articles—especially his work on the "Pym Particle.")

Ignoring Foster's hand for a panel, Hank glances suspiciously at Elihas and Warren.

Then Hank takes Foster's hand and welcomes him aboard. (Hank's thoughts will reveal his suspicion that Foster has been hired by the company to spy on him.)

## PAGE 8

Sometime later, as they leave the Egghead building, a pleased Warren claps a serious Hank on the back. (Warren is proud of Hank for getting his career back on track,)

With a serious expression on his face, Warren wonders if Hank is also interested in getting his social life back on track because his old friend Dr. Vernon Van Dyke has a beautiful single daughter—

—But Hank interrupts, saying it's only been six months since Maria's death and he isn't ready to start dating, again.

Holding his hands up in defeat, Warren heads back to the car as a suspicious Hank turns to look at the Egghead building.

This page ends with a close-up of Hank. His thoughts reveal that he is very conflicted about working for Maria's former employer.

## PAGE 9

Cut to a flashback that shows a crude drawing of the **Ant-Man helmet**.

Pulling back the camera, the flashback continues as a serious Maria explains the technology she is developing to communicate with insects to a curious Hank.

We have a focus shot of Maria when as she informs her husband that she intends to present this tech at the conference in Hungary.

Back in reality, Hank springs upward in bed. In his paranoia, he begins to wonder if Egghead murdered Maria for her tech.

## PAGE 10

Cut to an outdoor establishing shot of the Egghead Innovations building.

Inside their laboratory, Foster apologizes for being shoved down Hank's throat and also expresses his desire to learn more about Hank's theories. (We'll also discuss the commercial possibilities for the Pym Particles.)

We will have a series of panels showing the two of them working at computers, mixing chemicals and the sequence ends as Foster watches Hank sketch a crude drawing of chamber made of glass. (While this is happening, we'll explain the basic principles of Pym Particles.

## PAGE 11

Cut to days later and Hank and Foster are looking at the actual **glass enclosed chamber** which is about 6 feet high by 6 feet wide. It is also attached to a fancy gizmo so that the "shrinking gas" can be released into the confined space of the chamber.

Pleased with the day's work, Foster prepares to leave, but Hank says he's just going to check on a few things.

No sooner does Foster exit, then Hank gets down to the serious work of mixing chemicals. (Hank still doesn't trust Foster and has been doing his real work after Foster leaves at night.)

Cut to an image of Hank on a **video screen**.

Pulling back the camera, we see that a serious Elihas Starr has been secretly spying on Hank with hidden cameras because he knows these Pym Particles could be worth billions.

## PAGE 12

As the weeks follow, a montage shows a few images of Hank and Foster working together.
One night after Foster has gone, Hank places a chair in the shrinking chamber,
As he releases the shirking gas, we have a three-panel sequence that shows the chair shrinking.

## PAGE 13

Then an excited Hank releases a second gas as a three-panel sequence shows the chair enlarging.
An excited Hank realizes that his formula is a success.
Cut to Elihas Starr who turns from the monitor showing Hank toward the two security guards from **Page 6**. (Since it is obvious that Hank isn't going to share with Egghead, there's no need for Egghead to share this wonderful tech with him.)

## PAGE 14

Moments later, Hank is startled when the two guards burst into his laboratory and demand he turn over his research and the secure passwords for his computer.
Hank is defiant—
—And receives a punch in the gut for his resistance—
—Followed by a severe beating.
Savagely beaten and bruised, Hank gives them as secure passwords.

## PAGE 15

Having gotten what they want, the men decide to "disappear" him and throw Hank into the shrinking chamber.
Hank is horrified when he is exposed to the gas—
—And we have a multiple image sequence that shows Hank shrinking to the size of ant.

## PAGES 16-17

It's time for a little **Hoo-Ha** action as the guards try to finish Hank off. They enter the chamber and try to squash him.
We get some wild perspective panels shown from Hank's point of view as he runs for his life, trying to avoid the GIANT shoes crashing around him.
Laboratory tables are bumped into, beakers crash and chemicals splash around him as Hank tries to flee the lab and escape his GIANT attackers.

## PAGE 18

Reaching the outside hallway, Hank spots a **Giant janitor** in the distance.
The guards also reach the hallway.
Looking at the floor in search of Hank, they pass the janitor—
—Who pays them little mind as he continues to duties.

## PAGE 19

Sometime later, the janitor heads toward the building's back door.
Outside the building, the janitor tosses his trash bag into an open **dumpster**—
—And we cut to a tiny figure jumping off his shoe.
The figure is a desperate Hank who races toward the corner of the dumpster. (Beyond the dumpster we can see a patch of grass.)
Suddenly Hank freezes. Something is wrong!

## PAGE 20

Pulling back the camera, we see that Hank has gotten tangled in a **spider's web** that extends between the wall of the building to the bottom of the dumpster. A large, menacing spider is approaching Hank.

**To Be Continued!**

# ART PROCESS

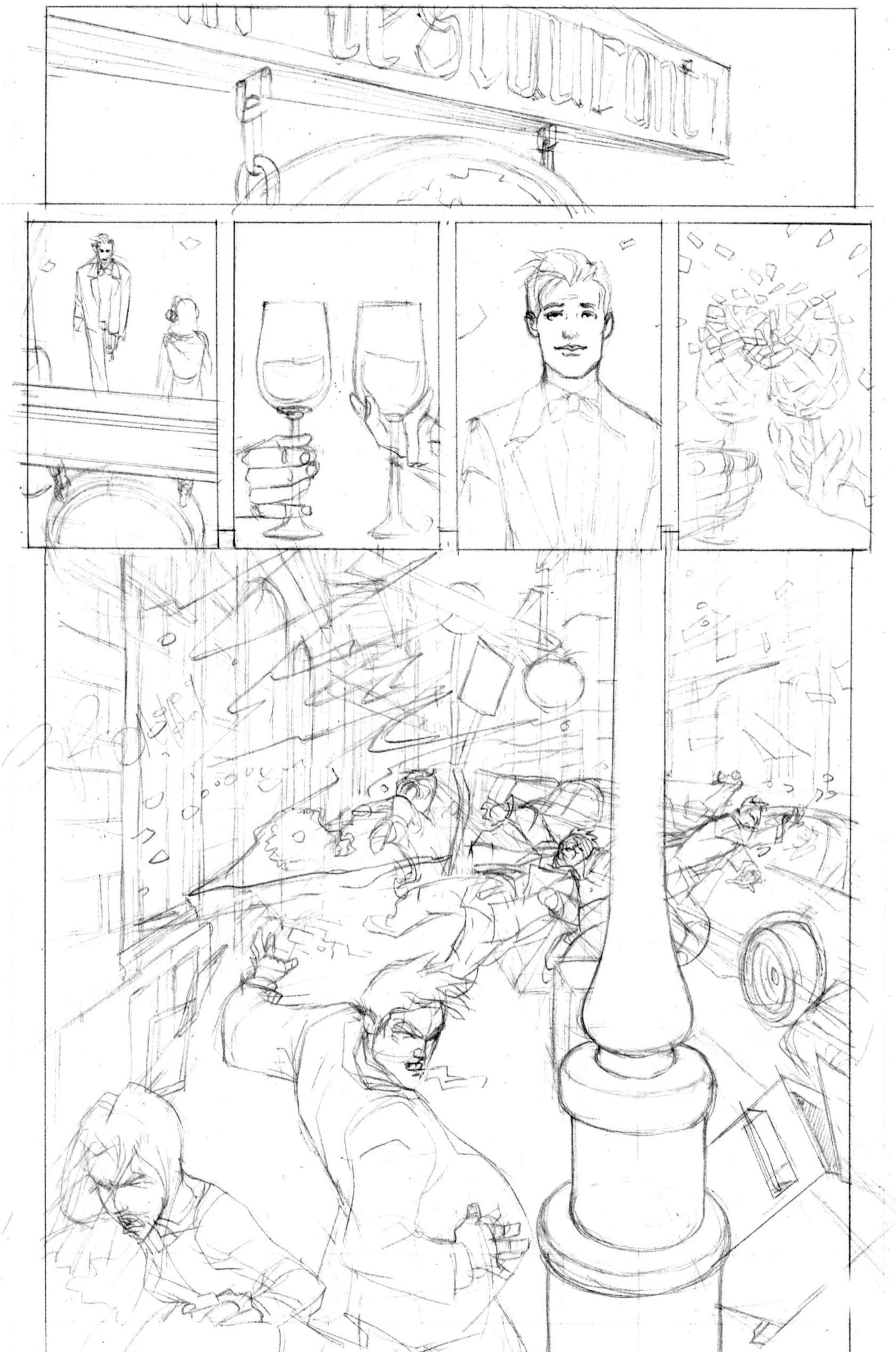
INSTRUCTIONS FOR DOUBLE PAGE SPREAD: CUT AS SHOWN, ABUT PAGE EDGES. TAPE ON BACK. DO NOT OVERLAP.

PAGE 1 ROUGHS

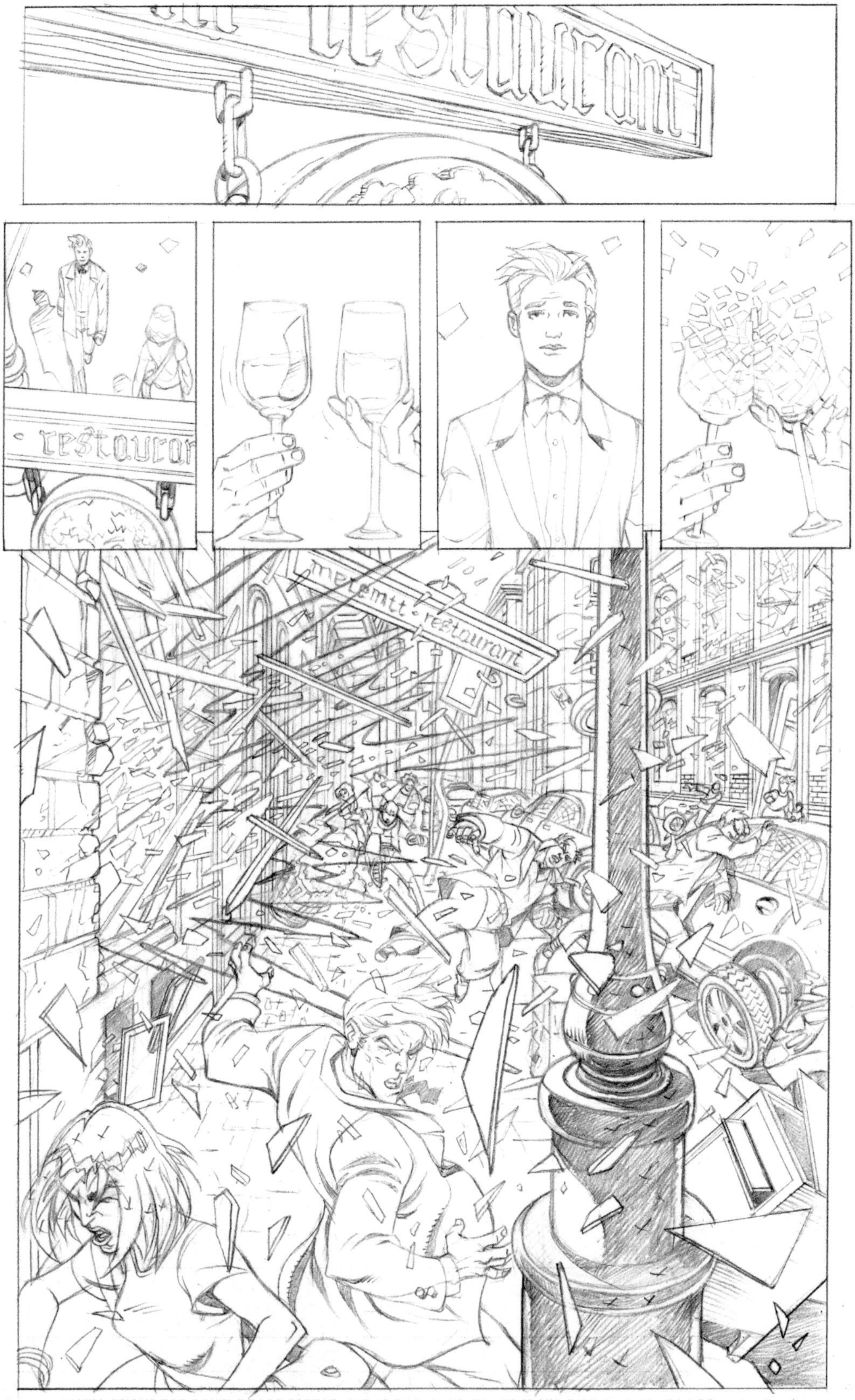
restaurant
restaurant
restaurant



PAGE 1 PENCILS

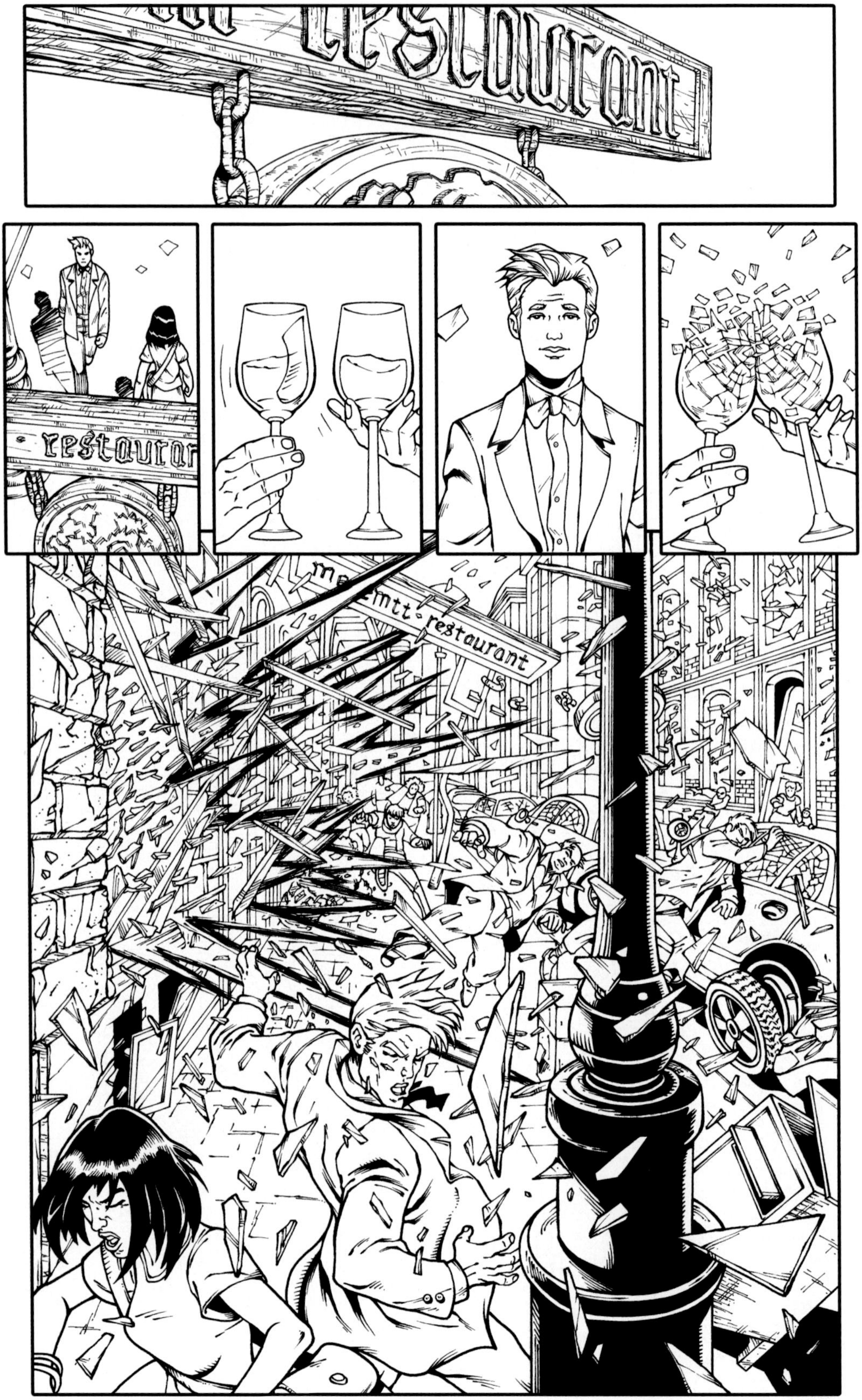
restaurant

PAGE 1 INKS

**PAGE 2 ROUGHS**

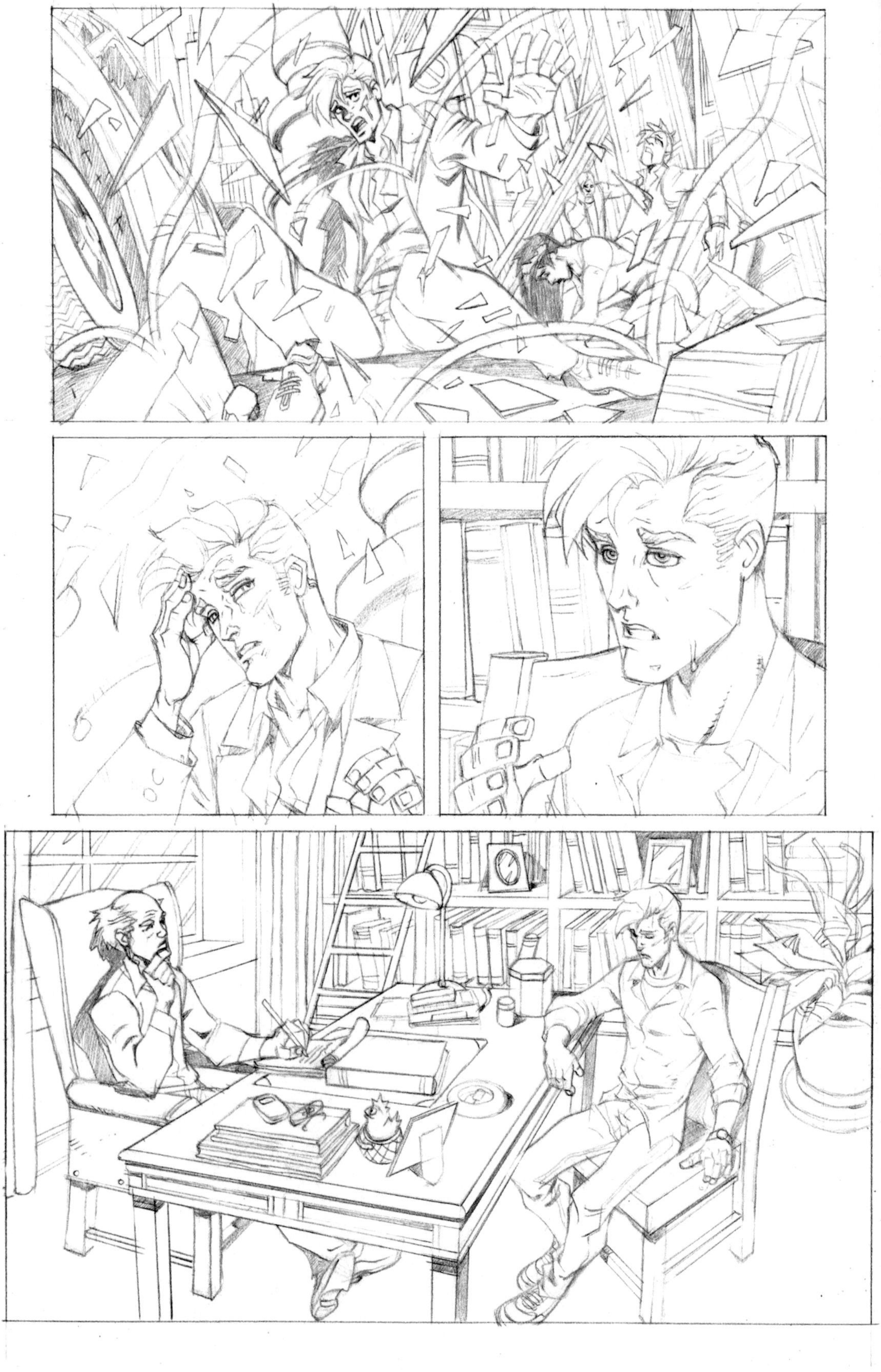

PAGE 2 PENCILS

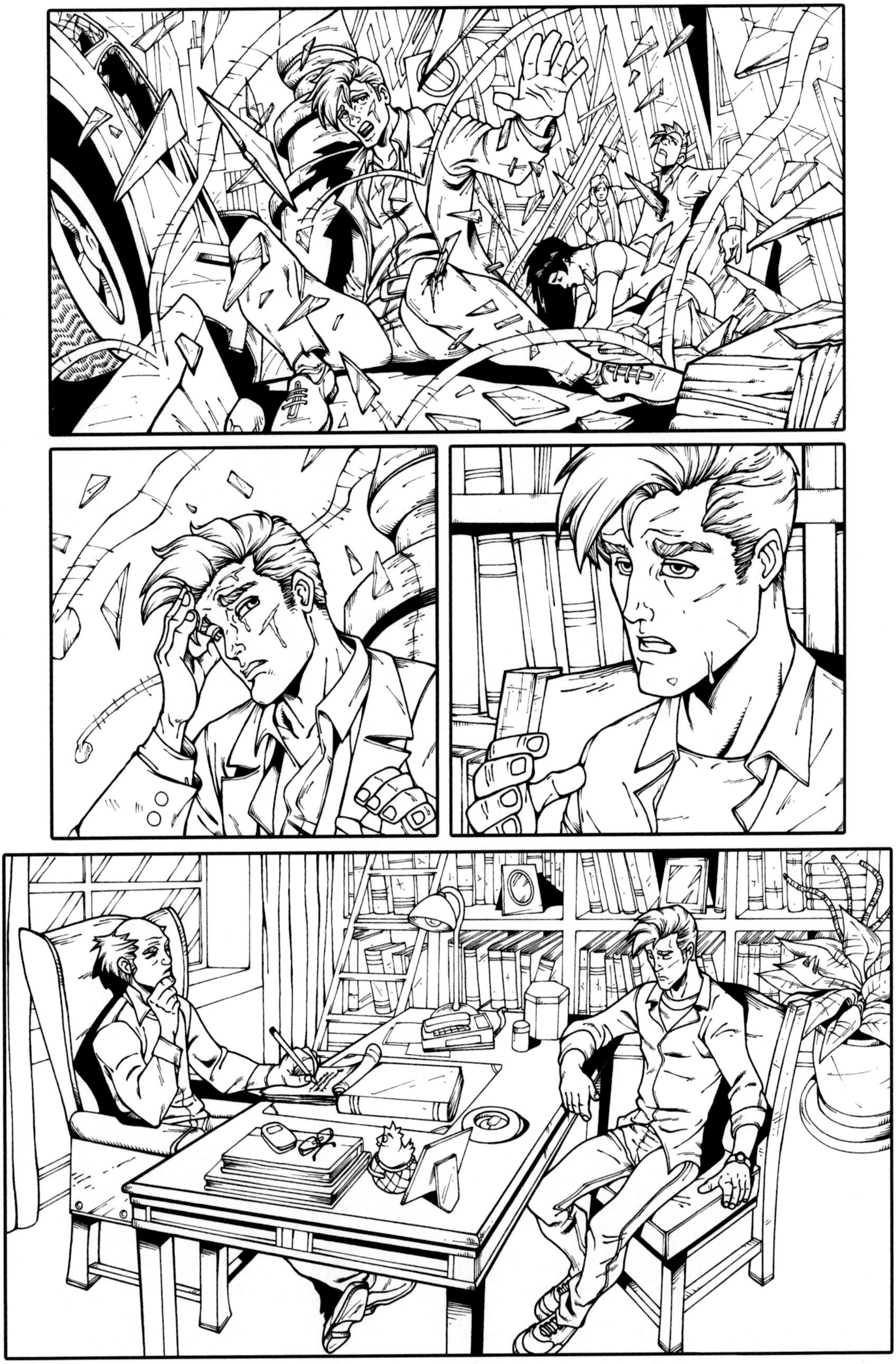

PAGE 2 INKS

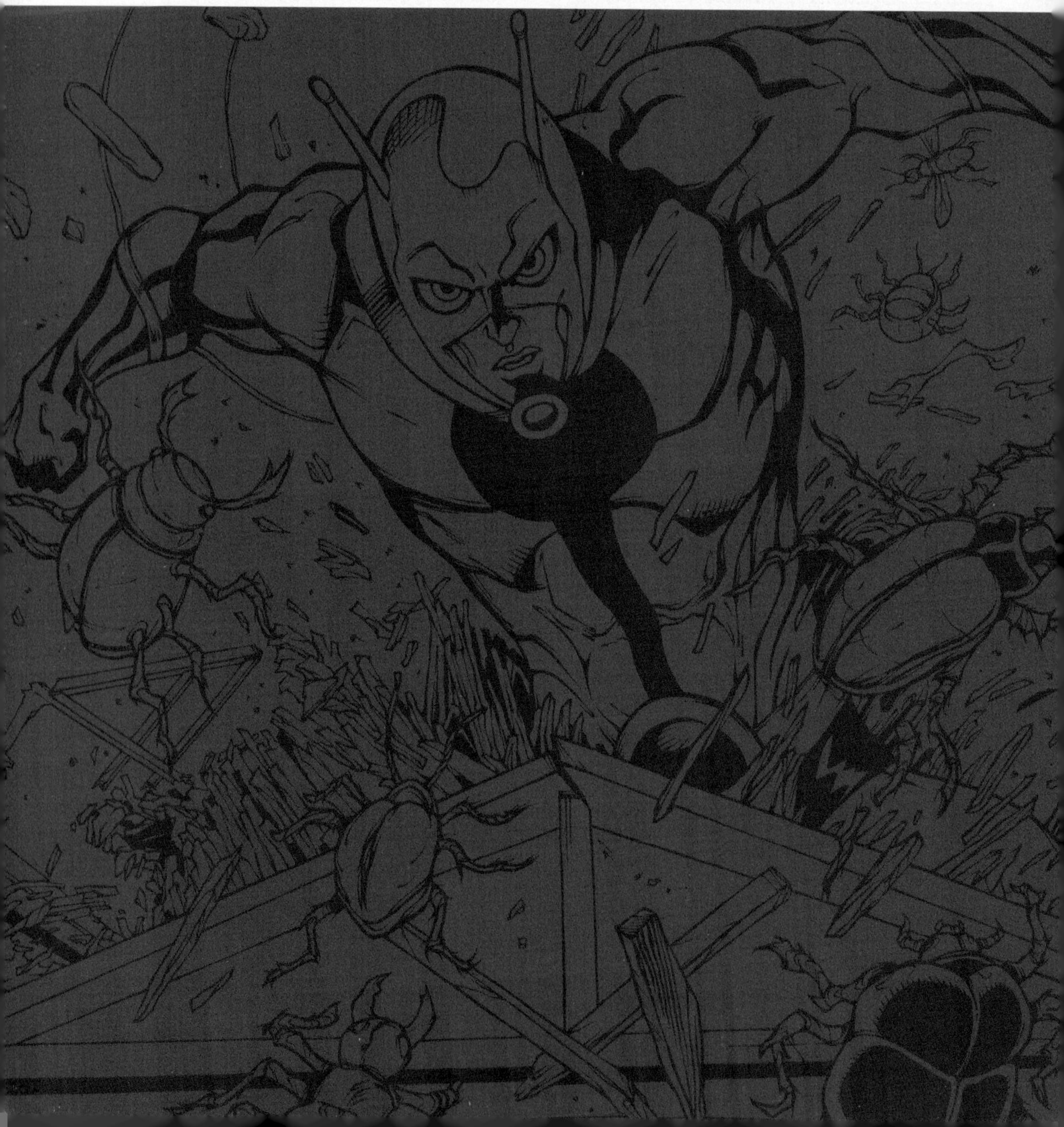